Resources for Preaching
and Worship—Year C

Also by Hannah Ward and Jennifer Wild
from Westminster John Knox Press

Resources for Preaching and Worship—Year B

The Westminster Collection of Christian Meditations

Resources for Preaching and Worship—Year C

QUOTATIONS, MEDITATIONS, POETRY, AND PRAYERS

Compiled by
Hannah Ward and Jennifer Wild

Westminster John Knox Press
LOUISVILLE • LONDON

Book design by PerfecType, Nashville, Tennessee
Cover design by Lisa Buckley

First edition
Published by Westminster John Knox Press
Louisville, Kentucky

This book is printed on acid-free paper that meets the American National Standards Institute Z39.48 standard. ∞

PRINTED IN THE UNITED STATES OF AMERICA

03 04 05 06 07 08 09 10 11 12 — 10 9 8 7 6 5 4 3 2 1

Library of Congress Cataloging-in-Publication Data

Resources for preaching and worship: quotations, meditations, poetry, and prayers / compiled by Hannah Ward and Jennifer Wild. — 1st ed.
     p. cm.
    Includes bibliographical references and indexes.
    Contents:—[2] Year B.
    1. Homiletical illustrations. I. Ward, Hannah. II. Wild, Jennifer.

  BV4225.3 .R47 2002
  264—dc21

2002066394

0-664-22508-X   vol. 2

CONTENTS

PREFACE

In the three volumes of *Resources for Preaching and Worship,* we are offering, for each Sunday or special day in the Christian year, a "hamper" containing various kinds of written material. Anyone who is concerned with preaching on Sunday—or leading study groups or prayer groups during the course of the week—can find here something to feed personal reflection, to stimulate ideas for sermon themes, and to provide stories and poems as well as prayers that in some way relate to the biblical readings for the day concerned. On the great days of the annual cycle, especially between Advent and Pentecost, the Bible readings clearly reflect the season. During large parts of the year, however—the "Proper" Sundays—there is little or no thematic matching of the Bible readings with each other; our choice of companion passages for these dates is at once more arbitrary and, we hope, perhaps even more useful. The passages we have chosen offer possible themes that the preacher might choose to fasten on, or that the person reading the Bible, alone or with others, might find leading to lines of thought not otherwise obvious. If we, in any way, can enlarge or sustain the range of themes and forms of expression open to the preacher or worship leader, we will feel that our aim has been accomplished. Although the writers from whom we have quoted are almost all from the Judeo-Christian traditions, we have tried, overall, to bear in mind that the great themes of Christian faith and practice are embedded in the basic experiences of human life, and the range of human experience is (perhaps) nearer to infinity than we might sometimes suspect.

Christians of many denominations now use the Revised Common Lectionary in one form or another. If you do not find exactly what your own church's lectionary prescribes for any given Sunday or special day, the biblical index at the end of this volume, or the theme index, may point to helpful ideas in another part of this book. One way or another, everyone can find something in here for them—even, sometimes, a point of view with which to disagree. As people who appreciate good sermons, we hope our "hampers" will stir the senses and memory of others who preach the Word of God.

Hannah Ward
Jennifer Wild

First Sunday of Advent

Jeremiah 33:14–16	1 Thessalonians 3:9–13
Psalm 25:1–10	Luke 21:25–36

The whole earth's a waiting room

We wait—all day long,
for planes and buses,
for dates and appointments,
for five o'clock and Friday.

Some of us wait for a Second Coming.
For God in a whirlwind.
Paratrooper Christ.

All around us people are waiting:
a child, for attention;
a spouse, for conversation;
a parent, for a letter or call.

The prisoner waits for freedom;
and the exile, to come home.
The hungry, for food;
and the lonely, for a friend.

The whole earth's a waiting room!
"The Savior will see you now"
is what we expect to hear at the end.

Maybe we should raise our expectations.
The Savior might see us now
if we know how to find him.
Could it be that Jesus, too, is waiting
for us to know he is around?

Joseph T. Nolan, *Let the Earth Rejoice! Scripture, Prayers, and Poems for the More Abundant Life* (Allen, Tex.: Thomas More Publishing, 2000), pp. 32–33.

Watching

Do you know the feeling in matters of this life, of expecting a friend, expecting him to come, and he delays? Do you know what it is to be in unpleasant company, and to wish for the time to pass away, and the hour strike when you may be at liberty? Do you know what it is to be in anxiety lest something should happen which may happen or may not, or to be in suspense about some important event, which makes your heart beat when you are reminded of it, and of which you think the first thing in the morning? Do you know what it is to have a friend in a distant country, to expect news of him, and to wonder from day to day what he is now doing, and whether he is well? Do you know what it is so to live upon a person who is present with you, that your eyes follow his, that you read his soul, that you see all its changes in his countenance, that you anticipate his wishes, that you smile in his smile, and are sad in his sadness, and are downcast when he is vexed, and rejoice in his successes? To watch for Christ is a feeling such as all these; as far as feelings of this world are fit to shadow out those of another.

John Henry Newman, from "Watching," *Plain and Parochial Sermons,*
vol. 4 (London, Oxford and Cambridge: Rivingtons, 1875), p. 323.

Love is his meaning

What, do you wish to know your Lord's meaning in this thing? Know it well, love was his meaning. Who reveals it to you? Love. What did he reveal to you? Love. Why does he reveal it to you? For love. Remain in this, and you will know more of the same. But you will never know different, without end.

So I was taught that love is our Lord's meaning. And I saw very certainly in this and in everything that before God made us he loved us, which love was never abated and never will be. And in this love he has done all his works, and in this love he has made all things profitable to us, and in this love our life is everlasting. In our creation we had beginning, but the love in which he created us was in him from without beginning. In this love we have our beginning, and all this shall we see in God without end.

Julian of Norwich (1343–after 1416), *Showings,*
trans. Edmund Colledge and James Walsh (New York: Paulist Press,
1978), chap. 86, pp. 342–43.

The communion of love

It is only deep calling unto deep, love calling unto love, heart calling unto heart, that can break the iron curtains that separate human beings. It is in sparing no effort in building a communion of love that the future of humanity lies.

This communion of love must be the vision of God as God moves on in fulfillment of the divine purpose for human history. This communion of love is communion in life and communion in hope.

A founder of an independent African church seems to share this vision of God for the communion of love when he tells us what he saw in his dream:

> I saw the world. A giant snake, enormously powerful, was coiling itself around the globe. The globe seemed too weak to withstand the pressure. I could see the first cracks in it. Then I saw a light at the center of the world. Enter into this light, I was told, but I resisted. I wanted to remain outside watching the drama. I was afraid, too, thinking the light would burn me to ashes. But the light was irresistible. I went towards it and, as I did so, I saw many others moving towards it, too. And the snake's grip gradually began to loosen.

Choan-Seng Song, *The Compassionate God: An Exercise in the
Theology of Transposition* (Maryknoll, N.Y.: Orbis Books/London:
SCM Press, 1982), p. 259. (*The quotation that ends this extract was
taken "from an unpublished private source."*)

The redemption of creation

In the Christian Church these weeks leading up to Christmas, this dark beginning of our new year, is also traditionally the time of thinking of the last things, of the "eschaton," the end. . . . That day when all nights will be spent, when time will end: we all know it's coming. . . . It has to happen sometime.

It was a long time before I could begin to think of this ending of all known things, all matter, the stars in their courses, music, laughter, sunrise, daisies and dynasties, starfish and stars, suns and chrysanthemums, as being in any way something to look forward to with joy and hope.

But annihilation is the opposite of what the eschaton is about. It is not nearly so much a going as a coming, an ending as a beginning. It is the redemption, not the destruction, of Creation.

Madeleine L'Engle, *The Irrational Season* (San Franciso:
Harper & Row, 1977), pp. 2–3.

Holding on to hope

The endurance of those who hold on to hope 'all the day long' becomes a strength to others, especially when they see faith in people who seem most vulnerable. . . .

The experience of God's past grace and present help gradually reveals a new horizon. That perspective must always remain partly unknown and the temptation to fill it with our own ideals or wants can only blind our vision of God. Hope cannot be placed in God just in case our plans do not work out even if we have to face the agnosticism which is an inevitable part of faith. [T. S.] Eliot claimed that, in contrast to the certainty of Marxists, his own beliefs were held with a scepticism which he never hoped to lose. Hope for the Psalmist is a quest of God's making. Anything else is a kind of ambition circumscribed by our limited horizons.

> I'll not reproach
> The road that winds, my feet that err.
> Access, Approach
> Art Thou, Time, Way, and Wayfarer.
>
> 'I am the Way' (Alice Meynell [1847–1922])

Brian Pickett, *Songs for the Journey: The Psalms in Life and Liturgy* (London: Darton, Longman & Todd, 2002), p. 65. © Darton, Longman & Todd Ltd., 2002. Used by permission of the publishers.

Advent prayer

Behold, You come. And Your coming is neither past nor future, but the present, which has only to reach its fulfilment. Now it is still the one single hour of Your Advent, at the end of which we too shall have found out that You have really come.

O God who is to come, grant me the grace to live now, in the hour of Your Advent, in such a way that I may merit to live in you forever, in the blissful hour of Your Eternity.

Karl Rahner, *Encounters with Silence*, trans. James M. Demske, S.J. (London and Glasgow: Sands & Co./Westminster, Md.: Newman Press, 1960), p. 87.

SECOND SUNDAY OF ADVENT

Malachi 3:1–4   Philippians 1:3–11
Luke 1:68–79   Luke 3:1–6

Prepare the way of the Lord

There is a voice that cries in the wilderness,
the prophet word demanding change:
'Prepare the way of the Lord;
fill in the gullies, level the ridges,
straighten the crooked, move the mountains.
God's glory shall be revealed
and every eye shall see it.'

Refrain:

Smooth the rough places,
move the mountains;
let God's glory be displayed!

In the wilderness of our cities,
furrowed by freeways and shaded by skyscrapers,
where hollow people jostle without love
or get lost in the wastes of suburbia,
where anonymous persons hide in flats,
or broken men queue up at hostels
for a bed and respite from dereliction:
Prepare the way of the Lord.

Refrain

In the wilderness of our countryside,
where little farmers eke out existence
while the rich accumulate massive farms
and city people play games on farmlets,
where once-proud towns shrink into shabbiness,
their sons and daughters drained off to the cities,

and unemployed blacks drink behind pubs:
Prepare the way of the Lord.

Refrain

. . . In the wilderness of our religions
where theological fashions come and go,
buildings and crowds persist as status-symbols,
and pomp and circumstance are high on the ratings,
where evangelism can be considered poor taste,
prayer and sacrifice as optional extras,
and even Jesus is feared as 'extremist':
Prepare the way of the Lord.

Refrain

Voice in the wilderness, what shall we do?
Prophet of the Lord, what is the word?
'Turn, turn, turn to the Lord;
you who have two suits, give to the naked;
if you eat well, share with the hungry;
in business and authority, deal with compassion—
and be ready for the One who comes with fire.'

Refrain

Bruce Prewer, in Bruce D. Prewer and Aub Podlich, *Australian
Accents* (Adelaide: Lutheran Publishing House
[Openbook Publishers], 1988), p. 38.

Expectation

Expectation—anxious, collective and operative expectation of an end of the world, that is to say, of an issue for the world—that is perhaps the supreme Christian function and the most distinctive characteristic of our religion. Historically speaking, that expectation has never ceased to guide the progress of our faith like a torch. We persist in saying that we keep vigil in expectation of the Master. But in reality we should have to admit, if we were sincere, *that we no longer expect anything.* The flame must be revived at all costs. At all costs we must renew in ourselves the desire and the hope for the great coming. But from where are we to look for the source of this rejuvenation? From the perception of *a more intimate connection* between the victory of Christ and the outcome of the work which our human effort here below is seeking to construct. . . .

The star for which the world is waiting, without yet being able to give it a name, or rightly appreciate its true transcendence, or even recognize the most spiritual and divine of its rays, is, necessarily, Christ himself, in whom we hope. To desire the Parousia, all we have to do is to let the very heart of the earth, as we Christianize it, beat within us.

Pierre Teilhard de Chardin, *Le Milieu Divin*, trans. Alick Dru and others (London: William Collins Sons & Co., Ltd./New York: Harper & Row, 1960), pp. 148–52.

Commitment to each other

In the face of all our realities:
We are the people who heal each other,
who grow strong together,
who name the truth,
who know what it means
to live in community,
moving towards a common dream
for a new heaven and a new earth
in the power of the love of God,
the company of Jesus Christ
and the leading of the Holy Spirit.

Dorothy McRae-McMahon, *Echoes of Our Journey: Liturgies of the People* (Melbourne: The Joint Board of Christian Education, 1993), p. 69. © Dorothy McRae-McMahon. Used by permission of the author.

The gift of discernment

Amma Theodora said that a teacher ought to be a stranger to the desire for domination, vain-glory, and pride; one should not be able to fool him by flattery, nor blind him by gifts, nor conquer him by the stomach, nor dominate him by anger; but that he should be patient, gentle and humble as far as possible; he must be tested and without partisanship, full of concern, and a lover of souls.

Benedicta Ward, *Sayings of the Desert Fathers* (London: A. R. Mowbray/ Kalamazoo, Mich.: Cistercian Publications, 1975), p. 72.

Spirit of love

Spirit of love, you move within creation,
drawing the threads to color and design:
life into life, you knit our true salvation,
       come, work with us,
       and weave us into one.

Though we have frayed the fabric of your making,
tearing away from all that you intend,
yet, to be whole, humanity is aching—
       come, work with us,
       and weave us into one.

Great loom of God, where history is woven,
you are the frame that holds us to the truth,
Christ is the theme, the pattern you have given—
       come, work with us,
       and weave us into one.

Toward the fullness of God's reign

Although Christianity developed many historical commemorations in its calendar . . . the core of the Christian calendar is eschatological or messianic. It builds upon the future dimension of Hebrew hope. But it also sees itself as already empowered by the advent of this final deliverance of the world from sin and death, even while still looking forward to its future completion. This element of a foretaste of things to come is the key dynamic of Christian ritual. One cannot understand the yearly reenactment of advent expectation, leading to the messianic birth, the Lenten preparation for the final passion and resurrection of Christ, and the feats of Christ's ascension into heaven and the outpouring of the Holy Spirit "in the last days," unless one understands that these are not simply remembrances of events completed in the past. Rather, they look back to experiences which themselves point forward to that final time when the bondage of evil and mortality is lifted from humanity and from all creation and the fullness of God's reign is established.

Rosemary Radford Ruether, *Women-Church: Theology and Practice of Feminist Liturgical Communities* (San Francisco: Harper & Row, 1985), pp. 103–4.

The Christian hope

The present demise of cultural optimism does not rob Christians of their hope. Their faith in the divine promises continues to nourish hope and love. Christians believe that since God is graciously acting in human history, good things always emerge in the midst of social and cultural crises, even if at first they touch only a minority. I have never forgotten a paragraph written . . . by . . . Maurice Blondel, which claims that because of God's redemptive immanence, humanity is, in every period, in labour giving birth to the new. Blondel spoke of "the stirrings of parturition." Christians, he wrote, must listen to the new ideas and practices, testing them with the gospel, and learn from them if they are compatible with it. In the same vein, the political economist, Karl Polanyi, also a Christian, has shown that when society has been threatened by economic forces, social movements emerge among ordinary people that try to protect the community and its environment from disintegration.

That God is redemptively at work in the world and sustains people struggling to create a more just and humane society was, we recall, the teaching of Vatican Council II. This Council, we noted, was carried by a certain cultural optimism which it passed on both to reformist Christians hoping to improve social democracy and to radical Christians hoping for revolutionary change and the creation of an alternative society. In the present situation this optimism has dissolved. Yet the collapse of optimism does not mean that Christians give up hope. Believing that God is graciously at work in the world, Christians scan society to detect "the stirrings of parturition" occurring in it. The drama of redemption, revealed in Jesus Christ, continues to be operative in the history of nations.

Gregory Baum, "Are We in a New Historical Situation?" in Gregory Baum et al., *Stone Soup: Reflections on Economic Injustice* (Toronto: Paulines, 1998), pp. 34–35.

Do not ask who the messenger is.
It is you.

Joseph T. Nolan

THIRD SUNDAY OF ADVENT

Zephaniah 3:14–20   Philippians 4:4–7

Isaiah 12:2–6   Luke 3:7–18

A great divine plan

Luke's concern is to emphasize that John has *not* come as a bolt out of the blue. There are social reasons why he had to preach at precisely that time and place rather than any other. Thus for Luke it is not an accident that the gospel begins in remote Galilee and then proceeds to Jerusalem and finally to Rome (at the end of the Acts of the Apostles). It is all part of a great divine plan. But it is a plan in which, though change is required of us, it is not to be a kind in which our social obligations to the particular society in which we are set may be forgotten. So in the second feature unique to Luke, it is he alone of the evangelists who reminds us that John preached, not that tax-collectors for the Empire should give up their jobs, but that they should refrain from extortion, and not that soldiers should leave the Imperial Army in response to the gospel but that they should use force with restraint. . . . So Luke, like Mark, certainly offers us a gospel of change, but unlike Mark, he insists that we take our setting in a particular social world with the maximum seriousness.

David Brown, *The Word to Set You Free: Living Faith and Biblical Criticism* (London: SPCK, 1995), pp. 119–20.

Bitter winter

Bitter winter, you crackle your fire
winter, you consume the woods, the roofs
winter, you slash and burn.

Whoever mourns, let him mourn; whoever suffers, let him suffer more;
whoever hates, let him hate more; whoever deceives, let him triumph:
this is the ultimate text and decree of our winter.

We didn't know what to do with
green life and the loving flowers.
That's why the ax is at the root of our hearts

and like writhing twigs we shall be burnt.

Franco Fortuni, in *New Italian Poetry 1945 to the Present, A Bilingual
Anthology*, ed. and trans. Lawrence R. Smith (Berkeley:
University of California Press, 1980). © 1981 The Regents
of the University of California.

Waiting

Our sense of urgency is balanced by the requirement to wait—to wait on the timing of God, which we can neither predict nor force. And the poor of the world have much to teach us about waiting—waiting with hope, purpose, and active preparation for change; waiting without falling into despair. For activists it may be hard but necessary to thank God for 'the darkness of waiting,' and for what we learn 'through failing where we hoped to succeed.'

Janet Morley, in *Bread of Tomorrow: Praying with the World's Poor*, ed.
Janet Morley (London: SPCK/Christian Aid, 1992), p. 14.

The longer we wait . . .

What strikes me is that waiting is a period of learning. The longer we wait the more we hear about him for whom we are waiting. As the Advent weeks progress, we hear more and more about the beauty and splendor of the One who is to come. The Gospel passages read during Mass all talk about the events before Jesus' birth and the people ready to receive him. In the other readings Isaiah heaps prophecy on prophecy to strengthen and deepen our hope, and the songs, lessons, commentaries, and antiphons all compete in their attempt to set the stage for the Lord who is to come.

There is a stark beauty about it all. But is this not a preparation that can only lead to an anticlimax? I don't think so. Advent does not lead to nervous tension stemming from expectation of something spectacular about to happen. On the contrary, it leads to a growing inner stillness and joy allowing me to realize that he for whom I am waiting has already arrived and speaks to me in the silence of my heart. Just as a mother feels the child grow in her and is not surprised on the day of the birth but joyfully receives the one she learned to know during her wait-ing, so Jesus can be born in my life slowly and steadily and be received as the one I learned to know while waiting.

This last week is indeed a happy one.

Henri J. M. Nouwen, *The Genesee Diary: Report from a Trappist Monastery* (New York: Doubleday, Image Edition, 1989), pp. 209–10.

Attention

Increasingly, prayer seems to be a waiting—and often, a goal-less waiting: it is sim-ply an end in itself. If some resolution, insight or peace comes, it comes as a gift, not as something I have angled for. I was at a loss to explain this to anyone until I remembered that the French for 'to wait' is 'attendre.' Then it became clear that waiting is giving one's complete and undivided attention . . . to the present moment, to the person or situation one wants to 'hold in the Light,' to the object before one's eyes, or the word arising in one's mind. To keep vigil is to be awake, waiting, attentive.

Kate Compston, in *A Restless Hope: Prayer Handbook 1995*, ed. Kate Compston (London: United Reformed Church of the United Kingdom, 1995), Advent 1.

Psalm 126

Laughter and song!
The Lord has done great things:
his people once were freed
from tyrant kings.

Yet now we wait
in sad captivity:
rise up, redeeming Lord,
to set us free!

Tears turn to joy!
The weeping farmer sows
and, slowly through the storms,
the harvest grows.

David Mowbray, in *Psalms for Today and Songs from the Psalms: Combined Words Edition*, ed. David Iliff, Michael Perry, and David Peacock (London: Jubilate, Hodder & Stoughton, 1990), no. 126A. © David Mowbray/Jubilate Hymns in the UK. © Hope Publishing Company in the USA, Canada, Australia, New Zealand, South Africa, Hungary, Mexico, and the Pacific-rim countries. Used by permission.

Without poverty of spirit, there can be no abundance of God.

Archbishop Oscar Romero

FOURTH SUNDAY OF ADVENT

Micah 5:2–5a	Hebrews 10:5–10
Psalm 80:1–7	Luke 1:39–45

Advent

Marvels can happen, we invite them all
Into a sudden state of wanting good.
Yes now every tall

Story comes true. A child is on his way. . . .

Elizabeth Jennings, *Timely Issues* (Manchester: Carcanet, 2001), p. 46.

Magnificat

My heart is bubbling over with joy;
with God it is good to be woman.
From now on let all peoples proclaim:
it is a wonderful gift to be.
The one in whom power truly rests
has lifted us up to praise;
God's goodness shall fall like a shower
on the trusting of every age.
The disregarded have been raised up:
the pompous and powerful shall fall.
God has feasted the empty-bellied,
and the rich have discovered their void.
God has made good the word
given at the dawn of time.

Phoebe Willetts in *Celebrating Women: The New Edition*, ed. Hannah
Ward, Jennifer Wild, and Janet Morley (London: SPCK, 1995), p. 37.

Celebration of new life

It took me some time to discover that the Church has unwritten rules. One of them is: 'Thou shalt not be happy. Joyful, thou mayest be, but remember: joy is no laughing matter.'

I realized this when the General Synod of the Church of England was debating a report called 'The Mystery of Salvation.' All of one summer's afternoon some of the best brains in the Church gnawed on this learned document like a dog with a bone.

Outside the sun was shining but, inside, things were different. Five hundred Christians were exploring nothing less than the gift of life. But never once was there a hint that we should enjoy exploring this astounding gift from God.

There were no balloons or party hats; not a hint of celebration. It was like a conference of undertakers discussing the price of embalming fluid.

My pal Peter Stoodely was furious about the title of the report: 'Salvation is not a mystery,' he said. And he was right. . . . Salvation is life, and life is as obvious as the flower on the stalk or the softness of a baby's bottom.

Amazingly, we may be able to pin-point the exact moment when salvation stopped being a mystery. . . . We have seen how Mary is confronted by what she believes to be an angel, and the whole purpose of her life opens up before her. She hurries off to see her cousin, Elizabeth, and their conversation seems to confirm and endorse what Mary is thinking.

Then it is as though there is a pause, during which the full implication of what is happening finally dawns on her. So far there has been fear, confusion, faith and obedience. But until now there has been not a hint of laughter, or celebration.

Now, quite suddenly, it is as though all this wells up in her heart. Perhaps remembering the song of Hannah from the Old Testament, she repeats those immortal words that we know as the Magnificat:

> My soul magnifies the Lord
> and my spirit rejoices in God my saviour.

David Rhodes, *The Advent Adventure* (London: Triangle, SPCK, 1998), pp. 27–28.

The visit

Loving God, maternal God,
You are indeed full of surprises,
You are always bringing to birth.
You visited Mary
and made of her
a model for all women.
Mary visited Elizabeth
and, touched by grace,
left us with
a legacy of praise,
a hint of future miracles,
experience of God's ways:
the lowly are uplifted,
the powerful overthrown,
the hungry offered sustenance,
the resources of the wealthy given
to the underprivileged class.
Thank You, God of people,
for revealing Your feminine face.
Visit us now, and always,
with Your renewing grace.
For this we pray.

Amen.

Miriam Therese Winter, *WomanPrayer, WomanSong: Resources for Ritual* (Oak Park, Ill: Meyer Stone Books, 1987), p. 72. © 1987 Medical Mission Sisters. Used by permission of The Crossroad Publishing Company.

The Visitation (Sunday, December 22, 1985)

I am deeply moved by this simple and mysterious encounter. In the midst of an unbelieving, doubting, pragmatic, and cynical world, two women meet each other and affirm in each other the promise given to them. The humanly impossible has happened to them. God has come to them to begin the salvation promised through the ages. Through these two women God has decided to change the course of history. Who could ever understand? Who could ever believe it? Who could ever let it happen? But Mary says, "Let it happen to me," and she immediately realizes that only Elizabeth will be able to affirm her "yes." For three months Mary and Elizabeth live together and encourage each other to truly accept the motherhood given to them. Mary's presence makes Elizabeth more fully aware of becoming the mother of the "prophet of the Most High" (Luke 1:76), and Elizabeth's presence allows Mary to grow in the knowledge of becoming the mother of the "Son of the Most High" (Luke 1:32).

Neither Mary nor Elizabeth had to wait in isolation. They could wait together and thus deepen in each other their faith in God, for whom nothing is impossible. Thus, God's most radical intervention into history was listened to and received in community.

The story of the Visitation teaches me the meaning of friendship and community. How can I ever let God's grace fully work in my life unless I live in a community of people who can affirm it, deepen it, and strengthen it? We cannot live this new life alone. God does not want to isolate us by his grace. On the contrary, he wants us to form new friendships and a new community—holy places where his grace can grow in fullness and bear fruit.

Henri J. M. Nouwen, *The Road to Daybreak: A Spiritual Journey* (New York: Doubleday/London: Darton, Longman & Todd, 1989), pp. 100–101. © 1988 by Henri J. M. Nouwen. Used by permission of Doubleday, a division of Random House, Inc., and of Darton, Longman & Todd Ltd.

Garment of glory

By providing the body of Christ, Mary . . . provided for all the garment of glory, the resurrection body.

> "Your mother put on,
> in her virginity, the garment of glory
> that suffices for all. I gave
> the small mantle of the body to the One who covers all."

Kathleen E. McVey, and Ephrem the Syrian, excerpt from introduction and text of "Hymn 17 on the Nativity," strophe 5, in *Ephrem the Syrian: Hymns*, trans. and intro. Kathleen McVey (New York/Mahwah, N.J.: Paulist Press, 1989), pp. 153 and 154. © Kathleen McVey 1989. Used by permission of Paulist Press. www.paulistpress.com.

"Thy will be done in earth, as it is in heaven" (KJ version)

Your one desire then acts with ours,
as in all light, so in
all forms.

Let all wills move together
in your vortex, as stars and planets
swirl through the sky.

Help us love beyond our ideals
and sprout acts of compassion
for all creatures.

As we find your love in ours,
let heaven and nature form
a new creation.

Unite the crowd within
in a vision of passionate purpose:
light mates with form.

Create in me a divine cooperation—
from many selves, one voice,
one action.

Let your heart's fervent desire
unite heaven and earth
through our harmony.

Your one desire then acts with ours,
as in all light, so in
all forms.

Neil Douglas-Klotz, from *Prayers of the Cosmos: Meditations on the Aramaic Words of Jesus*, trans. and with commentary by Neil Douglas-Klotz (San Francisco: HarperSanFrancisco, 1990), p. 22. © 1990 Neil Douglas-Klotz. Reprinted by permission of HarperCollins Publishers Inc.

Promised coming

Jesus comes today!
Prepare to meet your God!
  No Presidential cavalcade
  encircles him with might;
    the shepherds kiss a worker's child
    who loves till all are reconciled:
      Prepare to meet your God!

  Jesus comes today!
  Prepare to meet your God!
    No massed Convention roars its praise
    to hail the new messiah;
      love has no powers to lay aside,
      so crowds will have him crucified:
        Prepare to meet your God!

    Jesus comes today!
    Prepare to meet your God!
      No Primaries can pave his way
      to be the people's choice;
        he chooses us, and calls our name,
        and life can never be the same:
          Prepare to meet your God!

Brian Wren, *Piece Together Praise: A Theological Journey. Poems and Collected Hymns Thematically Arranged* (Carol Stream, Ill.: Hope Publishing Company/London: Stainer & Bell, 1996), no. 13, p. 15. © 1986 Hope Publishing Company for the USA, Canada, Australia and New Zealand, and Stainer & Bell for all other territories. Used by permission.

Who is God?

Who is God?

God is

the meaning for my joy.

God is

a gladsome joy in my being.

Mechtild of Magdeburg, in *Meditations with Mechtild of Magdeburg,*
versions by Sue Woodruff (Santa Fe, N.M.:
Bear & Company, 1982), p. 107.

Prayer

O God our deliverer,
you cast down the mighty,
and lift up those of no account:
as Elizabeth and Mary embraced
with songs of liberation,
so may we also be pregnant with your Spirit,
and affirm one another in hope for the world,
through Jesus Christ, Amen.

Janet Morley, *All Desires Known: Expanded Edition*
(London: SPCK, 1992), p. 27.

We are all meant to be mothers of God. For God is always needing to be born.

Meister Eckhart

CHRISTMAS, FIRST PROPER

| Isaiah 9:2–7 | Titus 2:11–14 |
| Psalm 96 | Luke 2:1–14 (15–20) |

Gazing

When I first met my friend, Donald Nicholl, after he had been told that he had terminal cancer, he said to me, 'I've been thinking. I think that thinking is part of the punishment for the Fall, so I have given up thinking and spend my days in gazing.'

Gazing is a most profitable occupation, for in gazing, instead of controlling our thinking and feeling, we allow thoughts and feelings to arise in us. For example, in gazing at a landscape, we may find ourselves at peace and delighting in the beauty and spaciousness of the scene. This experience of peace and delight may make us more aware of the lack of peace in our normal way of life. Gazing has deepened our awareness and so raised questions of fundamental importance for our well-being, questions which we are normally too busy or too afraid to consider....

In this reading [Luke 2:1–14 (15–20)], imagine the scene happening at this moment and that you are present in it. See the child in the manger, Mary, Joseph, and yourself, allowing your imagination to supply any other details. Just gaze at the scene and see what happens. You don't have to force anything, just be there. If you feel prompted to talk with Mary and Joseph, to ask them if you may hold the child, then do so. Talk to them about their lives and about your own.

Prayer

God, still our hearts and minds so that we can learn to gaze, and through gazing glimpse you, our soul's desiring.

Gerard W. Hughes, *God of Compassion* (London: Hodder &
Stoughton, 1998), pp. 57–58.

For Christmas

Opening Responses

God of creation, shaper of seas and stars
of planets and of people
GOD IS HERE WITH US

God, born in Bethlehem
gurgling, crying, laid in a manger
GOD IS HERE WITH US

God, breath of the universe
flickering, dancing in the candle flame
GOD IS HERE WITH US

God, Immanuel, amongst us, within us
WE BRING OURSELVES AND OUR DREAMS
FOR WE WANT TO BE HERE WITH YOU

Closing Responses

Mysterious God, confounding our expectations
meeting us where we least expect to find you
STAY WITH US NOW

Child of the manger, healing our pain
sharing our weakness
STAY WITH US NOW

Source of life
birth of God within our own experience
STAY WITH US NOW

Stay with us in our frailty
stay with us on our journey
WALK BESIDE US, LIVE WITHIN US
LEAD US TO GLORY, LEAD US HOME

Ruth Burgess, in *The Pattern of Our Days: Liturgies and Resources for Worship*, ed. Kathy Galloway (Glasgow: Wild Goose Publications, 1996), pp. 107–8. © Ruth Burgess.

Celebrating

> We celebrate this God
> who leaps free of our boundaries
> in love stretching out from horizon to horizon,
> and in mercy bending deep
> into fragile human hearts.

Dorothy McRae-McMahon, *Prayers for Life's Particular Moments*
(London: SPCK, 2001), p. 1.

Wrappings

We wrap our gifts in glittering paper and adorn them with ribbons, hoping to make what is really very ordinary look like something special. Your gift to us, your incarnate Word, comes barely wrapped at all. You give us that which is utterly special, but you wrap it in ordinariness, so that we won't be afraid to receive it.

Margaret Silf, *Daily Readings for a Life with God* (London: Darton,
Longman & Todd, 1999), p. 224.

Himself the Kingdom

Towards the end of his life Karl Barth was asked whether he had changed his mind on any important matter during the course of his life. He said that there was one point in particular on which he had shifted his opinions. Once he believed that Jesus of Nazareth came to preach the Kingdom of God. Now he knew that Jesus *was* that Kingdom. Origen had seen it all so many centuries before: *autobasileia*, himself the Kingdom. In his person Jesus was the reign of God in the world, God being gracious, God coming with healing and forgiveness. In meeting Jesus we encounter the Kingdom of God, as people found God-for-them when they met him in the streets and countryside of Palestine. When we meet Jesus in word, sacrament or neighbour, then we find the Kingdom of God. The man of flesh and blood like ours, in whom our human nature was taken into the Godhead, is personally the Kingdom. And so everything that served the en-fleshing of Jesus was a service of the Kingdom of God.

... [Mary] stands at the midmost point of the enmanment of God. By serving the taking of our nature by the Son of God, she put herself at the service of the Kingdom of God which we have entered and in another sense shall come to enter.

Geoffrey Preston, O.P., *Hallowing the Time: Meditations on the Cycle of the Christian Liturgy* (London: Darton, Longman & Todd, 1980), pp. 10–11.

Living at peace

To live at peace with others,
we have to leave them room
to love us or reject us,
to walk away or come.

To live at peace with others,
we have to leave them space
to question, challenge, know us,
oppose us to our face.

To live at peace with others,
we have to set them free
to choose to differ from us
in all they need to be.

Then, Prince of Peace among us,
come, help us to explore
new ways of love and living
as means to banish war,

and give us grace and wisdom,
while trying to be friends,
to use our inmost anger
for your creative ends.

Fred Kaan, *Planting Trees and Sowing Seeds* (Oxford: Oxford University Press/Carol Stream, Ill.: Hope Publishing Company, 1989), no. 12. © 1989 Hope Publishing Company for USA and Canada, and Stainer & Bell Ltd. for all other territories. Used by permission.

CHRISTMAS, SECOND PROPER

Isaiah 62:6–12	Titus 3:4–7
Psalm 97	Luke 2:(1–7) 8–20

Hear the angels sing

The frightened shepherds become God's messengers. They organize, make haste, find others, and speak with them. Do we not all want to become shepherds and catch sight of the angel? I think so. Without the perspective of the poor, we see nothing, not even an angel. When we approach the poor, our values and goals change. The child appears in many other children. Mary also seeks sanctuary among us. Because the angels sing, the shepherds rise, leave their fears behind, and set out for Bethlehem, wherever it is situated these days. The historic new beginning of 1990 [German reunification] does not represent the definitive farewell to the utopias, to spiritless life without angels, in which the poor shepherds are finally made invisible. On the contrary, we can now take the side of the poor without false compassion or distraction; we can become shepherds and hear the angels sing.

"Glory to God in the highest heaven,
and on earth peace among those whom God favors!"

Dorothee Soelle, *On Earth As in Heaven: A Liberation Spirituality of Sharing*, trans. Marc Batko (Louisville, Ky.: Westminster/John Knox Press, 1993), pp. 76–77.

A story from the community in Shepherds' Fields (Beit Sahour)

"We invited 25 Israeli families to come and spend the night with us, to share our homes and experiences. Our message was: 'Let us break bread not bones.' The visit was arranged for Friday night so that if the authorities discovered what was going on, nobody could travel back on the Sabbath.

"At 10am the next morning, the Jewish visitors were discovered by Israeli soldiers and told they were in danger, and should leave immediately. They refused. One of the visitors told the soldiers:

'For the first time in years, I slept well because I wasn't worried about Arabs
attacking me in my sleep!'"

Janet Morley, *Companions of God: Praying for Peace in the Holy Land*
(London: Christian Aid, 1994), p. 33.

An anti-carol

All they wanted was a shelter,
Just a place to call their own,
But there wasn't room to house them
In that overcrowded town:
For it seems the Welfare Service
Was the sort that soon breaks down.
So don't sing alleluia
And don't sing gloria!

They were strangers, Galileans,
And the man a carpenter,
Though not quite the helpless people
Who are permanently poor,
No one beckoned them to enter
As they knocked from door to door.
So don't sing alleluia
And don't sing gloria!

She was pregnant, more's the pity,
And her time was not far off.
It's the awkward complication
That upsets the planner's graph:
If it wasn't so pathetic
It would make the angels laugh.
So don't sing alleluia
And don't sing gloria!

As we know they found a lodging
In the backyard of an inn:
Not the best accommodation
She could have her baby in—

But it's all a God can hope for
When he's up against our sin.
So don't sing alleluia
And don't sing gloria!

But to know that his salvation
Is an all embracing care;
But to see what Christ is doing
And to find a way to share:
Is to sing our hymns and carols
As a challenge to despair.
Alleluia, alleluia
Alleluia, gloria!

Fred Pratt Green, in *The Hymns and Ballads of Fred Pratt Green*
(London: Stainer & Bell/Carol Stream, Ill.: Hope Publishing Company,
1982). © 1975 Hope Publishing Company for USA and Canada, and
Stainer & Bell Ltd. for all other territories. Used by permission.

Nativity scene

Some thirty years ago Fritz Eichenberg, the artist associated for so long with *The Catholic Worker*, published in those pages a wonderful and disturbing depiction of the nativity. In the center foreground lies the babe on hay and in swaddling clothes. Nestled round are an adoring donkey and a cow. Through the crossbeams above a star points down from the heavens. Hallmark, you would think, would snatch up the print for a comforting and conventional Christmas card.

But wait. A closer look through the archway reveals a village nearly off the edge of the frame. However, this is not the cozy skyline set on a Judean hillside as one might expect, but a bombed-out city in flames. One has the feeling that it's all coming this way, closing in on the child asleep, holy and innocent. Look again. Tucked beneath the hay is a soldier's helmet. He is born in a year of war, and violence is near.

This is a biblically accurate portrait. We suffer much from the static tableau of Christmas card and crèche. The biblical images of the incarnation are rendered flat and frozen. A quaint pastoral idyll is evoked.

Yes, the incarnation of Christ is a still point, a center for history, the presence of eternity in a moment of time. And the manger scene may signify well the dominion of Christ in creation, with all creatures gathered (at least by representation) and bowed down.

Nonetheless, it is a still point at the center of a furiously turning world, very nearly the eye of a hurricane, which implicates cosmic portents, the powers of history, forces marshalled and moving, threats and intrigues, journeys and exiles, and raging political violence. In our conventional manger scenes, these are pushed off the edge of the frame, out of sight and mind.

Bill Wylie Kellermann, *Seasons of Faith and Conscience*
(Maryknoll, N.Y.: Orbis Books, 1991), p. 141.

Christ the hope

South—North poles apart
East—West where do you start
    Men are killing—men are laughing
      Baby crying
        Mother sagging
    Youth are shouting
Children hungry
    Women slimming
Dole queue stretching
    Beer flowing
Bombs are sleeping quiet and waiting
    Church is singing
      Jesus weeping
        God is faithful to his people.
Be my eyes to see the suffering
    Love the children—feed their hunger
Be my hands and hold the dying
      Cleanse your ears and hear men speaking
    Strive for Peace—create some laughter
  Teach the young about the Master
      See my father and my mother
      hear my sister
        heal my brother

Sow each seed in expectation
    for Mary's child in adoration
    is Christ the Hope of every Nation.

Carys Humphreys, in *Dare to Dream: A Prayer & Worship Anthology
from Around the World*, ed. Geoffrey Duncan (London: Fount, 1995),
p. 130. © Carys Humphreys.

The Godward journey is a journey on which every individual is launched, all unknowingly, at birth.

Christopher Bryant

CHRISTMAS, THIRD PROPER

Isaiah 52:7–10   Hebrews 1:1–4 (5–12)

Psalm 98   John 1:1–14

God with us

"The Word was made flesh
and pitched a tent among us."

Not a temple, not a palace, but a tent,
pitched among us.
Eating our bread,
sharing our laughs,
crying our tears,
dying our death.

> Dorothy Brooker and others, *In Other Words: Worship Resources for Women's Groups* (Napier, New Zealand: Association of Anglican Women in the Diocese of Waiapu, 1993), p. 8. Used by permission.

Many words, one Word

Of old, God wrote a book by which in many words one Word has uttered. Today he has opened a book for us in which by one word many words are said. This is the book which has for its pages and for writing the word of the Father. The greatest of all books is the incarnate Son, because just as through writing words are joined to a page, so by assuming a human nature the Word of God is joined to flesh.

> Rupert of Deutz (c. 1070–1129), trans. Geoffrey Preston, in Geoffrey Preston, O.P., *Hallowing the Time: Meditations on the Cycle of the Christian Liturgy* (London: Darton, Longman & Todd, 1980), p. 54.

Hymn for the birthday of Jesus

My Lord, on this, Your day, that is near to us,
we have seen Your birth, that distant one.

Lord, let Your day be like You for us.

Let it be a means and a pledge of peace.

It is Your day that reconciled heaven and earth,

for on it the Heavenly One descends to the earthly ones.

. . . My Lord, Your day is great; let it not be diminished by us.

Let it have mercy on our follies, as is its custom.

And, my Lord, if every day pours forth Your forgiveness,

how much more will it increase on this day!

All of the days acquire glorious things

from the treasury of Your glorious day.

. . . In the winter that robs the branches of fruit,

the fruit sprang forth for us from the barren vine.

In the frost that stripped all the trees

a Shoot budded for us from the house of Jesse.

Ephrem the Syrian, from Hymn 4 on the Nativity, in *Ephrem the Syrian: Hymns*, trans. and introduction by Kathleen E. McVey (Mahwah, N.J.: Paulist Press, 1989), pp. 90 and 91. © Kathleen McVey 1989. Used by permission of Paulist Press. www.paulistpress.com.

Sing in jubilation

What does singing in jubilation signify? It is to realize that words cannot communicate the song of the heart. Just so singers in the harvest, or the vineyard, or at some other arduous toil express their rapture to begin with in songs set to words; then as if bursting with a joy so full that they cannot give vent to it in set syllables, they drop actual words and break into the free melody of pure jubilation. The *jubilus* is a melody which conveys that the heart is in travail over something it cannot bring forth in words. And to whom does that jubilation rightly ascend, if not to God the ineffable? Truly is he ineffable whom you cannot tell forth in speech; and if you cannot tell Him forth in speech, yet ought not to remain silent, what else can you do but jubilate? In this way the heart rejoices without words and the boundless expanse of rapture is not circumscribed by syllables.

Augustine of Hippo, from the *Second Discourse on Psalm 32 [33]*, in Dame Scholastica Hebgin and Dame Felicitas Corrigan, O.S.B. (trans.), *St. Augustine on the Psalms: Vol. II: Psalms 30–37*, Ancient Christian Writers No. 30 (Westminster, Md.: The Newman Press/London: Longmans, Green & Company, 1961), pp. 111–12.

Jesus shows us God

By his words and praxis, Jesus himself changed the content of the word 'God.' If we do not allow him to change our image of God, we will not be able to say that *he* is our Lord and our God. To choose him as our God is to make him the source of our information about divinity and to refuse to superimpose upon him our own ideas of divinity.

This is the meaning of the traditional assertion that Jesus is the Word of God. Jesus reveals God to us, God does not reveal Jesus to us. God is not the Word of Jesus, that is to say, our ideas about God cannot throw any light upon the life of Jesus. To argue from God to Jesus instead of arguing from Jesus to God is to put the cart before the horse. This, of course, is what many Christians have tried to do. It has generally led them into a series of meaningless speculations which could only cloud the issue and which prevent Jesus revealing God to us.

We cannot deduce anything about Jesus from what we think we know about God; we must now deduce everything about God from what we know about Jesus. Thus, when we say that Jesus is divine, we do not wish to *add* anything to what we have been able to discover about him so far, nor do we wish to *change* anything that we have said about him. To say now suddenly that Jesus is divine does not change our understanding of Jesus; it changes our understanding of divinity. We are not only turning away from the gods of money, power, prestige or self; we are turning away from all the old images of a personal God in order to find our God in Jesus and what he stood for.

Albert Nolan, *Jesus before Christianity: The Gospel of Liberation*
(London: Darton, Longman & Todd, 1977), pp. 136–37.

Humans and angels

My friends, let us take care not to let anything sordid defile us. In the eternal foreknowledge we are equal to God's citizens the angels. Let us claim our dignity by our way of life. We should not let dissipation corrupt us or base thoughts find us out. Wickedness shouldn't gnaw at our minds or envy consume us like rust. Pride shouldn't make us swell up or the search for earthly pleasures devour us or anger inflame us. Human beings have been called gods! You who are human, protect the dignity of God that is yours against vice: for your sake God became human!

Gregory the Great (c. 540–604), from a homily on Christ's birth (No. 8, 1–2), in an English version by John Leinenweber in John Leinenweber, *Be Friends of God: Spiritual Reading from Gregory the Great* (Cambridge, Mass.: Cowley Publications, 1990), p. 127.

Every creature is a divine word because it proclaims God.

Bonaventure

First Sunday after Christmas

1 Samuel 2:18–20, 26
Psalm 148

Colossians 3:12–17
Luke 2:41–52

Prayer

Lord of all power and might, let us not just suppose you to be of our company, but seek you out until we find you and rejoice in your presence; through Jesus Christ our Saviour, who lives and reigns with you and the Holy Spirit, one God, now and for ever. Amen.

David Adam, *Glimpses of Glory: Prayers for the Church Year (Year C)*
(London: SPCK, 2000), p. 16.

Parents and children

The greatest tragedy to me of my childhood is that everything that happened to me from about eight years old divided me from my parents. I mean they were not, how could they be, why should they be, very very well educated. They were intelligent people, they were working-class people, they were warm-hearted people, but everything I was interested in, everything that I became, everything that I learnt, made a huge gulf between them and me, and by the time I was in my twenties it was terribly difficult for me to communicate with them and for them to communicate with me. They were inordinately proud and supportive of me but we were like foreigners from different countries and it wasn't until much, much later (and they died a couple of years ago both in the same week) that I appreciated, I think, them and maybe they appreciated me, with the relaxation that comes with old age.

Sir Peter Hall in an interview with Professor Anthony Clare, in
Anthony Clare, *In the Psychiatrist's Chair* (London: Quality
Paperbacks Direct, 1992), p. 67.

The journey of Jesus

In the story of the losing and finding of the boy Jesus in the Temple the major obstacle to the journey of Jesus appears to be all that is meant by 'family.' Family gets Jesus to Jerusalem in the first, but it also tries to recover him prematurely once he had arrived. The day will come when it will try to prevent him returning there when it really matters. The experience that the *familiar* gets in the way is common to very many Christians. House, brothers, sisters, father, mother, children, are part of what Peter and the others had to leave in order to follow Jesus. The pattern goes back to Abraham, who had to leave his father and his father's house, and it goes on to our own time. It is the pattern of the dark night of mysticism and of the dark night of political involvement. Families are not ultimates. Of course, there can be no excuse for not following the Christian ways of justice and love with our families: but still, they are not absolutes. Modern psychology concurs with this when it suggests that we have to break with our families if we are to find ourselves. . . . Neither blood nor soil, neither nature nor nurture, can be allowed to have the last word in deciding who we are to be. We are not to allow any family to displace our direct and immediate relationship with God. The pilgrimage of Jesus led him to this discovery in the Jerusalem Temple when he was twelve years old. He found out that there was a higher claim on him than the claims of Mary and Joseph. For us, too, there is a sort of inbuilt principle of unpredictability in the Word of God that can divide our psyche from our true life. It can call us to something for which we are not programmed by our families, by all that is familiar to us. When it does call us, then we have to choose to save our lives or lose them, to remain settled or to involve ourselves with the destiny of Jesus of Nazareth, to join that pilgrimage to Jerusalem which was mapped out at his adolescence but trodden in deadly earnest in his manhood.

Geoffrey Preston, O.P., *Hallowing the Time: Meditations on the Cycle of the Christian Liturgy* (London: Darton, Longman & Todd, 1980), pp. 57–58.

Sing praise

God
who created
woman and man
to bear your image
and share your glory;
and through
a woman and a man
defeated all defeat
and set us free;

Renew in us
the faith of Mary,
the love of Jesus
and the joy of all
the saints;
that the creatures
of the earth
may sing your praise
for evermore. Amen.

Angela Tilby, in *Dare to Dream: A Prayer & Worship Anthology from
Around the World*, ed. Geoffrey Duncan (London: Fount Paperbacks,
1995), p. 97. © Angela Tilby.

The glory of God

It is . . . a doctrine of creation, properly understood, that grounds both our contemplation and our action. . . . We properly relate to God in gratitude and in
silence: before God, we can only celebrate the fact that we *are*, and are free to be
human with God for God and because of God; and wait without clear prediction
or absolute conceptual security for the further perception of and delight in God's
being God. Before the literally inconceivable fact of the divine difference and the
divine liberty, we have no words except thanksgiving that, because God's life *is
what it is*, we are. 'We give thanks to Thee for Thy great glory.' The contemplation
of God, which is among other things the struggle to become the kind of person
who can without fear be open to the divine activity, would not be possible if God
were seen as an agent exercising power over others, bending them to the divine

will. Contemplative prayer classically finds its focus in the awareness of God at the centre of the praying person's being—God as that by which I am myself—and, simultaneously, God at the centre of the whole world's being: a solidarity in creatureliness. It is the great specific against the myth of self-creation and isolated self-regulation. SaintJohn of the Cross speaks of the vision of God in the state of union as a vision of the creator, and thus of the beauty which each creature has of itself from God, as well as 'the wise, ordered, gracious and loving mutual correspondence' among creatures. To see God is to find place *in* this 'correspondence.' Contemplation, then, cannot properly be a prostration before a power outside us; it is a being present to ourselves *in* our world with acceptance and trust. Hence . . . the importance of attention to the praying *body*; the contemplative significance of taking time to *sense* ourselves in prayer, to perceive patiently what and where we materially are.

Rowan Williams, On Christian Theology (Oxford: Blackwell, 2000),
pp. 75–76.

Wonder is the basis of worship.

Thomas Carlyle

Glimpses of glory

God of the high and holy places
where I catch a glimpse of your glory,
above the low levels of life,
above the evil and emptiness which drags me down,
beyond the limits of my senses and imagination,
YOU LIFT ME UP.

In the splendour of a sunset,
in the silence of the stars,
in the grandeur of the mountains,
in the vastness of the sea,
YOU LIFT ME UP.

In the majesty of music,
in the mystery of art,
in the freshness of the morning,
in the fragrance of a single flower,
YOU LIFT ME UP.

Awe-inspiring God,
when I am lost in wonder
and lost for words,
receive the homage of my silent worship
but do not let me be content to bear your beauty and be still.
Go with me to the places where I live and work.
Lift the veil of reticence behind which I hide.
Give me the courage to speak of the things which move me,
with simple and unselfconscious delight.
Help me to share my glimpses of glory
until others are drawn to your light.

Jean Mortimer, in *Exceeding Our Limits: Prayer Handbook 1991* (London: United Reformed Church, 1991), March 10. © Jean Mortimer.

———————

The very act of praise releases the power of God into a set of circumstances and enables God to change them if this is his design.

Merlin R. Carothers

———————

Second Sunday after Christmas

| Jeremiah 31:7–14 | Ephesians 1:3–14 |
| Psalm 147:12–20 | John 1:(1–9) 10–18 |

The Word is made flesh

Leader: The Word was made flesh and lived among us
All: **Full of grace and truth, he lived among us**

Leader: When the glory of a sunset makes worshippers of people
When the High Street becomes holy ground
When there is room for things to grow
All: **The Word is made flesh and lives among us**

Leader: In attentive silence to another's story
In the first steps taken in forgiveness
In a disguise able to be left aside
All: **The Word is made flesh and lives among us**

Leader: In good bread on the table
In the loving embrace of a friend
In tears of anger for a homeless child
All: **The Word is made flesh and lives among us**

Leader: In a secret shared with confidence
In a child listened to with respect
In care that does not draw back from shame
All: **The Word is made flesh and lives among us**

Leader: When we put our money where our mouths are
When theory becomes practice
When intentions become actions
All: **The Word is made flesh and lives among us**

Leader: When the Word is made flesh and lives among us
All: **Satan has no power**

Kathy Galloway, in *Celebrating Women: The New Edition*, ed. Hannah
Ward, Jennifer Wild, and Janet Morley (London: SPCK, 1995),
pp. 103–4. © Kathy Galloway 1995.

A special tune

There is a story of a child who was taught a special tune in his native village. When he grew up and went out into the world, the rabbi said to him 'Don't forget the tune. But if you do forget it, then come right back home and learn it all over again.'

. . . There is a need to go beneath and behind and around our glib solutions to our terrible problems and perhaps select a much simpler and more primitive strand from the human heritage—the strand of wonder is the one that I suggest. Something that we observe in young children, and some of us remember from our own early childhood, is a capacity to find the world wonderful, to be reduced to breathless astonishment and joy by a flower or a tree or a stone, by something that shines or that emits a noise, by a vision of running water, or snow, or cloud or sun, by the movement of an animal or the flight of a bird, by the ringing of a bell or by the thump of a drum. Hidden in this experience, I suggest, is something even more wonderful than wonder, which is a capacity to find the world and the people in it sometimes numinous—to the baby at the breast the mother is numinous, to a child caught up in seeing its first Christmas tree the smell and the fragments of light and the brilliant colours are numinous, to a slightly older child a fairy at the pantomime may be numinous, to an adolescent or adult the person they are in love with may be numinous; it is only among those who have become dried and disappointed in life that numinosity is to be sought only in a direct experience of God. Our whole world shines with sacredness and we have forgotten how to see it; we have to learn from children, artists and primitive peoples for whom it has not yet become necessary to put God into a sort of isolation hospital.

Monica Furlong, from "Trying to Get Well: Trusting the God Who
Breaks In from the Future," in *20/20 Visions: The Futures of
Christianity in Britain*, ed. Haddon Wilmer (London: SPCK, 1992),
pp. 122, 124.

Dreams of an exile

The time when you feel least a stranger is when you return to yourself, even during your dreams, because when we dream I think we live more inside ourselves.

From time to time, I see in my dream a green hill—a hill of green grass where I spent time playing as a child, ten years old. That happened to be a place in northern Vietnam. And I have returned to that hill, that land, several times in dreams. Every time I leave, I leave things on that hill. I have grown trees here and there, and sometimes built something with the branches of the tree. Many dreams like that have been spaced in time. From time to time I have returned to that hill; and in the space between two dreams, the hill had grown. The hill is not a static image, it's growing like myself; and every time I come to the hill I see that's the place where I should be. And, each poem that I have written is in the form of a plant, a leaf, a flower.

Sometimes I meet friends in the form of a leaf or a plant or a tree. Each time I return I recognize these friends, and I see they have grown too. From time to time it has happened that something has stood in my way and I haven't been able to reach the hill. Very sadly I have returned, and each time like that I woke up with a feeling of sadness. Even in dreams you are not allowed to come back. I think the hill represents something like my homeland. And yet I know that homeland is not the hill where I played when I was ten. I know that if I were to go back and stand on that hill in northern Vietnam, I wouldn't say that it is the hill I have been dreaming of. One feels less a stranger when one returns to oneself, even in dreams.

Thich Nhat Hanh, in Thich Nhat Hanh and Daniel Berrigan, *The Raft Is Not the Shore: Conversations towards a Buddhist–Christian Awareness* (Maryknoll, N.Y.: Orbis Books, 2001 [originally published 1975]), pp. 52–53.

Dream

Behold, we know not anything;
I can but trust that good shall fall
At last—far off—at last, to all,
And every winter change to spring.

So runs my dream: but what am I?
An infant crying in the night:
An infant crying for the light:
And with no language but a cry.

Alfred, Lord Tennyson, *In Memoriam A. H. H.* (1950), from canto 54.

An upside-down Christmas

Carol our Christmas, an upside down Christmas:
snow is not falling and trees are not bare.
Carol the summer and welcome the Christ child,
warm in our sunshine and sweetness of air.

Sing of the gold and the green and the sparkle,
water and river and lure of the beach.
Sing in the happiness of open spaces,
sing a nativity summer can reach!

Shepherds and musterers move over hillsides,
finding, not angels, but sheep to be shorn,
wise ones make journeys, whatever the season,
searching for signs of the truth to be born.

Right side up Christmas belongs to the universe,
made in the moment a woman gives birth:
hope is the Jesus gift, love is the offering,
everywhere, anywhere, here on the earth.

Shirley Erena Murray, *In Every Corner, Sing* (Carol Stream, Ill.: Hope
Publishing Company, 1992), no. 2. © 1992 CopyCare International
for UK. © 1992 Hope Publishing Company for all other territories.
Used by permission.

Blessing

Go in peace,
for this is the gift of God to us all.
And may the God who spoke to an ordinary woman
speak in your life,
the God who came as a vulnerable child
touch you in your vulnerability,
and the Spirit join you in songs of joy.
Amen.

Dorothy McRae-McMahon, *Prayers for Life's Particular Moments*
(London: SPCK, 2001), p. 56.

EPIPHANY

Isaiah 60:1–6   Ephesians 3:1–12

Psalm 72:1–7, 10–14   Matthew 2:1–12

The gifts I bring

My singing heart, my days' doxology, my gold,
I bring for CELEBRATION.

My stillness, my glimpses of serenity, my frankincense,
I bring for MEDITATION.

My brokenness, my tears of rage and sorrow, my myrrh,
I bring for SACRIFICE.

Kate Compston, in *Bread of Tomorrow: Praying with the World's Poor*,
ed. Janet Morley (London: SPCK and Christian Aid, 1992), p. 58.
© Kate Compston.

We gentiles

Today's reading[s] lead us to reflect upon non-Jewish peoples, that is, the Gentiles, who are also brought to the fullness of grace in the Christian dispensation so that they become, as Paul says, "co-heirs with the Jews . . . sharers of the promise through the preaching of the gospel." . . . If this had not happened most of us would not be in the Church today. The wise men and women whom Matthew represents as coming to worship Jesus were probably Gentiles. They offered gold, frankincense and myrrh or as the gypsy in one of Robertson Davies' novels says, "Gold, frank innocence and mirth!" . . . Thus Epiphany is the feast *par excellence* of the universality of the Church.

J. Massyngbaerde Ford, *Days of the Spirit, Volume I: Advent to Lent*
(Collegeville, Minn.: The Liturgical Press, 1994), p. 88.

God's freedom

The power of tribalism has been drawn, and God's address to humankind is not in any way to be obstructed by it. Ethnicity, the diversity of people's origins, remains a fact within the community of faith but it has no determining influence on members' standing either before God or before the community. . . . The immense struggle which it took to accept this perception is in no way concealed in the New Testament. Specific issues within the life of the Church constantly raised the question of ethnicity. Which were the facts about people that belonged to their ethnicity: their history, culture, kinship, status and, indeed, their religion and morality? The life of the Church was to be built on the freedom of God to act irrespective of such matters. Which were the matters that belonged to the work of the Holy Spirit, addressing and converting people: the faith, hope, love and obedience that belonged to the heart of the gospel itself? On those there could be no compromise.

Peter Selby, *BeLonging: Challenge to a Tribal Church*
(London: SPCK, 1991), pp. 18–19.

From Psalm 72

Lord, judge your people in righteousness:
give justice to the oppressed.

Let the hills bring us prosperity:
the fruits of righteousness.

As long as the sun and the moon endure:
**let rain fall upon the mown fields,
let showers water the earth.**

Deliver the needy, who cry out for help:
the oppressed, who have no one to care for them.

Take pity on the poor and the helpless:
save them from death.

Rescue them from oppression and violence:
precious are their lives in your sight.

Bless the leaders of the people:
**let the people pray for them
and bless them every day.**

Let the harvests ripen throughout the land:
let corn ripple across the hills.

Let orchards and forests flourish:
let fields and pastures be beautiful.

Praise to the Lord our God:
praise his glorious name for ever!

Let the earth be filled with his glory:
Amen and amen!

Michael Perry, *Bible Prayers for Worship* (London: Marshall Pickering, 1997), pp. 143–44. Reprinted by permission of HarperCollins Publishers Ltd. © Michael Perry 1997.

Making the journey

Few people can make such a journey alone; even the shepherds needed to be encouraged by companions. Those who claim that finding and bearing the Christ child are easy may be on the wrong freeway. But when we finally see the lights of Bethlehem and see our star still shining there, after we have passed the last peaks and desert sands, then we see him lying there before us. We kneel and the sound of angelic music, the heavenly choir, breaks in on us, and we see the magnificent splendor, the ineffable glory of the Creator as a baby in a crib. Then we are embraced by divine love; we understand how little we have offered by our journey. The harbor is a million times worth the voyage.

Morton Kelsey, *The Drama of Christmas: Letting Christ into Our Lives* (Louisville, Ky.: Westminster John Knox Press, 1994), p. 64.

David's prophecy

David in Psalm 72 prophesies about our love for Christ and states it in three ways. He sings first: 'The kings of Tarshish and of the isles shall render tribute, and then

The kings of Sheba and Seba shall offer gifts.
Yea, all kings shall prostrate themselves before him.

Finally,

And blessed be His glorious name for ever;
And let the whole earth be filled with his glory.
Amen, and Amen. (Psalm 72:10, 19)

Such a deep love is rare enough. David expressed it powerfully and yet the truth is sometimes beyond words. Tribute, gifts, prostrated kings, glory that fills the whole earth, are only images and metaphors and however meaningful they still do not convey the fullness of mankind's love for Christ nor do they express the eternal love of the Father for His Son. We know there is no blessing outside Christ, no good thing that is not connected with Christ, no true happiness or bright future far from Christ.

Luis de Leon, *The Names of Christ*, trans. Manuel Duran and William
Kluback (London: SPCK/Mahwah, N.J.: Paulist Press, 1984), from
book 3, p. 327.

Epiphany

> There is a song in the air
> there is a star in the heavens
> there is a lowly stable
> there is a child to meet.
>
> Let us bring our gifts
> let us worship this child
> let us follow the light coming from where he sleeps
> let us seek blessing for our journey through the wilderness.
>
> May we be held in the palm of God's hand as we meet our Saviour
> may we keep the light before us.
>
> May we know the gift that the Christ child gives to us.
> May we know the love of the Messiah in our journeying!

Lisa Withrow, *Seasons of Prayer: Resources for Worship*
(London: SPCK, 1995), p. 81.

God-with-all-creation

The death of Jesus . . . shows to the world how alive God is, how actively God is involved in the saving work, and how vigorously God is engaged with human beings in their agony and suffering. The death of Jesus brings God close to the world—as close as God can be. It also makes God's presence in us real—as real as God can possibly be. The death of Jesus is the fulfillment of Immanuel, God-with-us, God-with-all-humanity, God-with-all-creation. God-with-all-nations-and-with-all-peoples is the meaning of the Word become flesh.

... Of course this God has been and will always be God for Israel and its people, but at the same time has always been and will always be God for all nations and all peoples. The God who caused the temple veil to tear in two is the God who is open to all, even to "pagans and gentiles."

Choan-Seng Song, *The Compassionate God: An Exercise in the Theology of Transposition* (London: SCM Press/Maryknoll, N.Y.: Orbis Books, 1982), pp. 94, 95.

Hymn for Epiphany

Son of the Father, born before time's dawn,
rise as our Daystar, hope of all the world.

O Star of Jacob, light of heav'n above,
light up our darkness, shine upon us all.

Kings, kneel in homage; give to Christ, your King,
gold, myrrh, and incense, faith and hope and love.

This day God's glory dawns on Zion's hill;
now shall all nations walk in Zion's light.

James Quinn, S.J., *Praise for All Seasons* (Kingston, N.Y.: Selah Publishing Company Inc. www.selhpub.com/London: Geoffrey Chapman, 1994), p. 8. Used by permission.

The woman's word

The wise ones knelt
to hear the woman's word
in wonder.
Holding up her sacred child,
her God in the form of a babe,
she said: "Receive and let
your hearts be healed
and your lives filled
with Love, for
this is my body,
this is my blood."

Alla Renée Bozarth, lines from "Before Jesus," in *Accidental Wisdom*, iUniverse.com, 2003.

First Sunday after Epiphany

(Baptism of the Lord)

Isaiah 43:1–7	Acts 8:14–17
Psalm 29	Luke 3:15–17, 21–22

Imago Dei

Jesus' baptism is the identifying "mark" of our discipleship. . . . In baptism, the Human One dies to the patriarchal forces which destroy the *imago Dei*. All hierarchical orders of sinful powers are washed away in the water. No question of walking on water here. Whoever accepts the baptism with which Jesus was baptized accepts the death of a socially structured identity and the resurrection of a free human being. *Imago Christi*.

Baptism is an enactment of liberation, effected by water and the Spirit. We are freed of our damaging debt to a Market mind-set, liberated from the tyranny of social location and inherited roles. In place of constricting labels, the community announces us as beloved of God, and pronounces our name.

Heather Murray Elkins, *Worshiping Women: Re-forming God's People for Praise* (Nashville: Abingdon Press, 1994), pp. 25, 26.

Reborn and unafraid

Lord of the Flood, wash us with your Spirit that we may be your ark of life, your peace in the sea of violence. Water is life; water cleans; water kills. Frightened, we are tempted to make a permanent home on the ark. But you force us to seek dry ground. We can do so only because you have taught us to cling to our baptisms, where we are drowned and reborn by the water and fire of your Spirit. So reborn, make us unafraid. Amen.

Stanley Hauerwas, *Prayers Plainly Spoken* (Grove, Ill.: InterVarsity Press, 1999; London: Triangle, 1999), p. 5.

The way of the servant

Living Christ,
this was *your* decisive moment.
Rising from the river of baptism
you began to discover
what it meant
to be committed
to the way of the servant.

In your moment
of seeing and hearing
the Spirit was preparing you for your mission:
you made the choice
and took the risk
of obedience
and the rippling reflection of a cross rose from Jordan.
In your baptism
you set the pattern for us;
help us to know,
and discover,
what it means
to be committed
to the way of the servant.

May your Spirit
open our eyes
and ears
that we may become
partners of your mission;
and in obedience,
take up the cross and follow you.

John Slow, in *Kneelers: Prayers from Three Nations,* Prayer Handbook
Advent 2001–2002, ed. Norman Hart (London: United Reformed
Church, 2001), p. 23. © United Reformed Church. Used by
permission of the publisher.

Pure water?

Since the beginning of the Christian era, theologians could take for granted that the water in its natural condition—rain, snow, running streams, lakes and oceans—was fresh, clean and life-giving. A book by Fred Powledge entitled *Water: The Nature, Uses and Future of Our Most Precious and Abused Resource* questions whether this assumption is still true. Much of the data, which I presented in my discussion of the polluted condition of water, both worldwide and in Ireland, raises the very same question. If the purity of water continues to deteriorate, will it still retain the power to symbolize new life and purification? This fear of destroying the symbolic power of water and other natural symbols should act as another spur to Christians to be particularly concerned about what is happening to our most precious resources. If the natural water systems, for example, are poisoned, water will come to symbolize death with no regenerative power. How can it then be an effective symbol for the transformative power of the life, death and resurrection of Jesus?

> Sean McDonagh, *To Care for the Earth: A Call to a New Theology*
> (London: Geoffrey Chapman/ Santa Fe, N.M.: Bear & Company,
> 1986), p. 171.

The water of life

Come to the waters,
all you that are thirsty:
children who need water
free from diseases,
women who need respite
from labour and searching,
plants that need moisture
rooted near the bedrock,
find here a living spring.
O God, may we thirst
for your waters of justice,
and learn to deny no one
the water of life.

> Janet Morley, in *Dear Life: Praying through the Year with Christian Aid*, ed. Janet Morley, Hannah Ward, and Jennifer Wild (London: Christian Aid, 1998), p. 78.

Dark ocean, light ocean

I was under great temptations sometimes, and my inward sufferings were heavy; but I could find none to open my condition to but the Lord alone, unto whom I cried night and day. And I went back into Nottinghamshire, and there the Lord shewed me that the natures of those things which were hurtful without, were within in the hearts and minds of wicked men. . . . And I cried to the Lord, saying, 'Why should I be thus, seeing I was never addicted to commit those evils?' And the Lord answered that it was needful I should have a sense of all conditions, how else should I speak to all conditions; and in this I saw the infinite love of God. I saw also that there was an ocean of darkness and death, but an infinite ocean of light and love which flowed over the ocean of darkness. And in that also I saw the infinite love of God; and I had great openings.

George Fox (1624–91), from his *Journal* (entry for 1647), ed. J. L. Nickalls (Cambridge: Cambridge University Press, 1952), p. 19.

For times of dryness

We ask your blessing mother God
on our times of dryness,
when the well of living water
seeps into barren land.

Help us to be, to listen in the waiting
for the still small voice
which speaks of promises unbroken
beneath our doubt and fear and forgetting.

And when the river returns to us, Creator God
teach us to praise the bounty of water,
to use its succour well, to succour others,
flowing with the love which comes from you.

Yvonne Morland, from *A Book of Blessings: And How to Write Your Own,* comp. Ruth Burgess (Glasgow: Wild Goose Publications, 2001), p. 86. Compilation © Ruth Burgess.

Blessing for those in distress

May you come safely to shore
across the dark ocean

and know
that even in the darkest depths

there is hope to be found
and peace.

Mary Taylor, in *A Book of Blessings: And How to Write Your Own*,
comp. Ruth Burgess (Glasgow: Wild Goose Publications, 2001), p. 91.
Compilation © Ruth Burgess.

SECOND SUNDAY AFTER EPIPHANY

| Isaiah 62:1–5 | 1 Corinthians 12:1–11 |
| Psalm 36:5–10 | John 2:1–11 |

Unity

We thank God for our unity in diversity:

There are different kinds of gifts:
but the same Spirit.

There are different kinds of service:
but the same Lord.

There are different kinds of working:
but the same God.

Praise to God almighty,
Father, Son and Holy Spirit,
who works in us
in all these ways. Amen.

Michael Perry, *Bible Prayers for Worship* (London: Marshall Pickering,
1997), p. 168. Reprinted by permission of HarperCollins Publishers
Ltd. © Michael Perry 1997.

Jesus learns from his mother

Jesus did not grow up in a vacuum. Jesus was nurtured and taught by a mother
who embodied his people's aspiration for liberation. Asian women theologians
claim that Mary announced 'what kind of messiah her son will be' through her
Magnificat. Mary's vision and life inspired Jesus. Mary's action in the wedding at
Cana (John 2) shows that 'she is a woman with all the compassionate sensitive-
ness to other people's needs, often lacking in men, especially those in power.' Asian
women assume that Mary became an exemplary human being who must have
mirrored her humanity to Jesus in the decisive years of his growth. 'From first
hand experience with his mother,' he was touched by her faith in God, her

historical consciousness, and her commitment to her people. Asian women name Mary's teaching to Jesus as 'compassionate justice':

> It was her [Mary's] openness and receptivity that Jesus showed when he made the blind see, healed the sick and dined with public sinners. It was her unambiguous solidarity with the poor he exercised when he shared their humble and oppressed lot. In his *compassionate justice* he put the good of humankind above the tyranny of perverted law in the same way she reached out to those who could not help themselves. In his fidelity to the perceived will of the Father, Jesus accepted the consequences of the cross (Jn. 2:1–12) just as she stuck it out with him through her darkest hour of life. Thus, if the scriptural image of Christ shows him to be the model of a new kind of humanity, then it would not be very wrong to say that Mary was his own model.

Chung Hyun Kyung, *Struggle to Be the Sun Again: Introducing Asian Women's Theology* (London: SCM Press, 1991; Maryknoll, N.Y.: Orbis Books, 1990), p. 79, quoting "Who Is Mary?" in *Proceedings: Asian Women's Consultation* (Manila: EATWOT, 1985), p. 155.

Footnote to John II.4

Don't throw your arms around me in that way:
    I know that what you tell me is the truth—
    yes I suppose I loved you in my youth
    as boys do love their mothers, so they say,
    but all that's gone from me this many a day:
    I am a merciless cactus an uncouth
    wild goat a jagged old spear the grim tooth
    of a lone crag . . . Woman I cannot stay.
Each one of us must do his work of doom
    and I shall do it even in despite
    of her who brought me in pain from her womb,
    whose blood made me, who used to bring the light
    and sit on the bed up in my little room
    and tell me stories and tuck me up at night.

R. A. K. Mason, *Collected Poems* (Christchurch, New Zealand: Pegasus Press, 1962), p. 58. Used by permission of The Hocken Library, Dunedin, New Zealand.

Cana

It might have been a neurotic's paradise,
With all that water there for endless washing,
The catering shaky, and most of us wondering
What sort of promise such a beginning held
For the couple's days and years. And then the wine
Ran out, clean out. What do you say—"One always
Likes to be moderate at these affairs"?—
When what you mean is, "There's more need than they
Can possibly provide for." Anyhow,
After a while they gave us wine in flagons,
The kind of thing it was a privilege
To drink, or think about. I still don't know
Where they had found it, how they bought it, why
They kept it until then. I do remember,
Late in the piece, a man who made some toasts
And drank as if he meant them, and the jars
For water, and the way they seemed to glow.

Peter Steele, *Marching on Paradise* (Melbourne, Australia: Longman
Australia Pty. Ltd. [now Pearson Education Australia], 1984). Used by
permission of the author.

"He saw to the supply of wine"

We can see that Baptism is a special sort of washing given to the Church and that the Eucharist is a special sort of eating and drinking. There is not in the same sense something called 'Christian marriage' which is a special sort of pairing. Christians have no right to colonize the marriage at Cana of Galilee as a Christian sacrament. It is worth reiterating that what 'Christ adorned and beautified with his presence' [1662 *Book of Common Prayer*] was a village wedding celebrated with folk rites. The bride and bridegroom were presumably unbaptized and uninstructed in Christian theology, and were subject to a law which allowed the bridegroom to divorce his wife if he found 'some unseemly thing in her.' As Austin Farrer pointed out, we are not told that the Lord preached to them their Christian duty: 'he saw to the supply of the wine.'

　　... Whatever we are supposed to learn from the story of the wedding at Cana about the wine of the Eucharist or the new wine of the Kingdom, the terms of reference and starting-point for all this exploration must be an ordinary human marriage.

Helen Oppenheimer, *Marriage* (London: Mowbray, 1990), pp. 59–60.

Seeing the glory

The first 'sign' of Jesus' glory in John's Gospel takes place at a wedding, and lifts the party to new heights. This 'sign' begins a series; John underlines the second one, too (4:54), and leaves us to work out the rest for ourselves. Though the point is debated, it seems likely that he intends the seventh (or perhaps it's the eighth, the first of a new sequence?) to be the resurrection. The present 'sign' takes place 'on the third day,' pointing forwards to that great fulfilment.

But of course Jesus' glory is fully revealed, as far as John is concerned, on the cross. There, when 'the hour has come' at last, Jesus' strange question (literally 'Woman, what is there to you and me?') is replaced by 'Woman, behold your son; son, behold your mother.' As at Cana Jesus takes the Jewish purification water and turns it into wine, so at Calvary he takes the Jewish Passover festival and transforms it into the great revelation-in-action of God's glory and love. . . . When we leave church . . . would people mistake us for wedding guests? As party-goers?

N. T. Wright, *Twelve Months of Sundays: Reflection on Bible Readings,*
Year C (London: SPCK, 2000), pp. 20–21.

When the wine of natural joy is spent and there is nothing left but the water of affliction, then doth Christ turn this water into wine.

Francis Rous (1579–1659)

Third Sunday after Epiphany

Nehemiah 8:1–3, 5–6, 8–10	1 Corinthians 12:12–31a
Psalm 19	Luke 4:14–21

Lives of passion

Without the ability to imagine, even just for a few moments, what life looks like seen through another's eyes, without the capacity to empathize with the pain or delight of another, to know that *there have I been, and there I am*, without the courage to go beyond the boundaries of our own self-interest, prejudices, cares, needs, and meet others without defences, how can we affirm, with Paul, that 'if one part of the body suffers, all the other parts suffer with it; if one part is praised, all the others share its happiness' (1 Cor. 12.26)? It is not just that we *have* bodies, we *are* a body, in which the divisions are the illusion and the barriers and the disease. Of all the divisions, the most damaging is that of one part of ourself from another part of ourself. As long as we are strangers to ourselves, then we will be deeply strangers to others. Sometimes it may be our experience of being deeply loved by another that will bring us home. Life is kinder than we let it be, for there are so many occasions for love, if we don't let fear overpower us. So many opportunities for healing, for wholeness, and all of them signs of the grace of God that desires to go on loving us and healing us and calling us home to ourselves and to each other. But without the facing of fear, even stumbling, even trembling, even sick to the pit of our stomachs, without these abandonments of jumping off the cliff into the arms of God, then we can only armour, repeat, retrench, self-protect, and whine at anyone who is different from us. And face lives without passion, without sap, without grace.

Kathy Galloway, *Getting Personal: Sermons and Meditations (1986–94)*
(London: SPCK, 1995), p. 23.

From Psalm 19

We see God's glory in the heavens:
the skies proclaim his skill.

Day after day, night after night: we see his wisdom on display:
all without voice or speech—
we hear no sound!

There is no language in which they cannot be understood:
yet their message reaches the ends of the earth.

Like a bridegroom arriving, like a champion athlete enjoying the race, is the
sun God has placed in the heavens; we see it rise in the east.
We see it set in the west:
nothing can be hidden from its heat.

God's law is perfect:
it renews our strength.

God's commandments are trustworthy:
they make the simple wise.

God's rules are right:
they bring joy to the heart.

God's insights are true:
they bring light to the eyes.

God's reign is holy:
it lasts for ever.

God's words are reliable:
they are absolutely right.

They are more precious than gold:
sweeter than honey.

Lord, all these are for our warning:
and for our reward when we obey you.

Rarely can we see our own failings:
Lord, forgive me for my hidden faults.

Free me from deliberate sins:
do not let them get a hold over me.

Lord, free me from the evil of sin:
make me holy.

O Lord, my refuge and my redeemer:
**let my thoughts and my words
always be acceptable to you. [Amen.**

**Glory be to God,
Father, Son and Holy Spirit,
for ever. Amen.]**

Michael Perry, *Bible Prayers for Worship* (London: Marshall Pickering,
1997), pp. 74–75. Reprinted by permission of HarperCollins
Publishers Ltd. © Michael Perry 1997.

Hearing the word of God

Really hearing the word of God is a moving experience. Think of the times when you have been deeply moved by the love of a friend, the death of a parent, the innocence of a child, the playfulness of a pet, the insight of a writer, the story of a preacher, a reading from scripture, a view from a mountain, the flight of a butterfly. I believe that the word of God comes in many forms, if only we have eyes to see, ears to hear, and hands to feel.

The people of Israel were deeply moved to hear the word of God addressed to them. Today widely diverse communities of faith hear the word of God in scripture personally addressed to them, and they too are moved.

A therapist friend once told me that tears are always a sign of grief. Even so-called "tears of joy" may represent some kind of grief: that joy is fleeting, that sorrow preceded the joy, that things should always be this way, that not everyone can share the joy. I believe it was tears not only of repentance but of joy that the people of Israel wept that day. That God would speak to *them!* And yet, in Yahweh's holy presence, how inadequate they felt, how many changes they wanted to make in their own lives and the life of their community.

But their spiritual leaders told them not to grieve about the past, but to take joy in God's strength, to eat and drink in celebration and send food and wine to others. May we also rejoice that we have heard God's words addressed personally to us, looking forward to the future rather than forlornly to the past. May we celebrate with food and drink and share our celebration with others.

Chris Glaser, *Reformation of the Heart: Seasonal Meditations by a Gay Christian* (Louisville, Ky.: Westminster John Knox Press, 2001), pp. 130–31.

I think the great difficulty about the *invisible* church is that one always chooses the members oneself. The invisible church is a kind of extension of the ego. The very essence of the church is that it is a visible body, and it is *one* body.

Lesslie Newbigin

An agenda for African spirituality

As an African and as a Christian, I need to contribute to the emergence of a relevant spirituality. The spiritual, it goes without saying, is central to all that we do. The God we worship is an extraordinary God, who dwells in light unapproachable, He is high and lifted up, and His train fills the temple. The angels and archangels and the whole host of heaven do not cease to worship and adore Him. Heaven and earth are full of His glory. He is the transcendent one who fills us with awe—the *mysterium tremendum et fascinans.* But He does not allow those who worship Him to remain in an exclusive spiritual ghetto. Our encounter with Him launches us into the world, to work together with this God for the establishment of His kingdom. This is a kingdom of justice, peace, righteousness, compassion, caring and sharing. We become agents of transfiguration, transformation and radical change. When Moses encountered God at the burning bush he heard the command, 'Go down to Pharaoh.' When Isaiah saw the Lord high and lifted up, it was to hear the summons 'Who will go for us?' When Jesus was baptised, He received the Spirit of God and it was this Spirit which propelled him into the wilderness to do battle with the evil one, and being anointed by the Spirit of the Lord meant being sent to preach the good news to the poor, the proclamation of release to those in captivity, and the year of the Lord's favour—a time when release was proclaimed to those indebted to others, and the return of the land to its rightful owner.

Desmond Tutu, from "Spirituality: Christian and African," in *Resistance and Hope: South African Essays in Honour of Beyers Naudé,* ed. Charles Villa-Vicencio and John W. de Gruchy (Grand Rapids: Wm. B. Eerdmans Publishing Co./Claremont, South Africa: David Philip, Publisher Pty., 1985), pp. 161–62.

The Canticle of the Sun

Most High, all-powerful, good Lord,
Yours are the praises, the glory, the honor, and all blessing.
To You alone, Most High, do they belong,
and no [one] is worthy to mention Your name.
Praised be You, my Lord, with all your creatures,
especially Sir Brother Sun,
Who is the day and through whom You give us light.
And he is beautiful and radiant with great splendor;
and bears a likeness of You, Most High One.
Praised be You, my Lord, through Sister Moon and the stars,
in heaven You formed them clear and precious and beautiful.
Praised be You, my Lord, through Brother Wind,
and through the air, cloudy and serene, and every kind of weather
through which You give sustenance to Your creatures.
Praised be You, my Lord, through Brother fire,
through whom You light the night
and he is beautiful and playful and robust and strong.
Praised be You, my Lord, through our Sister Mother Earth,
who sustains and governs us,
and who produces varied fruits with colored flowers and herbs.
Praised be You, my Lord, through those who give pardon for Your love
and bear infirmity and tribulation.
Blessed are those who endure in peace
for by you, Most High, they shall be crowned.
Praised be you, my Lord, through our Sister Bodily Death,
from whom no living [one] can escape.
Woe to those who die in mortal sin.
Blessed are those whom death will find in Your most holy will,
for the second death shall do them no harm.
Praise and bless my Lord and give Him thanks
and serve Him with great humility.

Francis of Assisi, in *Francis and Clare: The Complete Works*, trans. and
ed. Regis J. Armstrong, O.F.M. CAP, and Ignatius C. Brady, O.F.M.
(Ramsey, N.J.: Paulist Press, 1982), pp. 38–39. © Regis J. Armstrong
and Ignatius C. Brady 1982. Used by permission of Paulist Press.
www.paulistpress.com.

Fourth Sunday after Epiphany

Jeremiah 1:4–10	1 Corinthians 13
Psalm 71:1–6	Luke 4:21–30

Loving others

However trying we may find Paul's views on sex or the role of women, his defini-tion of *agape* is incomparable: that which is patient and kind, does not envy oth-ers, is not quick to take offence, keeps no score of wrongs, takes no pleasure in the sins of other people, delights in the truth. The opposite of love is not hate, but indifference, the failure to care—or to care enough. It is a want of imagination, a lack of empathy, an inability or a refusal to see in another human being a creature as frail and as easily hurt as I can be. Simone Weil wrote of how she loved the story of Perceval, who is the only Arthurian knight to attain the Grail because he was the only one to turn aside when it was within his grasp and ask its suffering guardian, 'What are you going through?' When someone is troubled, sick or dying, the caring love of people who also know themselves to be vulnerable has a strangely stabilising and anchoring power.

Michael Mayne, *Learning to Dance* (London: Darton, Longman & Todd, 2001), p. 195.

In artistic creation, as in human relationships, the authenticity of love is denied by the assurance of control. Love aspires for each that which, being truly an "other," cannot be controlled.

W. H. Vanstone

Made like unto us

And then our courteous Lord answered very mysteriously, by revealing a won-derful example of a lord who has a servant, and gave me sight for the under-standing of them both. . . . The servant stands before his lord, respectfully, ready to do his lord's will. The lord looks on his servant very lovingly and sweetly and mildly. He sends him to a certain place to do his will. Not only does the servant go, but he dashes off and runs at great speed, loving to do his lord's will. And soon he falls into a dell and is greatly injured; and then he groans and moans and tosses about and writhes, but he cannot rise or help himself in any way. And of all this, the greatest hurt which I saw him in was lack of consolation, for he could not turn his face to look on his loving lord, who was very close to him, in whom is all consolation; but like a man who was for the time extremely feeble and foolish, he paid heed to his feelings and his continuing distress. . . .

I was amazed that this servant could so meekly suffer all this woe; and I looked carefully to know if I could detect any fault in him, or if the lord would impute to him any kind of blame; and truly none was seen, for the only cause of his falling was his good will and his great desire.

Julian of Norwich, *Showings*, chap. 51 (Long Text), in *Julian of Norwich: Showings*, trans. and introduction by Edmund Colledge, O.S.A., and James Walsh, S.J. (New York: Paulist Press, 1978), pp. 267–68.

Mister God

When you're little you 'understand' Mister God . . . later on you understand him to be a bit different. . . . Even though you understand him, he doesn't seem to understand you! . . . In whatever way or state you understand Mister God, so you diminish his size. . . .

So Mister God keeps on shedding bits all the way through your life until the time comes when you admit freely and honestly that you don't understand Mister God at all. At this point you have to let Mister God be his proper size and wham, there he is laughing at you.

Fynn, *Mister God This Is Anna* (London: Collins, 1974), p. 118.

Another prophet

[The boy] Tarwater clenched his fists. He stood like one condemned, waiting at the spot of execution. Then the revelation came, silent, implacable, direct as a bullet. He did not look into the eyes of any fiery beast or see a burning bush. He only knew, with a certainty sunk in despair, that he was expected to baptize the child he saw and begin the life his great-uncle had prepared him for. He knew that he was being called to be a prophet and that the ways of his prophecy would not be remarkable. His black pupils, glassy and still, reflected depth on depth his own stricken image of himself, trudging into the distance in the bleeding stinking mad shadow of Jesus, until at last he received his reward, a broken fish, a multiplied loaf. The Lord out of dust had created him, had made him blood and nerve and mind, had made him to bleed and weep and think, and set him in a world of loss and fire to baptize one idiot child that He need not have created in the first place and to cry out a gospel just as foolish. He tried to shout, "NO!" but it was like trying to shout in his sleep. The sound was saturated in silence, lost.

Flannery O'Connor, The Violent Bear It Away (London: Faber
Paperbacks, 1980 [1955]), pp. 91–92.

You know the politicians will always ask the question "Is it expedient?" then the question "Is it right?" but the prophets ask the question "Is it right?" The Church must keep asking the question "Is it right?"

Jesse Jackson

The new route

Telling of a visit made some years ago to Archbishop Janani Luwum in Uganda, an English bishop describes sitting with his host on the verandah of the archbishop's house in Kampala a few weeks before Janani was killed; and speaks of the archbishop telling him that for some time now he had had to travel home each day by a different route to avoid being shot. The visitor suggested to the archbishop that for his own safety's sake he ought perhaps to consider leaving the country. A foolish and unworthy suggestion, reminiscent of Peter's words to Jesus, and one that he came to regret. The archbishop replied that in this re-ordering of his life, with all the uncertainties that it had brought, God had been at work in his heart. 'Every day I have been broken before him,' he said. 'How could I leave my people at this time?' 'And,' recalled the visitor, 'as he spoke those words his face shone with grace and power; this man who had been broken every day.' . . .

   This story gives sharp edge to 'the new route' that many Latin American Christians have felt called to follow in recent years; a new route which for them . . . also carries with it the real possibility of suffering and death. . . . For Jesus and his disciples this new route was inaugurated at his baptism, testing in the wilderness and proclamation in the synagogue at Nazareth; and led by a number of circuitous paths into desert places, up a mountain, across the lake; whilst healing, teaching, preaching and doing good wherever he went. Sometimes this involved back-tracking, taking alternative routes and rejecting the ways others would have him go.

John Carden, *A Procession of Prayers: Meditations and Prayers from Around the World* (London: Cassell/Geneva: WCC Publications, 1998), p. 114.

Prayer

O Lord, let the shelter of your wings give us hope. Protect us and uphold us. You will be the Support that upholds us from childhood till the hair on our heads is grey. When you are our strength we are strong, but when our strength is our own we are weak. In you our good abides for ever, and when we turn away from it we turn to evil. Let us come home at last to you, O Lord, for fear that we be lost. For in you our good abides and it has no blemish, since it is yourself. Nor do we fear that there is no home to which we can return. We fell from it, but our home is your eternity and it does not fall because we are away.

Augustine of Hippo, *Confessions*, book 4, chap. 16, in *Saint Augustine: Confessions*, trans. and introduction by R. S. Pine-Coffin (Harmondsworth, Middlesex: Penguin Books, 1961), pp. 89–90.

FIFTH SUNDAY AFTER EPIPHANY

Isaiah 6:1–8 (9–13)   1 Corinthians 15:1–11
Psalm 138   Luke 5:1–11

Haunted by God

"All my life I have been haunted by God," a character in one of Dostoevsky's books says. And that is the way it was for me.

≈

It began out in California, where the family had moved from New York a year before. We were living in Berkeley in a furnished house, waiting for our furniture to come around the Horn. It was Sunday afternoon in the attic. I remember the day was very chilly, though there were roses and violets and calla lilies blooming in the garden. My sister and I had been making dolls of the calla lilies, putting rosebuds for heads at the top of the long graceful blossoms. Then we made perfume, crushing flowers into a bottle with a little water in it. Even now I can remember the peculiar, delicious, pungent smell.

And then I remember we were in the attic. I was sitting behind a table, pretending I was the teacher, reading aloud from a Bible that I had found. Slowly, as I read, a new personality impressed itself on me. I was being introduced to someone and I knew almost immediately that I was discovering God. . . .

Of course I had heard of Him previous to this. Before we moved to California, my older brothers and I had gone to school in Bath Beach, and there every morning the teacher read something from the Bible and we bowed our heads on the desk and recited the Lord's Prayer. I had forgotten that until this moment of writing. It did not impress me then, and I remember now simply raising my head after the prayer to watch my breath fade upon the varnished desk.

Dorothy Day, in *Dorothy Day: Selected Writings: By Little and By Little*, ed. and introduction by Robert Ellsberg (Maryknoll, N.Y.: Orbis Books, 1999; first published 1983 by Alfred A. Knopf), pp. 9–10.

Homewards

Oh, that dreadful limiting of salvation! How can anyone who does it dare to take Our Lord's name on their lips again. As if His presence had not been with thousands who knew not who it was they entertained. You are right—we are *all* too narrow for God—and yet, to steer a clean course between bigotry and indifferentism is none too easy sometimes—for me, anyhow. But I cling to St. Paul—and seem to find his inmost teaching over and over again in all one's experience, and in everyone who cares for Christ—Catholic or Protestant or whatsoever he may be. Is it not amazing when one can stand back from one's life and look back down it—or still more, peep into others' lives—and see the action of the Spirit of God: so gentle, ceaseless, inexorable, pressing you bit by bit whether you like it or not towards your home? I feel this more and more as the dominating thing—it seems so odd that everyone does not feel and notice it happening, don't you think?

> Evelyn Underhill, from a letter dated 15 May 1911, in *The Letters of
> Evelyn Underhill*, ed. Charles Williams (London: Longmans, Green &
> Co., 1943), pp. 126–27.

Prophetic word

The prophetic word of criticism is addressed to the dominant community, but it will not be heard. . . . The prophetic word of energy is addressed never to the dominant community but only to those who are denied the pseudo-energy and power of the royal consciousness. . . . The ministry of Jesus, like the ministry of Second Isaiah, happens in the space between the clinging and the yearning. If there is only clinging, then the words are only critical. If there is yearning, there is a chance that the words are energizing. The staggering works of Jesus—feeding, healing, casting out, forgiving—happened not to those who held on to the old order but to those who yearned because the old order had failed them or squeezed them out.

> Walter Brueggemann, *The Prophetic Imagination*, 2d ed.
> (Minneapolis: Fortress Press, 2001), p. 111.

Verses for a commissioning of lay people for ministry

There is one body and one Spirit, just as you have been called in the one hope of your calling: one Lord, one faith, one baptism. Make your way in the world worthy of your calling.

Those who are planted in the house of the Lord
shall flourish in the courts of our God.
They shall bear fruit and abound in fresh growth.

Jesus said, 'I am the Vine, you are the branches. Whoever abides in me and I in them bears much fruit.'

The Book of the Gospels is held open before those to be commissioned. They may be sprinkled with holy water as all may say or sing:

Alleluia, your Word is a lamp to my feet, O Lord.
Alleluia, come to my help and I shall be safe.
Alleluia, visit us with your salvation, O Lord.

Alleluia, you have handed on to us the commandment to have your heart of love: do not forsake the work of your hands.

Brian Pickett, *Songs for the Journey: The Psalms in Life and Liturgy*
(London: Darton, Longman & Todd, 2002), pp. 47–48. © Darton,
Longman & Todd Ltd., 2002. Used by permission of the publishers.

The majesty of God

How shall I sing that majesty
    which angels do admire?
let dust in dust and silence lie;
    sing, sing, ye heavenly choir.
Thousands of thousands stand around
    thy throne, O God most high;
ten thousand times ten thousand sound
    thy praise; but who am I?

Thy brightness unto them appears,
    whilst I thy footsteps trace;
a sound of God comes to my ears,
    but they behold thy face.
They sing because thou art their Sun;
    Lord, send a beam on me;
for where heav'n is but once begun
    there alleluias be.

How great a being, Lord, is thine,
   which doth all beings keep!
Thy knowledge is the only line
   to sound so vast a deep.
Thou art a sea without a shore,
   a sun without a sphere;
Thy time is now and evermore,
   thy place is everywhere.

John Mason (c. 1645–1694)

The prayer of praise

One form of prayer that may help make the presence of the Risen Savior more real in your life and give you a reassuring sense of being supported and surrounded by God's loving providence, is the Prayer of Praise. It can bring you great peace and joy. This simple form of prayer consists of thanking and of praising God for everything whatever in your life. Its basis is the belief that nothing happens in your life that is not, or at least cannot be turned to God's glory—absolutely nothing, not even your sins—not even the murder of Jesus Christ.

When you have repented, you can praise God even for your sins because he will draw great good from them. Saint Paul encourages his disciples the Romans as follows, "Where sin increased, grace overflowed all the more." Again, he said, "What then shall we say? Shall we persist in sin that grace may abound? Of course not" (Rom. 5:20; 6:1). But having given thanks to God for your sins and his deliverance from them, you can learn to praise God for them. Peter surely repented his denial of Jesus and the fact that he was too weak to be a source of support to Jesus on his way to Calvary.

Too often people carry a lifelong burden of guilt in their hearts for sins they have committed. Even when convinced of God's forgiveness, many are unable to shake off their feeling of guilt. If you can express heartfelt thanks and praise to God for having sinned, you may feel that all is well, that all is in God's hands, and that your labors will be fruitful as a result.

James W. Skehan, S.J., *Place Me with Your Son: Ignatian Spirituality in
Everyday Life*, 3rd ed. (Washington, D.C.: Georgetown University
Press, 1991), p. 160.

I do not like to address God like some sort of sleepy donkey who really ought to wake up. I think God is mystery—loving mystery . . . a profound and depthless mystery, with whom we can have communion, but whom we cannot exactly comprehend.

Richard Holloway

Sixth Sunday after Epiphany

Jeremiah 17:5–10	1 Corinthians 15:12–20
Psalm 1	Luke 6:17–26

Words

Sometimes people today have difficulty with the words 'the poor' and 'the weak.' The gospel message talks about 'the poor' and this is frequently interpreted as the 'economically poor.' But a person without work and a parent who has lost a child are also poor. The poor person is one who is in need, who recognises this need and cries out for help. Weakness is frequently considered a defect. But are we not all weak and needy in some way? We all have our vulnerable points, our limits and our handicaps. When we recognise our weaknesses, we can ask for help; we can work together.

> Jean Vanier, *Our Journey Home: Discovering a Common Humanity beyond Our Differences*, trans. Maggie Parham (London: Hodder & Stoughton, 1997), pp. xvii–xviii.

With all our heart

'That was a beautiful prayer,' a voice called to me as I finished praying with one of my congregation. I crossed the hospital ward to meet a Jewess recovering from an operation, and, struggling to think of some appropriate response, I suggested we unite in saying the Hebrew *Shema*:

> 'Hear, O Israel: the Lord our God, the Lord is One.
> And you shall love the Lord your God
> with all your heart, and with all your soul,
> and with all your might.'
> (Deut. 6:4–5; cf Mk. 12:29–30)

It says it all. The oneness of God which we need to know and seek to show is found in the love of the heart. It is in the heart that we must stand before heaven and meet with God. Heart speaks to heart.

The heart here is not a souvenir shop of all our past sentimentality nor a barometer of our moods and emotions. It is the focus and centre of our whole life: our understanding and perception, our will and energy, our whole personality. The heart is where the Kingdom comes, where God's will is done and heaven is found on earth, because the heart is where we offer our whole selves to God.

Brian Pickett, *The Heart of Love: Prayers of German Women Mystics*
(Slough: St. Paul Publications, 1991), pp. 1–2.

The world of the poor

Beyond any possible doubt, the life of the poor is one of hunger and exploitation, inadequate health care and lack of suitable housing, difficulty in obtaining an education, inadequate wages and unemployment, struggles for their rights, and repression. But that is not all. Being poor is also a way of feeling, knowing, reasoning, making friends, loving, believing, suffering, celebrating, and praying. The poor constitute a world of their own. Commitment to the poor means entering, and in some cases remaining in, that universe with a much clearer awareness; it means being one of its inhabitants, looking upon it as a place of residence and not simply of work. It does not mean going into that world by the hour to bear witness to the gospel, but rather emerging from it each morning in order to proclaim the good news to every human being. . . .

We see with increasing clarity that it takes a great deal of humility for persons to commit themselves to the poor of our day. In this effort one experiences what Luis Espinal translated into a prayer in which he sought to express the mystery of life:

> Lord, a thin drizzle of humility is penetrating. We are not the axis of life, as our self-centeredness falsely claimed. . . . We travel through life like blind persons; we did not choose life before embarking on it, nor do we know the day when we will depart from it. . . . Life is larger than we are, and your ways extend beyond the horizon of our vision.

Gustavo Gutiérrez, *We Drink from Our Own Wells: The Spiritual Journey of a People*, trans. Matthew J. O'Connell (Maryknoll, N.Y.: Orbis Books/London: SCM Press, 1984), pp. 125–26.

The Lord speaks

Do not be afraid! It is not a high ideal or a lofty moral standard that I put before you and that you know yourself to be quite incapable of realising. I am not lecturing you. I know you too well. Agreed, you are a sinner, you are worthless, you don't know how to love or do great deeds. But don't you understand? That has no importance. I love you exactly as you are. I have taken your weaknesses upon myself, I shared them, all except your sin. . . . You are going to say that nothing in you seems changed. But yes, everything is changed, at a deeper level than that where you usually look. . . . Your weaknesses remain, so that my power in you may appear as coming from me and your pride may not appropriate it. The effort, the risk, the responsibility of your freedom remain . . . so that you may come to me of your own accord. . . . Your powerlessness to love truly with all your heart, that will also remain, but only to the extent that you must learn to climb the road of love, as a human being, a creature who makes himself, little by little, and above all, to the extent that you still have not learned not to count on your own strength to love, so that you let me love in you.

A Carthusian, *From Advent to Pentecost: Carthusian Novice Conferences*, trans. Carmel Brett (London: Darton, Longman & Todd, 1999), pp. 143–45.

The beatitude of truth

Witness to the fact that the Holy Spirit still continues to work even in our day . . . was given to my wife and me only three weeks ago. A Danish man with whom we have recently become friends was describing to us his experience in 1945 as a teenager in the Danish underground. He was captured by the Gestapo, and they tortured him in an effort to extract from him the names and plans of his underground comrades. Unlike almost everyone else in that situation, he did not pretend that he did not know of their names and future plans. 'Yes,' he said, 'I do know them. But you yourself must realise that I cannot tell you.' And so after further threats and torture, he was placed in the death-cell to await execution. Alone in the cell, so he told us, he had no fear, but was filled with such peace that is beyond human understanding—and his cell itself was completely filled with light—the light of the Holy Spirit. For us that was a sign that our friend had indeed received the Holy Spirit, the Consoler, who is promised to those who mourn for the truth's sake.

Donald Nicholl, *The Beatitude of Truth: Reflections of a Lifetime*, ed. Adrian Hastings (London: Darton, Longman & Todd, 1997), p. 11.

Dangerous memory

Jesus' vision burned through the external systems to the anxious human heart that lay beneath them and called for its transformation into a perfection of love. It is the impossibility of the vision, its eschatological hopelessness, that is the most compelling thing about it. . . . The Church exists to preserve the dangerous memory of a man who warned us against the idolatrous power that places its own survival before pity and truth, but it long ago gave up the attempt to order itself by the sublime impossibility of his vision.

Richard Holloway, *Doubts and Loves: What Is Left of Christianity*
(Edinburgh: Canongate, 2001), pp. 193–94, 234.

A cup of blessings

I found Trevor [a handicapped member of the L'Arche Daybreak community] in the hospital grounds, as always, looking for flowers. When he saw me his face lit up, and he ran up to me as if we had never been apart and said: "Henri, here are some flowers for you." Together we went to the [dining room]. The table was beautifully set, and about twenty-five people had gathered around it. Trevor and I were the last to sit down. . . .

People were making small talk. Many of the guests were strangers trying to get to know each other. The general atmosphere was quiet, somewhat solemn. . . . But suddenly Trevor stood up, took his glass of Coke, lifted it, and said with a loud voice and a big smile: "Ladies and gentlemen . . . a toast!" Everyone dropped their conversation and turned to Trevor with puzzled and somewhat anxious faces. I could read their thoughts: "What in the heck is this patient going to do? Better be careful."

But Trevor had no worries. He looked at everybody and said: "Lift your glasses." Everyone obeyed. And then as if it were the most obvious thing to do, he started to sing: "When you're happy and you know it . . . lift your glass. . . ." As he sang, people's faces relaxed and started to smile. Soon a few joined Trevor in his song, and not long after everyone was standing, singing loudly under Trevor's direction. . . .

Trevor's toast radically changed the mood in the Golden Room. He had brought these strangers together and made them feel at home. His beautiful smile and his fearless joy had broken down the barriers between staff and patients and created a happy family of caring people. With his unique blessing, Trevor had set the tone for a joyful and fruitful meeting. The cup of sorrow and joy had become the cup of blessings.

Henri J. M. Nouwen, *Can You Drink the Cup?* (Notre Dame, Ind.:
Ave Maria Press, 1996), pp. 65–66.

The ways of God

We praise you, Lord, that you have searched for us with humbleness,
We praise you, Lord, that you have cared for us with tenderness,
We praise you, Lord, that you have adorned us with lowliness,
We praise you, Lord, that you have guided us with gentleness,
We praise you, Lord, that you have ruled us with wiseness,
We praise you, Lord, that you have guarded us with powerfulness,
We praise you, Lord, that you have hallowed us with greatness,
We praise you, Lord, that you have counselled us with trustfulness,
We praise you, Lord, that you have lifted us to new heights with your love.

Mechtild of Magdeburg, in *Ein Vliessendes Licht der Gotheit:
Offenbarungen der Schwester Mechtild of Magdeburg,* ed. P. Gall Morel
(Regensburg, 1869), I, 6; trans. Brian Pickett in *The Heart of Love:
Prayers of German Women Mystics* (Slough: St. Paul Publications,
1991), pp. 36–37. © St. Paul Publications 1991.

Seventh Sunday after Epiphany

Genesis 45:3–11, 15   1 Corinthians 15:35–38, 42–50

Psalm 37:1–11, 39–40   Luke 6:27–38

Be merciful . . .

There should not be any brother in the world who has sinned, however much he may have possibly sinned, who, after he has looked into your eyes, would go away without having received your mercy, if he is looking for mercy. And if he were not to seek mercy, you should ask him if he wants mercy. And if he should sin thereafter a thousand times before your very eyes, love him more than me so that you may draw him back to the Lord. Always be merciful to such as these.

> Francis of Assisi, from "A Letter to a Minister," sent. 9, in *Francis and Clare: The Complete Works*, trans. and introduction by Regis J. Armstrong, O.F.M. CAP, and Ignatius C. Brady, O.F.M. (New York: Paulist Press, 1982), p. 75. © 1982 Regis J. Armstrong and Ignatius C. Brady. Used with permission of Paulist Press.

A father's prayer upon the murder of his son

O God,

We remember not only Bahram but also his murderers;

Not because they killed him in the prime of his youth

And made our hearts bleed and our tears flow,

Not because with this savage act they have brought further disgrace on the name of our country among the civilized nations of the world;

But because through their crime we now follow thy footsteps more closely in the way of sacrifice.

The terrible fire of this calamity burns up all selfishness and possessiveness in us;

Its flame reveals the depth of depravity and meanness and suspicion, the dimension of hatred and the measure of sinfulness in human nature;

It makes obvious as never before our need to trust in God's love as shown in the cross of Jesus and his resurrection;

Love which makes us free from hate towards our persecutors;

76

Love which brings patience, forbearance, courage, loyalty, humility,
    generosity, greatness of heart;
Love which more than ever deepens our trust in God's final victory and his
    eternal designs for the Church and the world;
Love which teaches us to prepare ourselves to face our own day of death.

O God,
Bahram's blood has multiplied the fruit of the Spirit in the soul of our
    souls;
So when his murderers stand before thee on the day of judgment
Remember the fruit of the Spirit by which they have enriched our lives,
And forgive.

Hassan B. Dehqani-Tafti, *The Hard Awakening* (London: Triangle,
1981), pp. 113–14.

A scary word

When we live according to our fears and our hates, our lives become small and
defensive, lacking the deep, joyous generosity of God. If you find some part of
your life where your daily round has grown thin and controlling and resentful,
then these texts are for you. Life with God is much, much larger, shattering our
little categories of control, permitting us to say that God's purposes led us well
beyond ourselves to live and to forgive, to create life we would not have imagined.

The story of Joseph is an affirmation about providence. "Providence" is scary
to "can-do" Americans. We fear we will lose free will and moral responsibility and
all of that. But consider, it will not do to reduce life to our moral calculus, because
we become grim and selfish and too sure, and then we die. The counterword on
the lips of Joseph and in the life of Jesus in the very heart of the gospel is this:

> You need not die. God has sent me to keep you alive.

The terms of life, however, are other than our own. They are the terms of the generous, merciful, giving, forgiving God. This God invites us to that new life, a second look, and a second life, forgiving, forgiven.

Walter Brueggemann, *The Threat of Life: Sermons on Pain, Power, and
Weakness*, ed. Charles L. Campbell (Minneapolis: Fortress Press,
1996), pp. 15–16.

Practical forgiveness

Joseph was not the nicest sibling you could hope to have. . . . But he didn't deserve to be seized by his brothers, roughed up, dumped down a well, and sold into slavery in a distant land.

. . . You remember how the story goes: Joseph rises, against all odds, to become the most powerful person in Egypt. . . . [His brothers] don't recognize [him] in his Egyptian clothes (even finer than what their father had given him long before), but he recognizes them. When he discovers that they still feel guilt over what they did to him, he is overcome with emotion.

And then he sets them up. He deals strictly but decently with them, and he sets up a situation in which they have to repeat the decision of earlier years. His little brother Benjamin is now their father's pet. What will the other brothers do with *him?*

. . . When push comes to shove, they prove to have changed. They walk through the door Joseph has opened for them, even though they don't in fact understand who has opened it. . . .

What Joseph did may seem like rather a hardheaded kind of forgiveness, but there's nothing wrong with that. It was completely genuine, and it opened the door to a shared future. That's all that's important. . . .

You may be thinking, "Yes, but doesn't Jesus set up a higher standard? Turning the other cheek. Going the extra mile. Ultimately, suffering martyrdom. Isn't that quite a different matter from this very practical approach to forgiveness?" Well, actually, no.

. . . Turning the other cheek doesn't mean complete passivity. It means we are not in a hurry to judge, that we give others the benefit of the doubt at first. It is a kind of test: Did you really mean that slap, or was it an act of passion that bypassed your mind and heart? Will you do it again, once it's been called to your attention? Turning the other cheek is a question addressed to the wrongdoer.

L. William Countryman, *Forgiven and Forgiving* (Harrisburg, Pa.:
Morehouse Publishing, 1998), pp. 67–69.

Transformed by love

Someone already transformed by love is needed, in order to convey an assurance of love sufficiently strong to penetrate the defences of the flesh in another and let loose the power of the spirit. This is the work of the community of love, but the particular group of human beings cannot, in itself, do this unless it has within it the power of renewal, which cannot reside in any one individual, at the risk of foundering when he founders, and of endangering even his own ability to love. Sometimes one person, sometimes another, can find the courage to go on, and so renew the rest. It happens in a marriage, it happens in a group. But the source of this courage is not the person himself, or herself. It is recognized as coming from the thing *shared*. It may be one person who renews faith, but it is not faith in himself that he renews but just faith—the given-ness, that at-riskness, of love. Even when faith is renewed by one person providing support, for a while, for the other or others, it is still support for the sake of love, or it doesn't work. Support given out of self-confidence becomes possessive, and does not allow further growth. Support given for love is willing to see the support no longer needed. So whatever form the renewal of faith takes it is the renewal of something shared. The centre, the heart of it, is never possessed but always given.

But this thing that is given is immensely powerful. . . . This [power] is the power that transforms.

Rosemary Haughton, *The Transformation of Man: A Study of
Conversion and Community* (London: Geoffrey Chapman, 1967),
pp. 114–15.

They say best men are molded out of faults,
   And, for the most, become much more the better
   For being a little bad.

William Shakespeare, *Measure for Measure*, 5.1.[440–42].

---

*Eleanore Milardo uses the spelling "Godde" to distinguish the object of her devotion
from the very male, patriarchal concepts surrounding the word in its usual spelling.*

Joy

   Joy is to be Goddes intention
   joy is a great big space
   open to the world

   joy is the space felt deep within
   formed by recognizing
   the dark and light in me

Godde then makes me a new creation
"new" in the realm of Godde
allowing now for abundant fruit

"I will not drink again of the fruit
until I drink it new in the realm of God"

Joy is the "New" in the realm of Godde
Joy is "Jesus drinking again of the fruit"

EIGHTH SUNDAY AFTER EPIPHANY

Isaiah 55:10–13   1 Corinthians 15:51–58
Psalm 92:1–4, 12–15   Luke 6:39–49

Don't change

I was a neurotic for years. I was anxious and depressed and selfish. Everyone kept telling me to change.

I resented them, and I agreed with them, and I wanted to change, but simply couldn't, no matter how hard I tried.

What hurt the most was that, like the others, my best friend kept insisting that I change. So I felt powerless and trapped.

Then, one day, he said to me, "Don't change. Don't change . . . I love you as you are."

I relaxed. I came alive. And suddenly I changed!

Now I know that I couldn't really change until I found someone who would love me whether I changed or not.

Is this how you love me, God?

Anthony de Mello, *The Song of the Bird* (New York: Doubleday, 1982).

A beautiful lesson

When I was in Bangladesh, I learned a beautiful lesson. After I had given a conference for a group of parents and friends of people with handicaps, a man got up. 'My name is Dominique,' he said. 'I have a son, Vincent, who has a severe handicap. He was a beautiful child when he was born, but at six months he had a terribly high fever which brought on convulsions. It affected his brain and his nervous system. Now, at sixteen, he has a severe mental handicap. He cannot walk, or talk, or eat by himself. He is completely dependent. He cannot communicate, except through touch. My wife and I suffered a lot. We prayed to God to heal our Vincent. And God answered our prayer, but not in the way that we expected. He has not healed Vincent, but he has changed our hearts. He has filled my wife and myself with joy at having a son like him.' Reality is not always changed. But by a gift of God, our barriers and preconceived ideas fall, doors are opened within us.

A new strength surges up permitting us not only to accept reality but to live it peacefully and even to love it.

Jean Vanier, Our Journey Home: Rediscovering a Common Humanity
beyond Our Differences, trans. Maggie Parham (London: Hodder &
Stoughton, 1997), pp. 166–67.

"All the trees of the field . . ."

Trees give me a 'functional' spirituality and theology. I spent twenty years thinking spirituality was 'up there' in the sky and that anything spiritual or holy was passed down from on high. This seems to me to be the classical approach of the church and its religious teaching. In fact most things that come 'down' to us in life with any intensity or force are things we need to avoid, like lightning, falling trees, monsoon rain or meteorites.

When I look at the world I see that life rises. The smallest seed rises from the soil and starts to climb. Rain rises from the ocean before it can fall. We are born helpless, and then with other creatures start our struggle to develop and grow. Trees teach me that life is dynamic and heroic. Each spring the sap rises: life force defying the odds. Everywhere there is a rising and falling of life in endless cycles, but it is the push upwards, against gravity and entropy, that is the exciting, surprising aspect of it. This teaches me not to sit waiting, head bowed in humble submission for blessings to arrive, but to walk tall and push against the sky.

Kirsten Hellier, "To Push Against the Sky: Trees, Mud and Music," in
Wrestling and Resting: Exploring Stories of Spirituality from Britain
and Ireland, ed. Ruth Harvey (London: Churches Together in Britain
and Ireland, 1999), p. 125.

Love at work

[God] shows me too that creating the truly human home, the human neighbourhood, the human city and a human world is about the reality of love at work in small as well as large things. The woman who takes the bank clerk a birthday cake in appreciation of his services, the *Big Issue* seller who gives his takings to the street collection for refugees in the Sudan, the Rastafarian youngster who guides a disabled white lady across an icy road, the bus conductor who always wishes his passengers 'a nice day': these, as well as the acts of the great and the good, are the very stuff of a truly human society, the sort of world which God loves and Christ lived for. Irenaeus *was* right: 'The glory of God is the human person fully alive.'

. . . And what of *eternal* life? . . . All I can say is that for me eternal life must be about the reality which lies at the heart of the universe. . . . If 'in the end' it is not faith or hope which are 'the greatest' but love, anything beyond this life of which I may be a part will be rooted and grounded in that love. In that love I trust, for myself and others whoever they are, Christians or not. My task, though much remains a mystery, is to go on practising as best I can how to love and be loved.

> David Clark, "From Mountain to Multitude," in *Wrestling and Resting: Exploring Stories of Spirituality from Britain and Ireland*, ed. Ruth Harvey (London: Churches Together in Britain and Ireland, 1999), pp. 132, 133.

Overcoming death

We're paying more attention to dying than to death. We're more concerned to get over the act of dying than to overcome death. Socrates mastered the art of dying; Christ overcame death as 'the last enemy' (1 Cor. 15:26). There is a real difference between the two things; the one is within the scope of human possibilities, the other means resurrection. It's not from *ars moriendi*, the art of dying, but from the resurrection of Christ, that a new and purifying wind can blow through our present world. *Here* is the answer to ['Give me somewhere to stand and I will move the earth']. If a few people really believed that and acted on it in their daily lives, a great deal would be changed. To live in the light of the resurrection—that's what Easter means. Do you find, too, that most people don't know what they really live by? This *perturbatio animorum* [disturbance of spirit] spreads amazingly. It's an unconscious waiting for the word of deliverance, though the time is probably not yet ripe for it to be heard.

> Dietrich Bonhoeffer, *Letters and Papers from Prison: The Enlarged Edition*, ed. Eberhard Bethge, trans. Reginald Fuller, Frank Clarke, and others; with additional material trans. John Bowden (London: SCM Press, 1971), pp. 240–41.

Life must be lived

> I have begotten life and taken away
> Life lent to others. I have thought of death,
> And followed Plato to eternity,
> Walked in his radiant world; have trod the fields

My fathers' sins have trampled richly down,
Loam warmed by a sun that burns at the world's heart,
Sol of the underworld. My heart is steady,
Beats in my breast and cannot burn or break,
Systole and diastole for seventy years.

Set up the bleak worn day to show our sins,
Old and still ageing, like a flat squat herd
Crawling like sun on wall to the rim of time,
Up the long slope for ever.

                    Light and praise,
Love and atonement, harmony and peace,
Touch me, assail me; break and make my heart.

> Edwin Muir, from "Soliloquy," in *Edwin Muir: Collected Poems*, 2d ed.
> (London: Faber & Faber, 1984), pp. 196–97. © 1960 Willa Muir.
> Used by permission of Faber & Faber Ltd. and Oxford
> University Press, Inc.

Made in God's image

Human beings made in God's image could appropriate their heritage as sub-creators: makers as well as contemplators. People would still ask 'What shall I do?' and even struggle to find the best answer; but their struggles would not be sinful struggles with one another but strenuous efforts to glorify God as excellently as possible. To praise our Creator who at great cost has made all this possible would be to enter into an infinite diversity of value.

> Helen Oppenheimer, *Making Good: Creation, Tragedy and Hope*
> (London: SCM Press, 2001), p. 124.

Getting acquainted with death

Now that my mother's older, she speaks louder and I couldn't help hearing her on the telephone. An elderly admirer of hers had died and his son was breaking it gently to her. 'Oh, he died on Monday,' boomed my mother in deep distress. 'And the funeral's on Friday.' She paused and then said briskly, 'Now, what's news?' How that son's jaw must have dropped! Later on I explained to him that my mother wasn't being evasive; her Father in heaven has the same warm indulgent love for her as her Yiddish father and mother on earth. So, like many Jews, she dislikes death but doesn't fear it and has no time for hell, even for her enemies. I have inherited her matter-of-factness.

A lady complimented me on my pastry. 'You can't beat marble for rolling it out,' I said enthusiastically. 'Cadge a bit of tombstone from the stonemason!' Well, she had another cuppa but no more cake.

Now, I don't want to put you off your food too, but death is the one certainty for us all, so it's prudent to get acquainted. . . .

I'm not trying to glamorise death. I dislike pain and all the functions of the body are messy, whether it's birth, death, making love or masticating food, but a foretaste of your own mortality brings a lot of benefits. It makes you appreciate the present, stops you hoarding, and helps you work out what's worthwhile and what's silly in your life, which is very practical.

Lionel Blue, *Tales of Body and Soul*
(London: Hodder & Stoughton, 1994).

Last Sunday after Epiphany

(Transfiguration Sunday)

Exodus 34:29–35	2 Corinthians 3:12–4:2
Psalm 99	Luke 9:28–36 (37–43)

A feast of light?

Too often we think of the Transfiguration as a feast of light only, one that dazzles like the sun reflected off the mothering sea. Too often we seek to fix our feet in light alone, unrealistically or pridefully thinking that our transformation has reached a point where we will not be burned by uncreated light. . . .

The story of the Transfiguration is surrounded by darkness: it is no mere ecstatic vision. It is surrounded by losing one's life to gain it, by denial of prophets, by being tossed between fire and water by the fits of our sins writhing under the light of God, and in the end by the glory of crucifixion.

Mere ecstatic vision is vain and ephemeral, and if like Peter we wish to fix our feet in that light, we will perish.

Maggie Ross, *The Fountain and the Furnace* (Mahwah, N.J.:
Paulist Press, 1987), p. 154.

Transfiguring light

Before I joined the Franciscans, I lived for a year with the Community of the Transfiguration in Roslin, near Edinburgh. At that time the community had charge of the Sunday eucharist in the famous and mysterious Roslin Chapel. I say 'mysterious' because I felt some strange influences there—a place where light and darkness seemed in conflict. There were some dark stories about the Battle of Roslin and the bloodshed which was carried into the church of that time, and down into the crypt.

It was the crypt which was most solemn in its light and darkness. You became aware of the descent below ground level, and if there was no heat it was both dark and damp. But as you descended, you were faced with a glorious window, the base of which was at ground level, while you further descended into the crypt. It depicted the wonderful light and colour of the transfiguration, the effulgent Christ radiating rays of glory towards the dazed disciples, while underneath were the words: 'In Your light shall we see light.' I felt a creepy sense of historical darkness in that crypt, but also a theological and spiritual sense of glory.

Our text is like that. It is a place of dazzling glory, but also of impending darkness, for here it is that Jesus sets his face and heart toward the cross. Here it is that law and prophet in the person of Moses and Elijah appear in glory, and speak with him about his exodus, the passion which he was to accomplish at Jerusalem.

Brother Ramon, *When They Crucified My Lord: Through Lenten Sorrow to Easter Joy* (Oxford: The Bible Reading Fellowship, 1999), pp. 37–38.

Confession

If we have believed that we have seen
the only Christ and all of Christ:
Forgive us and open our eyes,
O God who is beyond our seeing.

When we believe that the word
is only heard in truth in our own church:
Forgive us and open our ears,
O Spirit who is beyond our knowing.

If we have stopped looking for you
in surprising places and unexpected people:
Forgive us and open our hearts,
O Christ, who is beyond our imagining.

Dorothy McRae-McMahon, *Prayers for Life's Particular Moments* (London: SPCK, 2001), pp. 10–11.

Seeing the world as one

You never enjoy the world aright, till the Sea itself floweth in your veins, till you are clothed with the heavens, and crowned with the stars: and perceive yourself to be the sole heir of the whole world, and more than so, because men are in it who are every one sole heirs as well as you. Till you can sing and rejoice and delight in God, as misers do in gold, and Kings in sceptres, you never enjoy the world.

Till your spirit filleth the whole world, and the stars are your jewels; till you are as familiar with the ways of God in all Ages as with your walk and table; till you are intimately acquainted with that shady nothing out of which the world was made: till you love men so as to desire their happiness, with a thirst equal to the zeal of your own; till you delight in God for being good to all: you never enjoy the world. Till you more feel it than your private estate, and are more present in the hemisphere, considering the glories and the beauties there, than in your own house: Till you remember how lately you were made, and how wonderful it was when you came into it: and more rejoice in the palace of your glory, than if it had been made but to-day morning.

Thomas Traherne (1637–74), *Centuries*, 29 and 30 (First Century)
(London: The Faith Press, 1963), pp. 14–15.

Transfiguration

Was it a vision?
Or did we see that day the unseeable
One glory of the everlasting world
Perpetually at work, though never seen
Since Eden locked the gate that's everywhere
And nowhere?

Edwin Muir, from "The Transfiguration," in *Edwin Muir: Collected
Poems*, rev. ed. (London: Faber & Faber, 1984), p. 199. ©1960 Willa
Muir. Used by permission of Faber & Faber Ltd. and Oxford
University Press, Inc.

Sermon on 6 August
(kept as the Feast of the Transfiguration and Hiroshima Day)

The light of the transfiguration shines on the church, and in that light we can see many shadows—for the church follows the world so often, in that glory belongs not to selfless achievement, but to petty ambition—and the church on which falls the mantle of Christ's authority is rent apart by conflicting authorities.

This feast reminds us who are the church, how urgent is the task of prayer for the church—that we may learn what makes for true glory—a life of selfless love in obedience to the authority of the Lord Jesus Christ.

On this day, we must go further, and view our world, God's world, in the light of Christ's transfiguration. On this day in 1945 a blinding light shone on the city of Hiroshima, the light which accompanied the exposure of an unsuspecting population to shock and radiation from that first nuclear explosion. However the bomb may be justified strategically, politically—it has to be seen as a judgment not on its victims but on the rest of the human race—in its light we can see the worth of human values.

> Brother Anselm, S.S.F., *Sermons Preached at the Sung Eucharist, St.*
> *Bene't's Church, Cambridge* (privately printed, no date), pp. 18–29.

Fear of the unknown

O Lord, we beseech thee to deliver us from the fear of the unknown future; from fear of failure; from fear of poverty; from fear of bereavement; from fear of loneliness; from fear of sickness and pain; from fear of age; and from fear of death. Help us, O Father, by thy grace to love and fear thee only, fill our hearts with cheerful courage and loving trust in thee; through our Lord and Master Jesus Christ.

> Akanu Ibaim, Nigeria, in Desmond Tutu, *An African Prayer Book*
> (London: Hodder & Stoughton/New York: Doubleday, 1996), p. 104.

Without a veil

> Our needy souls sustain
> With fresh supplies of love,
> Till all thy life we gain,
> And all thy fulness prove,
> And, strengthen'd by thy perfect grace,
> Behold without a veil thy face.

> John Wesley (1703–91)

The cloud imports both Majesty and Obscuration . . . if a light to cheer us, we must have a cloud to humble us.

> Joseph Hall (1574–1656)

Ash Wednesday

Joel 2:1–2, 12–17

Psalm 51:1–17

2 Corinthians 5:20b–6:10

Matthew 6:1–6, 16–21

Ashes

—powdery-grey
from keeping on trying
to get a spark from two stones

—streaky black
from relighting a candle
that keeps going out

—soft white
from a fire that burned down to its heart
and kept everyone warm

these are the ashes worth wearing.

© Kathy Galloway, *Coracle* 3, no. 12 (1992).

Fasting

There is [a] way, perhaps a surprising one, in which we can improve our relationship with food, and that is through fasting. Many people are not aware of the positive aspects of fasting. They see it primarily as a tool for losing weight or as an ascetic discipline that means little in today's world.

A one-day juice fast, though, can give us a more objective awareness of eating. Afterward we are more alert to the tendency to consume food mindlessly. When we break the fast, we taste food as if for the first time. The natural flavor of an apple, a banana, or an orange, for example, comes alive in our mouth after a fast.

Fasting also wakes us up to our inner life. By temporarily paying less attention to food, we reconnect with a deeper hunger. Instead of being led by desires, we see that we have the freedom to live our life according to an ultimate sense of truth. Through the ages holy men and women fasted not because they disliked food or wanted to inflict pain on themselves, but because they wanted to stay connected with the love that they found within.

Wayne Simsic, *Pray without Ceasing: Mindfulness of God in Daily Life*
(Winona, Minn.: St. Mary's Press, 2000), p. 79.

The meaning of fasting

The most searching and profound prayer any of us can make is to eat our dinner. To eat at all is to recognize—if we are humble enough to admit it—our total dependence.

The trouble is that, in the West, something frightful has happened to our attitude to food. For all sorts of economic and other reasons our appetite for food is grossly overstimulated, with the result that many of us over-consume it.

I find that there are three levels on which I need to tackle the problem.

On the first level I need to 'tune in' much more patiently and attentively to what my body is saying to me about its hunger or lack of it. Over the years I have developed the dangerous trick of using food to achieve other ends apart from fulfilling simple physical needs—to tranquillize me when I am anxious, to cheer me when I am sad, to pep me up still further when I am jolly. In the end it is hard to know any longer whether I am hungry or not, hard too to break out of 'automatic' eating at regular times.

The next level is what we actually *do* about reforming our eating habits. I recently decided that I wanted to shake up my ideas about food from top to bottom, trying to throw modish ideas about slimming out of the window but to cherish the cross little infant inside me whose fierce rebellion has stymied more than one sensible eating plan; working mainly from the idea of what my body *needs*, in terms of nutrition, but also respecting what it *likes*.

The third level on which we have to care about food . . . is on the political level. What has to be redeemed here is the uncaringness, the cynicism, the blind commercialism which affects on the one hand the hungry millions but also the way food is prepared, marketed and advertised here. In this area, as in others, our need to learn to love matter is part of the kit for survival.

To fast is to learn to love and appreciate food, and one's own good fortune in having it.

Monica Furlong, in *The Church Times*, 4 March 1983. Reprinted by
permission of the author.

Choose

Leader:	Choose this day whom you will serve;
All:	**we will choose the living God.**

Leader:	The road is narrow that leads to life;
All:	**we will walk the way of Christ.**

Leader:	Faith is not our holding on;
All:	**faith is letting go.**

Leader:	We offer more than words, O God;
All:	**we offer you our lives.**

Brian Woodcock, from an Ash Wednesday Service, Michael Chapel,
Iona, in *Lent & Easter Readings from Iona*, ed. Neil Paynter (Glasgow:
Wild Goose Publications, 2002), p. 18. © Brian Woodcock.

Choose life, choose love

This poem/hymn was written on 6 July 1985 for the Choose Life Conference in Uppsala.

Choose life, choose love—the hour is late!
Say 'yes' to Christ and 'no' to fate.
Join hands with people of the faith,
reach out in hope to all who live.

In seeking space and life for each,
we need to practise what we preach,
to turn into creative deeds
the inner urges of our creeds.

With Christ-the-Least, renouncing power,
we face the challenge of this hour,
we rise against the death of earth,
the end of life, the end of birth.

The hour is late! Choose life, choose love,
with Christ into God's future move:
life to the full, the earth a feast,
through making, speaking, *being* peace!

Fred Kaan, *The Only Earth We Know* (London: Stainer & Bell Ltd.
Carol Stream, Ill.: Hope Publishing Company, 1999), p. 93. © 1989

Hope Publishing Company for USA and Canada, and Stainer & Bell
Ltd. for all other territories. Used by permission.

First love

Grace must come before sin can be confessed but Christians are not always good
at affirming God's love for themselves or anyone else. The Church, by its nature
and calling, attracts people who are aware of their own insecurity, lovelessness and
failure. Though religion should be a way to work through these experiences, insecurity may opt for a safer, rigid discipline of worship and behaviour which
represses difficulties and drives us to repress others whose openness threatens us.

More than any other, Psalm 51 has come to express our need of forgiveness and
it begins with the love of God, expressed in that combination of enduring faithfulness (*hesdh*) and the compassion that wells up from a mother's womb (*rah-
mim*).

> Have mercy on me, O God,
>   according to your faithful love:
>   according to the abundance of your mother-love,
>   blot out my transgressions.
>
> *Psalm 51.1*

Here is the lasting commitment of a caring parent who cannot stop loving. . . .

Love is the antidote to the disintegration of our personality. If we see ourselves
and our sins only in our own light or in the opinion of the friends we choose to
agree with us, we have chosen the road to self-despair. . . . The philosopher Martin Buber understood that we only discover our own identity in our friendship
and conversation with God, for 'all real living is meeting.' The believer is free to
grow in their knowledge of truth because they have not imposed their own conditions.

Brian Pickett, *Songs for the Journey: The Psalms in Life and Liturgy*
(London: Darton, Longman & Todd, 2002), pp. 70–71. © Darton,
Longman & Todd Ltd., 2002. Used by permission of the publishers.

Invocation for Lent

Into a dark world
a snowdrop comes
a blessing
of hope and peace
carrying within it
a green heart
symbol of God's renewing love

Come to inhabit our darkness
Lord Christ, for dark and light
are alike to you

May nature's white candles of hope
remind us of your birth
and lighten our journey
through Lent and beyond

Kate McIlhagga, in *The Pattern of Our Days: Liturgies and Resources for Worship*, ed. Kathy Galloway (Glasgow: Wild Goose Publications, 1996), pp. 115–16. © Kate McIlhagga. Used by permission of Donald McIlhagga.

Hypocrites we are: but we are on the way to liberation even from our own hypocrisy.

Charles Elliott

First Sunday in Lent

Deuteronomy 26:1–11	Romans 10:8b–13
Psalm 91:1–2, 9–16	Luke 4:1–13

The temptation to become someone other than ourselves

[Satan] is no archfiend seducing Jesus with offers of love, wealth, and carnal pleasures. Satan's task is far more subtle. He presents Jesus with well-attested scriptural expectations which everyone assumed were God's chosen means of redeeming Israel. Satan throws up to Jesus the collective Messianic hopes, and by so doing brings them for the first time to consciousness as options to be chosen rather than as a fate to be accepted. Tested against his own sense of calling, they did not fit. Jesus could perceive them to be "yesterday's will of God," not what was proceeding out of the mouth of God.

Satan offers him, in short, not outright evils but the highest goods known to Israel. That is when the satanic is most difficult to discern—when it offers us the good instead of the best. That does not mean Satan is benign. By no means! We have so moralized him that we fail to see that the most satanic temptation of all is the temptation to become someone other than ourselves. When people try to be "good Christians"—what is that but Satan's crowning victory? For "being a good Christian" is always collectively defined by some denomination or strong religious personality or creed. One does not need to "live by every word that proceeds from the mouth of God" in order to be a "good Christian"; one need only be pliant, docile, and obedient. Is it not easier to "let Jesus do it all for us," or imitate Christ, rather than embark on the risky, vulnerable, hazardous journey of seeking to find God's will in all its mundane specificity for our own lives? That harder way will certainly entail mistakes and failures, false starts, and sin masquerading as innovation. Perhaps the collective way is better—but what am I doing, my friends? With whose voice am I speaking?

Walter Wink, *Unmasking the Powers: The Invisible Forces
That Determine Human Existence* (Philadelphia:
Fortress Press, 1986), pp. 18–19.

And lead us not into temptation, but deliver us from evil

Don't let surface things delude us,
But free us from what holds us back
(from our true purpose).

Don't let us enter forgetfulness,
the temptation of false
appearances.

(To the fraud of inner vacillation—
like a flag tossed in the wind—
alert us.)

But break the hold of unripeness,
the inner stagnation that
prevents good fruit.

(From the evil of injustice—
the green fruit and the rotten—
grant us liberty.)

Deceived neither by the outer
nor the inner—free us to
walk your path with joy.

Keep us from hoarding false wealth,
and from the inner sham of
help not given in time.

Don't let surface things delude us,
But free us from what holds us back.

Prayers of the Cosmos: Meditations on the Aramaic Words of Jesus,
trans. and with a commentary by Neil Douglas-Klotz (San Francisco:
HarperSanFrancisco, 1990), p. 34. © 1990 Neil Douglas-Klotz.
Reprinted by permission of HarperCollins Publishers Inc.

Temptations, when we first meet them, are as the lion that roared upon Samson; but if we overcome them, the next time we see them we shall find a nest of honey within them.

John Bunyan

The companionship of difference

When I came to work in Northern Ireland as a Chaplain at Queen's University Belfast, I quickly discovered that working within my denomination's Chaplaincy buildings was a very effective way of institutionalising Northern Ireland's sectarian divide. With the other Chaplains we formed the Inter Chaplaincy Group, where Catholics and Protestants could explore together those topics which are taboo for polite conversation in 'mixed' company: religion and politics. We went to Corrymeela and the 'safe place' they offered for such a meeting was a powerful liberation for the students and Chaplains alike.

Soon after that experience, I became a member of the Corrymeela Community. Corrymeela has 180 members, Catholics and Protestants who commit themselves to follow the path of reconciliation. The importance is that the exploration is ecumenical, whereas the context in which we live, and the attitudes which form our actions, are so often sectarian. To join Corrymeela is to choose an alternative context for our life. Corrymeela members are not free of sectarianism, violence, rivalry and scape-goating which represent the fault line of fear which runs between Protestant and Catholic communities here. But when we find that our 'instinctive reactions' are hurting valued friends from the 'other' community, we are given an opportunity to change. We discover that prejudice is not just 'other people's problem,' but is lying deep and hidden within our hearts; that attitudes which are as normal as the air we breathe within our own communities contain the elements of fear, hatred and violence. We need to bring the enemy close, to walk with them, and be changed by their company, if either of us is to find the path to peace.

Ecumenical spirituality is living with the companionship of difference and discovering freedom, together. . . .

The experience among members and at the Corrymeela Centre has altered my spirituality. Christian Community can no longer be a grouping of the like-minded. It is a group defined by a single focal point, Jesus Christ, rather than a circle which is defined by its circumference, when the emphasis is on who is inside the line and who is outside. . . . Ecumenical spirituality encourages us to recognise the differences between us, and discover that those differences can be a cause for celebration, rather than a source of fear.

Trevor Williams, in *Wrestling and Resting: Exploring Stories of Spirituality from Britain and Ireland*, ed. Ruth Harvey (London: CTBI, 1999), pp. 184–86. © Trevor Williams and CTBI 1999.

"Lent"

Lent is a time to learn to travel
Light, to clear the clutter
From our crowded lives, and
Find a space, a desert.
Deserts are bleak: no creature
Comforts, only a vast expanse of
Stillness, sharpening awareness of
Ourselves and God.

Uncomfortable places, deserts.

Most of the time we're tempted to
Avoid them, finding good reason to
Live lives of ease; cushioned by
Noise from self-discovery,
Clutching at world's success
To stave off fear.
But if we dare to trust the silence
To strip away our false security,
God can begin to grow his wholeness in us,
Fill up our emptiness, destroy our fears.
Give us new vision, courage for the journey,
And make our desert blossom like a rose.

Ann Lewin, from *Candles and Kingfishers: Reflections on the Journey* (Ann Lewin, 1993; Peterborough: Methodist Publishing House, Foundery Press, 1997). © Ann Lewin 1997. Reprinted by permission of the publishers.

From the heart

Let the Lord see that we are prepared to let him do what he likes with us. Our cry to God comes from the depths of our heart and so is part of our simplest self-knowledge. We should learn to recognise it. . . . We must consent to it. Pay attention to it. Not let ourselves be distracted from it. If our cry to our father in heaven is in the depths of our heart, this is because we are living in communion with Christ. What is deepest in us only lives in and through this communion, it does not belong to us alone. We should live believing in Christ who lives in us.

If the Lord is really everything to us, this means he must be present in our whole life. We should live this simply trusting in his grace. It is a gift. We must humbly accept it in peace and trust. Our trust leads us towards the mystery of God, leads us to live in its light. Our act of faith brings us a peace which, even if we can hardly feel it, is like no other peace, because it comes from God.

Metropolitan Anthony and Georges Lefebvre, O.S.B., *Courage to Pray*,
trans. Dinah Livingstone (London: Darton, Longman & Todd, 1973),
pp. 108–9.

Lenten prayer

Servant Christ,
help us to follow you into the desert,
with you to fast, denying false luxury,
refusing the tempting ways of self-indulgence,
the way of success at all costs,
the way of coercive persuasion.

Servant Christ, help us to follow you.

From "Litany of the Disciples of Christ the Servant" (India), in
Worship in an Indian Context, ed. Eric J. Lott (Bangalore: United
Theological College, 1986), p. 60. Used by permission.

Second Sunday in Lent

Genesis 15:1–12, 17–18   Philippians 3:17–4:1
Psalm 27   Luke 13:31–35

8 October 1941, Jerusalem

I feel dreadfully restless. Except for dinner occasionally, I seldom leave Government House and must be on hand always for coded messages which I decipher in the billiard room—often at night. When I can find time I walk round the big garden inside the high wire fence. My work is interesting; I live in great comfort; and yet I am unhappy and long to go away. It seems to be sometimes that there is a curse on Jerusalem—I so seldom meet anyone who is happy here. There is a tense atmosphere, not only over religions but as if the turmoils of centuries are still alive. Perhaps these thoughts stem from my own sadness yet I suspect Jerusalem must remain, for ever, a place of conflict.

Countess of Ranfurly, *To War with Whitaker: The Wartime Diaries of the Countess of Ranfurly 1939–45* (London: Mandarin, 1997).

Pilgrimage

Making a pilgrimage to Jerusalem today can be one of the most sobering of all experiences. Of course, it is possible to visit the city, see the sites, contemplate on the sacred places, and be almost totally blind to the tragic dynamic of the city today. A pilgrim, however, who learns to reflect on the meaning for the present of the religious events to which the city bears witness is confronted by all the complex and baffling questions of faith. Is there a hope for the future? Can faith be a partner of such hope or will it be a hindrance? Jerusalem is a critical challenge to those who believe it possible for peoples with conflicting histories and beliefs to live together creatively in peace, freedom and justice. It also bears witness to a pivotal issue for religion—must religion always serve power and so deepen division?

John Gladwin, *Love and Liberty: Faith and Unity in a Postmodern Age* (London: Darton, Longman & Todd, 1998), p. 63.

Pathos

St Thérése of the Child Jesus tells how, one day when she came upon a hen with her brood of chickens, she could not restrain her tears. That familiar sight reminded her of how intimate and complete is the love of Jesus for us, which enfolds us to himself. The words of Jesus came vividly to life for her at that moment.

"O Jerusalem, Jerusalem, killing the prophets and stoning those who are sent to you! How often would I have gathered your children together, as a hen gathers her brood under her wings, and you would not!" (Matthew 23:27).

So many deep and consoling truths are presented by the familiar image of a hen and her brood of chickens.

The love of Jesus, so all-embracing. St Augustine says that there is no bird which conveys so completely the idea of an all-enfolding care. Her wings gather her whole brood till they are totally covered. Such is the spread of the love of Jesus for his whole flock.

The caring gesture of the hen is constantly repeated—an unending gathering. How often does Jesus extend his arms in a universal embrace; yet how often is his gesture rejected!

St John Chrysostom describes the pathos of that moment. "Even the killing of the prophets could turn not my love away from you. And, not once but often, he shows the greatness of his love through the example of the hen."

John Moloney, The Time Is Now: Thoughts for the Day (Blackrock, Co
Dublin: The Columba Press, 2001), p. 17.

A psalm for the unloved

I saw you in the doorway.
You were black
and bruised
and broken.
I knew you were someone's daughter.

You are your mother's daughter.
If she could,
she would sit with you
and say how much she loved you.

I saw you in the shelter.
You looked much older
than your years.
Your kids were tired
and making a fuss.
I knew you were someone's daughter.

You are your mother's daughter.
Imagine her here,
as a sister and friend,
saying how much she loves you.

I saw you on the news last night
on a dirt road in Soweto.
They were screaming at you.
You had no shoes.
I knew you were someone's daughter.

You are your mother's daughter,
and she is her mother's daughter.
She has put up with so much abuse;
that shows how much she loves you.

I saw you in the delivery room
in drug withdrawal, writhing.
They say you have AIDS.
You are three hours old,
and I knew you were someone's daughter.

You are your mother's daughter
and she needs you to forgive her.
She doesn't know how to love you as yet,
but when she does,
I promise you
she will say how much she loves you.

I saw you in the orphanage.
How sad you looked
and lonely.

They say you are hard to place,
but I know you are someone's daughter.

You are your mother's daughter
and a foster mother's daughter,
and one of these days
she will come for you
and say how much she loves you.

I saw you in a nursing home.
You were slumped on a chair
with a vacant stare.
I knew you were somebody's daughter.

You are your mother's daughter,
your Mother God's own daughter.
Soon, very soon,
She will come for you
and say how much she loves you.

M. T. Winter, *WomenWitness* (New York: Crossroad Publishing
Company, 1992). © 1992 Medical Mission Sisters. Used by permission
of the Crossroad Publishing Company.

"Things are not always what they seem"

One day a church worker involved with homeless people was sitting in the congregation at a service in a city-centre church. As he sat listening to the reading, a homeless man came and sat beside him. He knew what would happen next—the homeless man, finding a captive audience, would beg some money. He waited in anticipation for the question of money to be raised.

Sure enough, after a few minutes, the homeless man leaned across. 'Here,' he said, 'I can't stay. Will you put this in the collection for me? They often give me sandwiches at this church and I just want to say thank you.' He pressed two pound coins into the church worker's hand and slipped away. Looking down on other people, it is so easy to think we know best.

David Rhodes, *Lenten Adventure: Daily Reflections from
Ash Wednesday to Easter Day* (London: SPCK, 2000), p. 11.

Prayer to Jesus

And you, Jesus, are you not also a mother?
    Are you not the mother who, like a hen,
    gathers her chickens under her wings?
Truly, Lord, you are a mother;
    for both they who are in labour
    and they who are brought forth
        are accepted by you.
You have died more than they, that they may labour to bear.
    It is by your death that they have been born,
    for if you had not been in labour,
        you could not have borne death;
and if you had not died, you would not have brought forth.
    For, longing to bear sons into life,
        you tasted of death,
    and by dying you begot them.
You did this in your own self,
    your servants by your commands and help,
    you as the author, they as the ministers.
So you, Lord God, are the great mother.

Anselm of Canterbury (c. 1033–1107), from "Prayer to St Paul," in
The Prayers and Meditations of St Anselm, trans. and introduction by
Benedicta Ward, S.L.G. (Harmondsworth, Middlesex: Penguin
Classics, 1973), pp. 153–54. © Benedicta Ward, 1973.
Used by permission of the publishers.

Jerusalem

[Jerusalem] remains a unique focus of hope, in the beauty of human aspiration, and of despair, in the intransigence of human folly; a potential flashpoint for war and yet the place to which all nations may one day be drawn in peace, as Isaiah's towering vision proclaimed when the fortunes of the earthly city were at a nadir.

Hugh S. Pyper, "Jerusalem," *The Oxford Companion to Christian
Thought,* ed. Adrian Hastings, Alistair Mason, and Hugh S. Pyper
(Oxford: Oxford University Press, 2000), p. 338.

THIRD SUNDAY IN LENT

Isaiah 55:1–9   1 Corinthians 10:1–13

Psalm 63:1–8   Luke 13:1–9

The road back

There is a song with the title 'The Emigrant's Return,' celebrating the joy of home-coming.

Like a strong rhythm, increasing in intensity, four words of the Prophet Isaiah reach us—seek, call, forsake, return. Like a theme with variations, they express one thought—an urgent invitation to the sinner to take the road back.

All of us, by sin, have to some degree left our Father's house. But there need never be a point of no return. At some moment grace stirs us. Already a change of heart is bringing a change of direction. How do we proceed? The prophet tells us.

Seek: The honest search for God is never in vain. He shows us the way.

Call: We may feel that our prayer is but a plaintive cry. Yet ours is not a feeble call from the dark. We call with hope, for God is near.

Forsake: Well for us that God whom we have forsaken, whose Son was forsaken on the Cross, does not forsake us. All he asks is that we break with the past.

Return: The rest is easy. The road back is shorter. For our heavenly Father is already coming out to greet us. We approach without fear, for we realise that he who loves us excessively '. . . will abundantly pardon' us.

John Moloney, *The Time Is Now: Thoughts for the Day* (Blackrock, Co
Dublin: The Columba Press, 2001), p. 135.

The bright field

> I have seen the sun break through
> to illuminate a small field
> for a while, and gone my way
> and forgotten it. But that was the pearl
> of great price, the one field that had
> the treasure in it. I realize now
> that I must give all that I have
> to possess it. Life is not hurrying

105

on to a receding future, nor hankering after
an imagined past. It is the turning
aside like Moses to the miracle
of the lit bush, to a brightness
that seemed as transitory as your youth
once, but is the eternity that awaits you.

R. S. Thomas, *Collected Poems 1945–1990* (London: J. M. Dent, 1995),
p. 302. Used by permission of the Orion Publishing Group.

Choosing joy

Joy is what makes life worth living, but for many joy seems hard to find. They complain that their lives are sorrowful and depressing. What then brings the joy we so much desire? Are some people just lucky, while others have run out of luck? Strange as it may sound, we can choose joy. Two people can be part of the same event, but one may choose to live it quite differently from the other. One may choose to trust that what happened, painful as it may be, holds a promise. The other may choose despair and be destroyed by it.

What makes us human is precisely this freedom of choice.

Henri J. M. Nouwen, *Bread for the Journey* (London: Darton, Longman & Todd, 1996), p. 38.

Joy and sorrow

Then a woman said, Speak to us of Joy and Sorrow.

And he answered:

Your joy is your sorrow unmasked.

And the selfsame well from which your laughter rises was oftentimes filled with your tears.

And how else can it be?

The deeper that sorrow carves into your being, the more joy you can contain.

Is not the cup that holds your wine the very cup that was burned in the potter's oven?

And is not the lute that soothes your spirit the very wood that was hollowed with knives?

When you are joyous, look deep into your heart and you shall find that it is
   only that which has given you sorrow that is giving you joy.
When you are sorrowful, look again in your heart, and you shall see that in
   truth you are weeping for that which has been your delight.

Kahlil Gibran, *The Prophet* (London: Heinemann [1926],
1972), p. 24.

Joy dwells with God

Joy belongs not only to those who have been called home, but also to the living,
and no one shall take it from us. We are one with them in this joy, but never in
sorrow. How shall we be able to help those who have become joyless and fearful
unless we ourselves are supported by courage and joy? I don't mean by this something fabricated, compelled, but something given, free. Joy dwells with God; it
descends from him and seizes spirit, soul and body, and where this joy has grasped
a person it grows greater, carries them away, opens closed doors. There is a joy
which knows nothing of sorrow, need and anxiety of the heart; it has no duration,
and it can only drug one for the moment. The joy of God has been through the
poverty of the crib and the distress of the cross; therefore it is insuperable,
irrefutable. It does not deny the distress where it is, but finds God in the midst of
it, indeed precisely there; it does not contest the most grievous sin, but finds forgiveness in just this way; it looks death in the face; yet it finds life in death itself.

Dietrich Bonhoeffer, *True Patriotism* (London: William Collins,
1965), p. 189.

Remembering

   On my bed I will remember you,
   and through the night watches I will meditate on you.

(Psalm 63:6)

According to a Hebrew myth, an angel comes down from heaven when a child is
born, takes the child under his wing, and recites the Torah. At the end of the recita-
tion, the angel places a finger on the upper lip of the child, creating the indenta-
tion that each human being possesses there, and says, 'Forget.' The child, then,
journeys through life trying to remember.

This is the story of each of our lives. We forget God, and, like the prodigal sons and daughters, we go off and seek our own way. . . . We search for God in the far country while God waits for us at home, observes Meister Eckhart. At some point, perhaps in midlife, we wake up to the presence of Something More and attempt to find our way home. . . .

The search for truth that occurs when we wake up and remember that God lives at the center of our being changes our perception of prayer. Instead of praying at given times and then taking a vacation from God during other activities, we see prayer as ongoing attentiveness or mindfulness. In that sense prayer is an attitude, a way of living. Rather than creating a corner of our life with our selves and our goals as the center, we choose to make God central.

Wayne Simsic, *Pray without Ceasing: Mindfulness of God in Daily Life*
(Winona, Minn.: St. Mary's Press, 2000), pp. 19–20.

A prayer for right judgment

Christ our companion,
you came not to humiliate the sinner
but to disturb the righteous.
Welcome us when we are put to shame,
but challenge our smugness,
that we may truly turn from what is evil,
and be freed even from our virtues,
in your name, Amen.

Janet Morley, *All Desires Known*, expanded ed.
(London: SPCK, 1992), p. 10.

FOURTH SUNDAY IN LENT

Joshua 5:9–12   2 Corinthians 5:16–21
Psalm 32   Luke 15:1–3, 11b–32

The Prodigal's request

The evangelist Luke tells it all so simply and so matter-of-factly that it is difficult
to realize fully that what is happening here is an unheard-of event: hurtful, offensive, and in radical contradiction to the most venerated tradition of the time. Kenneth Bailey, in his penetrating explanation of Luke's story, shows that the son's
manner of leaving is tantamount to wishing his father dead. Bailey writes:

> For over fifteen years I have been asking people of all walks of life from
> Morocco to India and from Turkey to the Sudan about the implications of
> a son's request for his inheritance while the father is still living. The answer
> has always been emphatically the same . . . the conversation runs as follows:
> Has anyone ever made such a request in your village?
> Never!
> Could anyone ever make such a request?
> Impossible!
> If anyone ever did, what would happen?
> His father would beat him, of course!
> Why?
> The request means—he wants his father to die.

Bailey explains that the son asks for the division of the inheritance, but also for
the right to dispose of his part. 'After signing over his possessions to his son, the
father still has the right to live off the proceeds . . . as long as he is alive. Here the
younger son gets, and thus is assumed to have demanded, disposition to which,
even more explicitly, he has no right until the death of his father. The implication
of "Father, I cannot wait for you to die" underlies both requests' (Bailey, p. 164).

The son's 'leaving' is, therefore, a much more offensive act than it seems at first
reading. It is a heartless rejection of the home in which the son was born and nurtured and a break with the most precious tradition carefully upheld by the larger
community of which he was a part. When Luke writes, 'and left for a distant

country,' he indicates much more than the desire of a young man to see more of the world. He speaks of a drastic cutting loose from the way of living, thinking, and acting that has been handed down to him from generation to generation as a sacred legacy. More than disrespect, it is a betrayal of the treasured values of family and community. The 'distant country' is the world in which everything considered holy at home is disregarded.

Kenneth E. Bailey, *Poet and Peasant and Through Peasant Eyes:*
A Literary-Cultural Approach to the Parables (Grand Rapids: Wm. B.
Eerdmans, 1983), pp. 161–62, quoted in Henri Nouwen, *The Return*
of the Prodigal Son: A Story of Homecoming (London: Darton, Longman & Todd, 1994), pp. 35–36.

Unconditional love

In today's reading from Luke's Gospel we are given an insight into what it is to be loved unconditionally. The younger son in the story was totally responsible for his own downfall. When he decided to return home he was motivated by feelings of self-pity and self-preservation rather than by any sense of sorrow for what he had done. The father allowed none of this to get in the way of his desire to re-admit his wayward son into the family circle. At the risk of looking foolish in the eyes of the rest of his household, he runs out to greet his son. There is no wagging finger or prolonged interrogation, no 'I hope you learnt your lesson.'

The returned prodigal does not have to prove his readiness to change, to per-form and to pull his weight this time round before he regains his father's trust. The ring, the sandals, the cloak, are the signs of his restored dignity and status. Their reconciliation is immediate and unconditional.

The story is about God's love for us, a love that we should try to reflect in all our human relationships. God's is a love that allows us space to make mistakes, a love that is not possessive, jealous, or intrusive. That does not mean that God is indifferent to our plight. Whatever our human condition, be it self-induced through ignorance or arrogance, we remain loveable in the eyes of a God who is always ready to embrace us unconditionally.

Oliver McTernan, in *Fruits of the Earth: The CAFOD/DLT Lent Book*
2002 (London: CAFOD/Darton, Longman & Todd, 2001), pp. 36–37.

A missionary in China

These first days, left so utterly alone in such dark and filthy confinement; subjected to it so suddenly and without reason; cut off from the outside world by immense distances and hedged in by a foe, who as yet did not deign even to speak sensibly to me; together with the absolute shattering of my highest expectation of years, my work amongst the Tibetans cruelly snatched from me, my position of opportunity in Tibet destroyed and myself brought back to Batang a helpless prisoner, now sinking lower and lower in a mire of fateful circumstance in this dismal dungeon out at the back of beyond; all this created an unbearable pressure weighing down upon me, crushing my spirit and rending my soul. The spiritual poverty of my life and service suddenly came before me. All my Christian life seemed just to crumble away. So much of all that I had said and done, ostensibly for his Kingdom, was now, under his rebuke, revealed to be nothing but wood, hay and stubble. With tears, I broke down and knelt trembling on the dusty floor. My mind in a turmoil and overcome by a sense of sin and unworthiness, I wept my way afresh to Calvary. There God met me again. His love to me was wonderful. I thought of the way behind as the way of a prodigal but now, as I knelt in the dust, the Father came running out to meet me where I was. There was no rebuke. I had come to where I had found him at the first. I tried to blurt out: 'I have sinned. . . . I am not worthy. . . . I am not worthy,' but was only conscious of his great arms around me and his kiss of pardon on my dirty cheeks. And there I knelt and knelt until I heard those matchless words: 'Bring forth the best robe. . . . Bring forth the best and put it on him.' It will live with me for ever. Into my heart came a peace and a joy in God's grace and forgiveness, in a measure I had never known before.

Geoffrey T. Bull, *When Iron Gates Yield* (London: Hodder & Stoughton, 1976), p. 40.

"Mysterious Wealth"

> Feeling today like the Prodigal Son
> just arrived back in his father's arms,
> I observe the world and all it contains.
>
> June's milky sky glimpsed through a window,
> the sunlight dancing over fresh green leaves,
> clusters of sparrows that scatter, chirping,
> full-blown petunias in pots on verandas,

all strike me as infinitely new,
astonishing and miraculous.

My grandson, too, rushing round the living-room
and chattering away for all he's worth,
my wife, with her glasses on,
embroidering a pillow-case,
and the neighbours, each with their particularities,
coming and going in the lane below,
all are extremely lovable,
most trustworthy, significant.

Oh, mysterious, immeasurable wealth!
Not to be compared with storeroom riches!
Truly, all that belongs to my Father in Heaven,
all, all is mine!

Ku Sang (b. 1919, Korea), *Wasteland of Fire: Selected Poems of Ku
Sang*, trans. Brother Anthony of Taizé (London and Wayland, Mass.:
Forest Books, 1990), p. 53. © Ku Sang and Anthony Teague, 1990.
Used by permission.

The edge of chaos

There should be a rational response to everything, we thought; it should be possible to make a better world.

It hasn't worked. Management and control are breaking down everywhere. The new world order looks very likely to end in disorder. We can't make things happen in the way we want them to at home, at work or in government, certainly not in the world as a whole. There are, it is now clear, limits to management. We thought that capitalism was the answer, but some of the hungry and homeless are not so sure.

Scientists call this sort of time the edge of chaos, the time of turbulence and creativity out of which a new order may jell. The first living cell emerged, some four million years ago, from a primordial soup of simple molecules and amino acids. Nobody knows why or how. Ever since then the universe has had an inexorable tendency to run down, to degenerate into disorder and decay. Yet it has also managed to produce from that disorder an incredible array of living creatures, plants and bacteria, as well as stars and planets. New life is forever springing from the decay and disorder of the old.

At the Santa Fe Institute, where a group of scientists are studying these phenomena, they call it 'complexity theory.' They believe that their ideas have as much relevance to oil prices, race relations and the stock market as they do to particle physics. In his book about their work, *Complexity*, Michael Waldrop describes the edge of chaos as the one place where a complex system can be spontaneous, adaptive and alive. It is also uncomfortable if you are in the middle of it, as so many of our social institutions are right now.

Charles Handy, *The Empty Raincoat* (London:
Arrow Books, 1995), p. 16.

I am his daughter. He said so. Oh the infinite gentleness of my God!

Margaret of Cortona (1247–97)

FIFTH SUNDAY IN LENT

Isaiah 43:16–21   Philippians 3:4b–14
Psalm 126   John 12:1–8

The goodness of God

Second Isaiah gives his people a remarkable gift. He gives them back their faith by means of rearticulating the old story. He gives them the linguistic capacity to confront despair rather than be surrounded by it. And he creates new standing ground outside the dominant consciousness upon which new humanness is possible. A cynic might argue that nothing has really changed. And indeed, nothing really changed if only the fall of empires is anything and if it must happen immediately. But prophets are not magicians. Their art and calling are only with words that evoke alternatives, and reshaped hardware will not overcome despair in any case. That will come only with the recognition that life has not been fully consigned to us and that there is another who has reserved for himself his sovereign freedom from us and for us. He is at work apart from us and apart from Babylon. The goodness of God takes the form of liberation for exiles. So Gerhard von Rad settled on that most remarkable of all texts that we should not speak until we decide if we trust it:

> Remember not the former things
> > nor consider the things of old.
> Behold, I am doing a new thing;
> > now it springs forth, do you not perceive it? (Isa. 43:18–19)

Those not comforted can hardly believe such a thing can be uttered. But clearly they will have no personal joy, no public justice, no corporate repentance, and no family humaneness until the community receives a newness it cannot generate for itself.

Walter Brueggemann, *The Prophetic Imagination*, 2d ed.
(Minneapolis: Fortress Press, 2001), p. 77.

Approaching the Passion

The Passion of Jesus comes, not just at the end of the gospel: rather, the evangelist has taken major elements of the passion tradition and woven them back into the story of Jesus as a whole. The temple cleansing comes in chapter 2, the eucharistic elements of the last supper come in chapter 6, the decision to put Jesus to death is linked to the raising of Lazarus in chapter 11. The anointing of Jesus at Bethany takes place before the triumphal entry, and a reminiscence of the agony in the garden comes before the last supper. The effect of this is to make the gospel as a whole a gospel of the passion. The coming of Jesus provokes conflict and division from the beginning. Likewise, believing in Jesus provokes conflict and division from the beginning.

Stephen C. Barton, *The Spirituality of the Gospels* (London: SPCK, 1992), p. 121.

Only the passion and death of Jesus can reconcile those two apparently irreconcilable truths: that God is in love with us, and that at some point in our lives we all experience suffering, pain and dereliction.

Michael Mayne

The meal at Bethany

Martha was serving; Lazarus was sharing; Mary was adoring; Judas was complaining. They were all involved in this process of dynamic movement, for none of us stands still in life. We have to move backwards or forwards, not only in our great decisions, but in the simple acts of ordinary living.

The action that became the centre of attention was that of Mary kneeling at the feet of Jesus, anointing them with the expensive ointment of pure nard, and wiping them with her unbound hair. This was a dramatic action, beautiful in the eyes of Jesus, remarkable in the eyes of the onlookers, but disreputable, displeasing and discomforting in the eyes of Judas.

The consequence of this action was twofold: the whole house was filled with the fragrance of the perfumed ointment, and a duplicitous and grating challenge was voiced by Judas. . . .

Prayer

Jesus anointed at Bethany: I find myself present in this company today. With Martha I desire to serve you; with Lazarus to sit at table with you; with Mary to kneel at your feet in costly devotion. Can it be true that with Judas I discover within myself a carping spirit of criticism, sarcasm, and at times cynicism, towards others, towards myself? Arrest any process of deterioration and corruption in my soul, Lord, for I realize that only by your grace can such a deliverance be effected, and I want to rely on that grace today.

Brother Ramon, *When They Crucified My Lord: Through
Lenten Sorrow to Easter Joy* (Oxford: The Bible Reading
Fellowship, 1999), pp. 79, 81.

Mary of Bethany

Yes, it was this that day, which shocked them!
Not the extravagance of the gesture, but that I,
a woman, should pour out perfume over his feet,
filling the room with the scent of my love
for him. Was it hysteria in me? Shameless
display? Even careless contempt for the poor?

The anonymous *they* will always say such things.
Anointing his body for burial, he said.
A truth I had not understood until he spoke it.
My salute to one about to die! My passionate
uncomprehending "yes" to his incarnate flesh!
Just so do acts of love precede our understanding.

Alan Gaunt, from "Mary of Bethany," in *Textures of Tomorrow: Words
and Images on the Theme of Reconciliation*, ed. Kate Compston
(London: United Reformed Church, 1996), p. 20. © Alan Gaunt,
1992. Used by permission of the author.

Let me love you

Take my gifts and let me love you,
God who first of all loved me,
Gave me light and food and shelter,
gave me life and set me free,
Now because your love has touched me,
I have love to give away,
now the bread of love is rising,
Loaves of love to multiply!

Take the fruit that I have gathered
from the tree your Spirit sowed,
harvest of your own compassion,
juice that makes the wine of God,
Spiced with humor, laced with laughter—
flavor of the Jesus life,
tang of risk and new adventure
taste and zest beyond belief.

Take whatever I can offer—
gifts that I have yet to find
skills that I am slow to sharpen,
talents of the hand and mind,
things made beautiful for others
in the place where I must be:
take my gifts and let me love you,
God who first of all loved me.

Shirley Erena Murray, *In Every Corner Sing: The Hymns of Shirley
Erena Murray* (Carol Stream, Ill.: Hope Publishing Company, 1992),
no. 66. © CopyCare International for the UK. © Hope Publishing
Company for all other territories. Used by permission.

Love brought it down

The girls' High School and the boys' Grammar School in Chesterfield were adjacent to each other and separated by a strong stone wall. The large stones of this wall were held together by mortar. When I started at that school, the wall was complete; and by the time that I left, the wall was breached in many places. That wall was broken down, not out of anger or frustration and not by our using brute force on it. No heavy instruments were used against it. But over the years we carefully and persistently loosened the mortar between the stones in order to pass through notes making assignations, and letters declaring our undying love. Before I left, that wall fell down all by itself. It was love that brought it down.

Kathleen M. Richardson, in *Textures of Tomorrow: Words and Images on the Theme of Reconciliation*, ed. Kate Compston (London: United Reformed Church, 1996), p. 20.

A thought about Lent

Nobody warns, "So many shopping days to Easter!"
No costly gifts, no monetary loss.
Easter seems too easy.
It is—if you forget the cross.

Joseph T. Nolan, *Let the Earth Rejoice: Scripture, Prayers, and Poems for the More Abundant Life* (Allen, Tex.: Thomas More Publishing, 2000), p. 66. © Joseph T. Nolan, 2000. Used by permission of the publisher.

SIXTH SUNDAY IN LENT

(Palm Sunday or Passion Sunday)

Isaiah 50:4–9a	Philippians 2:5–11
Psalm 118:1–2, 19–29	Luke 19:28–40

King Jesus

Jesus, King of the universe;
ride on in humble majesty,
ride on through conflict and debate,
ride on through sweaty prayer and betrayal of friends,
ride on through mockery and unjust condemnation,
ride on through cruel suffering and ignoble death,
ride on to the empty tomb and your rising in triumph,
ride on to raise up your Church, a new body for your service,
ride on, King Jesus, to renew the whole earth in your image:
in compassion come to help us.

> From *Service for All Seasons*, ed. E. J. Lott (Hyderabad, India: Andhra
> Theological College, 1973), p. 12. Used by permission.

The path to paradise

Our participation in Christ's Easter journey transfigures every threshold we have to cross, including the frontier of life and death. Early Christian tradition drew upon the imagery of Psalm 118 and its association with the Eucharist to affirm that those who shared his supper were also led by him in a procession of triumph through the gates of death. By the eighth century Psalm 118 was sung during the funeral procession from the church to the grave, accompanied by lights and incense. . . .

The glory of the risen Christ sheds light on all our journeys, not only that of our ending. We know that coming home and leaving home are often moments of potential joy or sorrow, excitement, anger, even depression. And we, in the West, sometimes have no idea how to express our confused emotions and reactions in a safe way because we have lost the rituals which many religions have. . . . Irish Christians would celebrate their homecoming with the same words from Psalm 118 which took their departed home to God. In such ways we become aware that every homecoming, every leave-taking, has the potential to carry a significance beyond opening or closing the door behind us.

> Brian Pickett, *Songs for the Journey: The Psalms in Life and Liturgy* (London: Darton, Longman & Todd, 2002), pp. 10, 13. © 2002 Darton, Longman & Todd Ltd. Used by permission of the publishers.

The form of a servant

In the incarnation God 'emptied himself, taking the form of a servant' (Phil. 2:7, RSV), thus exposing himself to all the buffeting that was the slave's lot, including crucifixion itself. But we must not confine that image of God as slave to the life of Jesus. For it was also with the weak and marginalized that he identified in that central Old Testament event of the Exodus, bringing the Israelite slaves to freedom. Not only that, he allowed himself to be buffeted again and again throughout Israel's history by a rebellious people who frequently misunderstood him, wanting to be Egyptian tyrants in their turn. Yet God's only response was the response of the weakness of the slave—not honouring power, but continuing to love even as their fortunes declined. Paradoxically, however, precisely because of that love it was this same people, the Jews, who were able to preserve sufficient of the vision for the continuity in due course to be seen.

> David Brown, *The Word to Set You Free: Living Faith and Biblical Criticism* (London: SPCK, 1995), p. 21.

Affirming our faith

Equal with God:
Jesus is Lord.
Emptied himself:
Jesus is Lord.
Came as a slave:
Jesus is Lord.
Found as a man:
Jesus is Lord.
Humbly obeyed:

Jesus is Lord.
Went to his death:
Jesus is Lord.
Death on a cross:
Jesus is Lord.

(*getting gradually louder:*)
God raised him up:
Jesus is Lord.
Gave him the name:
Jesus is Lord.
Higher than all:
Jesus is Lord.
Every knee bow:
Jesus is Lord.
All tongues confess:
'Jesus is Lord!'

Glory to God! **Amen!**

Michael Perry, *Bible Prayers for Worship* (London: Marshall Pickering, 1997), p. 129. Reprinted by permission of HarperCollins Publishers Ltd. © Michael Perry 1997.

The burden of the other person

The other person is a burden to the Christian, in fact for the Christian most of all. The other person never becomes a burden at all for the pagans. They simply stay clear of every burden the other person may create for them. However, Christians must bear the burden of one another. They must suffer and endure one another. Only as a burden is the other really a brother or sister and not just an object to be controlled. The burden of human beings was even for God so heavy that God had to go to the cross suffering under it. God truly suffered and endured human beings in the body of Jesus Christ. But in so doing, God bore them as a mother carries her child, as a shepherd the lost lamb. God took on human nature. Then, human beings crushed God to the ground. But God stayed with them and they with God. In suffering and enduring human beings, God maintained community with them.

Dietrich Bonhoeffer, *Life Together*, trans. John Doberstein (New York: Harper & Row, 1954), pp. 100–101.

Having the mind of Christ

The exhortation to suffer like Christ in expectation of future salvation was frequently used to admonish Christian women and slaves to submit to abusive husbands or masters. Christians who believe that the present world will soon end often find the idea of a reward for suffering like Christ to be an excuse for failing to struggle against injustice in this world. They forget that the hymn starts not with the suffering Christ but with the Christ who is equal to God. The poor in Latin America who are told to suffer like Christ rather than struggle for freedom, or abused women whose ministers tell them to submit to husbands, are not in the position to copy the Christ of this hymn. Its challenge is addressed to persons of some status and power, just as Christ had the status of God. In order to preach a gospel that centers on a crucified person and that brings persecution in its wake, such people must empty themselves.

Pheme Perkins, from "Philippians," in *Women's Bible Commentary*,
expanded ed., ed. Carol J. Newsom and Sharon H. Ringe (Louisville,
Ky.: Westminster John Knox Press, 1998), pp. 434–35.

———

Let us imitate those who have gone out to meet [Jesus], not scattering olive branches or garments or palms in his path, but spreading ourselves before him as best we can, with humility of soul and upright purpose.

Andrew of Crete (c. 660–740)

———

Holy Thursday

Exodus 12:1–4 (5–10) 11–14   1 Corinthians 11:23–26
Psalm 116:1–2, 12–19   John 13:1–17, 31b–35

The body of Christ

I shall always remember visiting Mother Teresa's home for the dying in Calcutta and being shown round by the sister-in-charge, Sister Luke. The dying lie on thin palliasses of straw, the men in one section of the extended ward, the women and children in the other. Between the two wards is a small cubicle with a plastic curtain drawn across the front of it. Just before I reached the home an old woman had been brought in from the streets in a filthy condition. She was barely recognisable as human.

'Come and see,' said Sister Luke, and took me across to the curtained-off trough. She drew back the curtain. The trough was filled with a few inches of water, in which was lying the stick-like body of the old woman. Two Missionaries of Charity were gently washing her clean and comforting her at the same time. Above the trough, stuck to the wall, was a simple notice containing four words: 'The body of Christ.' It is an image I can never forget.

> Michael Mayne, *A Year Lost and Found* (London: Darton,
> Longman & Todd, 1987), p. 69.

Offering

Since once again, Lord—though this time not in the forests of the Aisne but in the Steppes of Asia—I have neither bread, nor wine, nor altar, I will raise myself beyond these symbols, up to the pure majesty of the real itself; I, your priest, will make the whole earth my altar and on it I will offer you all the labours and sufferings of the world.

Over there, on the horizon, the sun has just touched with light the outermost fringe of the eastern sky. Once again, beneath this moving sheet of fire, the living surface of the earth wakes and trembles, and once again begins its fearful travail. I will place on my paten, O God, the harvest to be won by this renewal of labour.

Into my chalice I shall pour all the sap which is to be pressed out this day from the earth's fruits.

My paten and my chalice are the depths of a soul laid widely open to all the forces which in a moment will rise up from every corner of the earth and converge upon the Spirit. Grant me the remembrance and the mystic presence of all those whom the light is now awakening to the new day.

Pierre Teilhard de Chardin, *Hymn of the Universe* (London: William Collins and Co. Ltd.; New York: Harper & Brothers, 1965), p. 19.

A life shared

The life we share with God . . . is the life of people in relationship. Christ proclaims this fact in the revelation of his own presence; for where Christ is, there is the relationship of people, the community of Love. It could be said that the principles according to which the Eucharist is organised constitute the underlying structure of personhood itself, for they correspond to the action of self-giving whereby the individual becomes the person, moving out of isolation into community. The action of abandoning the self for the other, the glorious primal movement—original and inevitable when it happens in God, for it is his expression of his joy in the nature of his being, but difficult and terrifying for men and women, as for the Son who took their nature upon himself—is eternally presented in the Eucharist. It is presented to us not as an idea or a proposition, but as a living event in which we are ourselves deeply and essentially involved: a fact, the fact, of our common life.

Roger Grainger, *The Message of the Rite: The Significance of Christian Rites of Passage* (Cambridge: Lutterworth Press, 1988), p. 82.

"The Foot-Washing"

They kneel on the slanting floor
before feet white as roots,
humble as tree stumps.
Men before men
women before women
to soothe the sourness
bound in each other's journeys.
Corns, calluses, bone knobs

all received and rinsed
given back clean
to Sunday shoes and hightops.

This is how they prepare
for the Lord's Supper,
singing and carrying a towel
and a basin of water,
praying while kids put soot
in their socks—almost as good
as nailing someone in the outhouse.

Jesus started it: He washed feet
after Magdalen dried His ankles
with her hair. "If I wash thee not,
thou hast no part in me."

All servants, they bathe
flesh warped to its balance.
God of the rootwad,
Lord of the bucket in the well.

George Ella Lyon, in *Appalachian Journal* 9, no. 4 (summer 1982).
©1982 by Appalachian State University/Appalachian Journal. Used by
permission of the publisher and author.

Washing the feet of the poor

This afternoon I took the train to Paris to celebrate the Holy Thursday liturgy with the L'Arche community, 'Nomaste.' It was a very moving celebration. We gathered in the community room of Nomaste. There were about forty people. In his welcome, the director of the community, Toni Paoli, expressed his vision that L'Arche should be not simply a comfortable place for handicapped people, but a Christian community in which people serve one another in the name of Jesus. After the Gospel reading, he again proclaimed his deep love for Jesus. Then he stood up and washed the feet of four members of his community.

After the Eucharist, a rice dish, bread, and wine were brought and put on the altar. In silence, deepened by three short Gospel readings about God's love, we shared this simple food.

Sitting in the basement room in Paris surrounded by forty poor people, I was struck again by the way Jesus concluded his active life. Just before entering on the road of his passion he washed the feet of his disciples and offered them his body and blood as food and drink. These two acts belong together. They are both an expression of God's determination to show us the fullness of his love. . . .

What is even more astonishing is that on both occasions Jesus commands us to do the same. . . . Jesus calls us to continue his mission of revealing the perfect love of God in this world. He calls us to total self-giving. He does not want us to keep anything for ourselves. Rather, he wants our love to be as full, as radical, and as complete as his own. He wants us to bend ourselves to the ground and touch the places in each other that most need washing. He also wants us to say to each other, 'Eat of me and drink of me.' By this complete mutual nurturing, he wants us to become one body and one spirit, united by the love of God.

Henri J. M. Nouwen, *The Road to Daybreak: A Spiritual Journey*
(London: Darton, Longman & Todd, 1989; New York: Doubleday,
1988), pp. 158–59. © 1988 Henri J. M. Nouwen. Used by permission
of Doubleday, a division of Random House, Inc., and of Darton,
Longman & Todd Ltd.

Cleansing and deliverance

Great God, your love has called us here,
as we, by love for love were made.
Your living likeness still we bear,
though marred, dishonoured, disobeyed.
We come, with all our heart and mind
your call to hear, your love to find.

We come with self-inflicted pains
of broken trust and chosen wrong,
half-free, half-bound by inner chains,
by social forces swept along,
by powers and systems close confined,
yet seeking hope for humankind.

Great God, in Christ you call our name
and then receive us as your own,
not through some merit, right or claim,

but by your gracious love alone.
  We strain to glimpse your mercy seat
  and find you kneeling at our feet.

Then take the towel, and break the bread,
and humble us, and call us friends.
Suffer and serve till all are fed,
and show how grandly love intends
  to work till all creation sings,
  to fill all worlds, to crown all things.

Great God, in Christ you set us free
your life to live, your joy to share.
Give us your Spirit's liberty
to turn from guilt and dull despair
  and offer all that faith can do
  while love is making all things new.

Brian Wren, in *Piece Together Praise: A Theological Journey* (London: Stainer & Bell; Carol Stream, Ill.: Hope Publishing Company, 1996), no. 84, p. 79. © 1975, 1995 Hope Publishing Company for the USA, Canada, Australia and New Zealand, and Stainer & Bell Ltd. for all other territories. Used by permission.

"Round table" leadership

This leadership ["in the round"] begins as women once more take up their ancient heritage as Spirit-filled leaders in Christian community. The impetus for this reversal of "things as they are" is the recognition of the need for forms of organization that connect us to those at the margin of society. One such leader is a Korean woman named Henna Yogumhyun Han, an ordained United Methodist pastor who has found her own way in Korean-American ministry by founding the Rainbow Church. This church is a faith community of Korean-American women in international marriages affiliated with the Seaford (New York) United Methodist Church. The Rainbow Church invites the whole family to attend church at the same time so that the fathers and children can attend English-language worship and Sunday school and the women can attend their Women-Church in the Korean language. Following the services the families share a meal and discussion.

These women, many of them G.I. brides, have great difficulty in the United States and often run into misunderstanding and abuse from husbands who do not speak the same language or share the same culture. They are lonely and isolated, often rejected by Korean congregations because the women were formerly bar women and entertainers who lived outside U.S. bases in Korea. They and their children face discrimination in the United States because of racism. Henna Han has a crisis hot line for the women and is planning to establish a shelter for battered women and children. As part of her ministry of partnership with those considered to be nobodies, and who themselves have very low self-esteem, she has created a worship in the round. The women gather around a low round table, where they look down on a cross. Here they learn that Christ came to share life with them, that he welcomes those who are the lowest in society and inspires them by the Spirit of his love to lift them up for new life and service. The women gather as a community of the Spirit, and through Henna Han's leadership in solidarity with the margin they discover that the tables have been overturned and that Christ has made them welcome!

Letty M. Russell, *Church in the Round: Feminist Interpretation of the Church* (Louisville, Ky.: Westminster/John Knox Press, 1993), p. 63.

When Christ serves, he serves perfectly.

Brook Foss Westcott

GOOD FRIDAY

| Isaiah 52:13–53:12 | Hebrews 4:14–16; 5:7–9 |
| Psalm 22 | John 18:1–19:42 |

"Friday"

We nailed the hands long ago,
Wove the thorns, took up the scourge and shouted
For excitement's sake, we stood at the dusty edge
Of the pebbled path and watched the extreme of pain.

But one or two prayed, one or two
Were silent, shocked, stood back
And remembered remnants of words, a new vision.
The cross is up with its crying victim, the clouds
Cover the sun, we learn a new way to lose
What we did not know we had
Until this bleak and sacrificial day,
Until we turned from our bad
Past and knelt and cried out our dismay,
The dice still clicking, the voices dying away.

> Elizabeth Jennings, *Collected Poems* (Manchester:
> Carcanet Press, 1986), p. 193.

The cross

If Jesus is indeed what God communicates to us, God's language for us, his cross is always both ours and not ours; not a magnified sign of our own suffering, but the mark of God's work in and through the deepest vulnerability; not a martyr's triumphant achievement, but something that is there for all human sufferers because it belongs to no human cause.

> Rowan Williams, *Writing in the Dust: Reflections on 11th September
> and Its Aftermath* (London: Hodder & Stoughton, 2002), pp. 77–78.

Luke XXIII

Gentile or Jew or simply a man
Whose face has been lost in time,
We shall not save the silent
Letters of his name from oblivion.

What could he know of forgiveness,
A thief whom Judea nailed to a cross?
For us those days are lost.
During his last undertaking,

Death by crucifixion,
He learned from the taunts of the crowd
That the man who was dying beside him
Was God. And blindly he said:

Remember me when thou comest
Into thy kingdom, and from the terrible cross
The unimaginable voice
Which one day will judge us all

Promised him Paradise. Nothing more was said
Between them before the end came,
But history will not let the memory
Of their last afternoon die.

O friends, the innocence of this friend
Of Jesus! That simplicity which made him,
From the disgrace of punishment, ask for
And be granted Paradise

Was what drove him time
And again to sin and to bloody crime.

Jorge Luis Borges, "Luke XXIII," trans. Mark Strand, in Jorge Luis
Borges, *Selected Poems*, ed. Alexander Coleman (New York: Viking
Penguin; London: Allen Lane, The Penguin Press, 1999). © 1999
Maria Kodama. Translation © 1999 Mark Strand. Used by permission
of Viking Penguin, a division of Penguin Putnam Inc., New York, and
Penguin Books, Ltd. London.

Simon carries the cross

The door of Sam's room had been left open by the nurses. His family's distress was obvious—his wife holding his hand, his daughter with her arm round her mum, his son staring out of the open window—as they waited for Sam to die. I wanted to go in and meet this family in their sorrow. But I had nothing to offer, no clever words to say. I only glanced into the room as I passed, a spectator of their pain and grief.

It could not and would not last. Eventually, I felt compelled to go in. I was scared, ill-equipped, tongue-tied, out of my depth. But for a moment or two, and on two or three other occasions throughout the day, I offered what I could—a stumbling word, a shared silence, a comforting touch—each time overwhelmed by the pain of it all and my uselessness to make it any different.

Sam died that night. Next morning, the door of his room was still open. But there was no patient or distressed family, only the empty bed and the stillness of the aftermath of death. . . . Later that morning, the family came to collect Sam's belongings and the death certificate—and asked to see me, to say thank you for my help during yesterday. My help? I murmured some words of protest. But Sam's wife persisted: 'No, you did good yesterday. . . . You came into the room—and I know how hard that was for you.' . . . My own inadequacies had been transparent. . . . But with the compulsion to go in and the fearfulness of being there, in the transition from spectator to participant, something good—of God—had taken place.

Simon, too, looked through a wide-open door and witnessed a journey to death. And he too . . . was forced to enter the drama. What good could he possibly do? . . . The good is God saying 'Thank you, Simon,' for being there when you were needed and others had turned away.

When the ultimate is beyond you, but you still step over the threshold into the distress and pain, you are Simon for Christ, and God says 'Thank you' for your healing presence.

Tom Gordon, in *Lent and Easter Readings from Iona*, ed. Neil Paynter
(Glasgow: Wild Goose Publications, 2002), pp. 91–92.
© Tom Gordon.

The Mother

People are kind.
Come away, they cry.
No need to put yourself through this.
He'll understand.

But I am his mother,
and though nails pierce his body,
and a sword sunders my soul,
I must stand with him,
I must stand by him,
I must stand up in this his hour of dying.

And yet, and yet,
there's more at stake than that.

From somewhere within
this horror of great darkness,
Gabriel-haunted still,
I dream dreams, hear voices, see visions.
I see others.

Mothers, sons, brothers, daughters,
sisters, fathers, friends, lovers,
a vast army who will not turn away;
clad in the armour of fidelity
and hollow-eyed courage,
they will stand by,
stand with,
stand up,
in those slow, dimming,
dove-grey hours of dying. . . .

Sylvia Sands, "The Second Word: The Mother," from "Seven Words,"
in Rowan Williams et al., *Darkness Yielding: Angles on Christmas, Holy
Week, and Easter* (Sheffield: Cairns Publications, 2001), p. 155.

God of the cross

O God of the Cross,
keep us passionate through our wrestling with your ways,
and keep us humble before the mystery of your great love,
    known to us in the face of Jesus Christ.

> Jim Cotter, from "Darkness at Noon: The Crucifixion and Death of
> Jesus Christ," in Rowan Williams et al., *Darkness Yielding: Angles on
> Christmas, Holy Week, and Easter* (Sheffield: Cairns Publications,
> 2001), p. 197.

Unavoidable suffering

Love does not cause suffering or produce it, though it must necessarily seek confrontation, since its most important concern is not the avoidance of suffering but the liberation of people. Jesus' suffering was avoidable. He endured it voluntarily. There were other ways out, as is stressed again and again in mythical language: it would have been possible for him to come down from the cross and allow himself to be helped. To put it in political terms, he didn't need to go to Jerusalem and could have avoided the confrontation. To avoid confrontation by giving up certain goals is one of the most common forms of apathetic behavior; to seek confrontation is a form of behavior necessary for those who suffer and aspire. This can be demonstrated through many experiences in the civil rights movements. . . . The officials in charge usually practice a policy of appeasement, delay, and cover-up. The citizens who are taking part, on the other hand, seek and produce confrontation as they make suffering visible. Their suffering would be avoidable only under conditions they neither can nor want to fulfill. To reconcile God with misery means precisely avoiding confrontation and, in fear of being formed in the image of Christ, which includes pain, putting off liberative love.

> Dorothee Soelle, *Suffering*, trans. Everett R. Kalin (Philadelphia:
> Fortress Press, 1984), pp. 164–65.

The cross

We focus on the cross. Let us pray in the words of a tenth-century African hymn.

The cross is the way of the lost
the cross is the staff of the lame
the cross is the guide of the blind
the cross is the strength of the weak
the cross is the hope of the hopeless
the cross is the freedom of the slaves
the cross is the water of the seeds
the cross is the consolation of the bonded labourers
the cross is the source of those who seek water
the cross is the cloth of the naked.

All   **O God,**
you have made us for yourself,
and against your longing there is no defence.
Mark us with your love,
and release in us a passion for your justice
in our disfigured world;
that we may turn from our guilt and face you,
our heart's desire.

Janet Morley, *All Desires Known* (London: SPCK, 1992), p. 10, quoted in Rebecca Dudley and Janet Morley, *Praying for a Change: A Christian Aid Lent Course* (London: Christian Aid, 1996), p. 41.

EASTER

Acts 10:34–43   1 Corinthians 15:19–26

Psalm 118:1–2, 14–24   John 20:1–18

Easter Even—10 April 1982

This day—Easter Even—as the Prayer Book calls it—has an empty, dead feel about it: suspended between the tragedy of Crucifixion and the triumph of Resurrection. It is a day, surely, when Christians ought to stay indoors. For the past week has been almost too much, and what happened yesterday was the end of all our hopes—or so it seemed. He descended into Hell. . . . Not quite the place of eternal punishment, I think; more of a Limbo, or the ancient Hebrew *Sheol*, where the souls of those who had died before Christ slept uneasily, awaiting his coming to judge them. A friend of mine suggested the dramatic scene of the arrival there of the hanged Judas Iscariot—to find the gates burst open, and the Lord whom he had betrayed confronting him. Judas, of all the disciples, the first to know the real truth. . . .

Gerald Priestland, *Gerald Priestland at Large* (London: Fount, 1983), p. 188.

From "The Flowering of the Rod"

Yet resurrection is a sense of direction,
resurrection is a bee-line,

straight to the horde and plunder,
the treasure, the store-room,

the honeycomb,
resurrection is resurrection,

food, shelter, fragrance
of myrrh and balm.

H.D. [Hilda Doolittle], "The Flowering of the Rod [7]," in *Trilogy*
(Manchester: Carcanet Press, 1973); and in *Collected Poems
1912–1944*, © 1944, 1945, 1946 by Oxford University Press, renewed
1973 by Norman Holmes Pearson. Reprinted by permission of
Carcanet Press and New Directions Publishing Corp.

135

Easter Prayer

Christ our life,
you are alive   in the beauty of the earth
   in the rhythm of the seasons
   in the mystery of time and space
   Alleluia

Christ our life,
you are alive   in the tenderness of touch
   in the heartbeat of intimacy
   in the insights of solitude
   Alleluia

Christ our life,
you are alive   in the creative possibility
   of the dullest conversation
   of the dreariest task
   the most threatening event
   Alleluia

Christ our life,
you are alive   to offer re-creation
   to every unhealed hurt
   to every deadened place
   to every damaged heart
   Alleluia.

You set before us a great choice.
Therefore we choose life.
The dance of resurrection soars and surges through the whole creation,
It sets gifts of bread and wine upon our table.
This is grace, dying we live.
So let us live.

Kathy Galloway, in *Celebrating Women: The New Edition*, ed. Hannah
Ward, Jennifer Wild, and Janet Morley (London: SPCK, 1995), pp.
144–45. © Kathy Galloway.

Knowing and loving

Today we heard the story of the encounter between Jesus and Mary of Magdala, two people who love each other. . . . This simple and deeply moving story brings me in touch with my fear as well as my desire to be known. When Jesus calls Mary by her name, he is doing much more than speaking the words by which everybody knows her, for her name signifies her whole being. Jesus knows Mary of Magdala. He knows her story: her sin and her virtue, her fears and her love, her anguish and her hope. He knows every part of her heart. Nothing in her is hidden from him. He knows her even more deeply and profoundly than she knows herself. Therefore, when he utters her name he brings about a profound event. Mary suddenly realizes that the one who truly knows her truly loves her. . . .

I can see what a healing moment this encounter must have been. Mary feels at once fully known and fully loved. The division between what she feels safe to show and what she does not dare to reveal no longer exists. She is fully seen and she knows that the eyes that see her are the eyes of forgiveness, mercy, love, and unconditional acceptance.

Henri J. M. Nouwen, *The Road to Daybreak: A Spiritual Journey* (New York: Doubleday, 1988; London: Darton, Longman & Todd, 1989), pp. 164–65. © 1988 Henri J. M. Nouwen. Used by permission of Doubleday, a division of Random House, Inc., and of Darton, Longman & Todd Ltd.

African Easter: Easter Morning

. . . Yet you Christ are always there.
You are the manyfaceted crystal
Of our desires and hopes,
Behind the smoke-screen of incense,
Concealed in mumbled European tongues
Of worship and of praise.
In the thick dusty verbiage
Of centuries of committees
Of ecumenical councils.
You yet remain revealed
To those who seek you.
It is I, you say.

You remain in the sepulchre
Of my brown body.

Christ is risen, Christ is risen!

You were not dead.
It was just that we
Could not see clearly enough.
We can push out the rock from the inside.
You can come out now.
You see we want to share you
With our masters, because
You really are unique.

The great muddy river Niger
Picks up the rising equatorial sun,
Changing itself by slow degrees
Into thick flowing molten gold.

Abioseh Nicol (Sierra Leone, 1924–), from "Easter Morning," in *Poems from Black Africa*, ed. Langston Hughes (Bloomington: Indiana University Press, 1963). Used with permission of David Higham Associates Ltd.

Easter Sunday

Holy Week is the world's sacred Winter:
    The earth is a widow, the skies are sere,
There's a sound of scourging and nailing in the vinegary wind;
    And the darkness chokes the Son of Man.

But spring, two springs, are coming to the world
    From the depths on the third morning:
The lily, the primrose and the daffodil
    Will follow the Saviour from the Egypt of soil.

The rejoicing is green and white, the praise is yellow
    Because the new Adam has risen alive from the grave;
And the ivy, tying itself round the tree like the old serpent,
    Is for us eternal life with God.

D. Gwenallt Jones, in Donald Allchin and D. Densil Morgan with translations [from Welsh] by Patrick Thomas, *Sensuous Glory: The*

Poetic Vision of D. Gwenallt Jones (Norwich: Canterbury Press, 2000),
p. 125. Translation used by permission of Gomer Press.

Easter is not a part of the old accustomed divine order, of the ordered world in which we live, but it is an absolutely new, unexpected act of the living God, which interrupts and runs counter to the uniform rise and fall of the world's rhythm. Here we have the beginning of something new.

Martin Niemoller

SECOND SUNDAY OF EASTER

Acts 5:27–32	Revelation 1:4–8
Psalm 150	John 20:19–31

The place of good news

After thirty years of living and working ecumenically, I am convinced that[,] in every circumstance[,] where the Holy Spirit leads us, if we choose to follow, is to the place of gospel, of good news. This is the place where the marks are visible, where people hear their names called with love, where people break open their lives to share them, where people bear witness. This is where Jesus finds us, knows us, heals us, sets us free and calls us to follow him. Furthermore, I am convinced that the place of the gospel is rarely inside a church. The place of the gospel is the world.

> Kathy Galloway, from "Put Your Hand into My Side," in *For God's Sake . . . Unity: An Ecumenical Voyage with the Iona Community,* ed. Maxwell Craig (Glasgow: Wild Goose Publications, 1998).

A way of believing

Yes—I trust in AbbaAmma,
Source of all that comes to be,
Goodness, Truth, and marvellous Beauty,
Surging Life—Love's Mystery.

And I trust in Love embodied,
Jesus born in Galilee,
Healing outcasts, eating with them,
Crucified upon the Tree:

Bearing pain with all creation,
Willing love to victory,
Loosening evil's grip for ever,
Death no more the enemy.

Foe and friend, in Love's acceptance,
Each and all alike are formed,
Freed by touch and word and water,
Fed by bread and wine transformed.

And I trust the Hidden Spirit
In and through our common life
Weaving threads all torn and broken,
Shaping justice out of strife.

So I trust in Love's Communion,
Lover, Loved, and Mutual Friend,
Seated at the welcoming table,
Gently bidding us attend.

[Therefore:]

Pilgrim-soul, I make Love's Journey,
Striving with the Powers of Night,
Named and blessed by awesome Stranger,
Limping from the crucial fight.

I embrace the law of Loving:
Dying to possessive need;
Squeezed through eye of true compunction,
Into spacious freedom breathed;

Crushed to death by cruel winepress,
Following in the Way of Scorn;
Stigma's wounds in glory shining,
Joy of resurrection dawn.

Jim Cotter, in Jim Cotter and the Cairns Network, *By Heart for the Millennium* (Sheffield: Cairns Publications, 1998), pp. 16–17.

Blessed are they who have not seen and have believed. Certainly this refers to us. We hold in our hearts one whom we do not see in his body. He refers to us, but only if we follow up our faith with our works. Those people truly believe who express their belief through their works.

Gregory the Great (540–604)

We have not seen . . . and we believe

We believe in God whom we do not see
because of Jesus who was seen
and people who live by his Spirit.

We believe in God whom we do not see
because of truth and beauty,
love, goodness, and integrity,
which make the divine a part of human life.

We believe in a heaven we have not seen
because love is stronger than death
and all our hopes
cannot find fulfillment in this life.

We believe in the Spirit we cannot see
because we see the Creator Spirit
at work in our lives
and hear the Spirit's voice in our silence.

We believe in the earth and its people
in spite of the evil we see
because we have shared their goodness.

We believe in the church we see
with its saints and sinners
because it has given us the Word
and gathered us in the breaking of the bread.

We believe in a providence we do not always see
because God made us,
and here we are,
with ten billion years behind us.

We believe in the resurrection
in spite of the death we see
because we have been raised up many times,
and passed from death to life.

We believe in God whom we do not see
because of the One who said,
"He who sees me sees the Father."

We have seen him in our humanity,
in his risen body,
and we believe.

Joseph T. Nolan, *Let the Earth Rejoice: Scripture, Prayers and Poems for the More Abundant Life* (Allen, Tex.: Thomas More Publishing, 2000), pp. 23–24. © Joseph T. Nolan, 2000.

"And the Glory"

The silence breaks the morning.
The One Star lights the world.
The lily springs to life and
     not even Solomon . . .

Let it begin with singing
     and never end!
Oh, angels, quit your lamenting!
Oh, pilgrims,
     upon your knees in tearful prayer,
          rise up
               and take your hearts
                    and run!

We who were no people
     are named anew
          God's people,
for he who was no more
     is forevermore.

Ann Weems, *Kneeling in Jerusalem* (Louisville, Ky.: Westminster/John Knox Press, 1992), p. 94.

"Mother" does not mean being the woman who gives birth to and cares for a child; to be a mother is to feel in your own flesh the suffering of all the children, all the men, and all the young people who die, as though they had come from your own womb.

Luz Beatriz Arellano (Nicaragua)

THIRD SUNDAY OF EASTER

Acts 9:1–6 (7–20)   Revelation 5:11–14
Psalm 30   John 21:1–19

Looking for something?

Easter Sunday started at 6.30—we had a joint service with the chapel on Barrington Hill. There were about twenty-five of us in a circle. I was without the usual six o'clock start that Jonson and Harris normally provide. I must have slept through the alarm clock, so I arrived looking as though I had just got out of bed, which was the truth of it. Both churches were pretty full. A basket full of eggs came down from the bell chamber in Haslingfield to the charismatic children's arms below. Harlton was awash with flowers. The singing at Harlton is amazing—it can fill the place.

This is it: salt marshes, avocets, the sea breeze, Merlin's woods, North Norfolk and muddy waters. We're staying in a house in Cley. Freedom: the dog-collar's in the kennel. The boundary between the priest and the person is more relaxed now; they can coexist quite happily or they can come together without pressure. It's a wonderful job, but it makes too many martyrs, the parochialism is killing: cleaning the cobwebs, managing the money, mending the windows . . . making sure the grass is mown, sorting out the raffle, keeping the nettles down, all this becomes defining, it sticks in your throat. The North Sea is grey. I've rarely seen it blue, it's a leeward sea, wrestling with purgatory. This is the Church of England; there is always nothing exciting about it, is there? It's got Could Do Better stamped all over it, come on, love one another, make a scene about it; we have forgotten how to dance.

The sky on the sea was dragged off the Fens, the luminous edges outlining Constable colours. We sat on the beach, our hair crashing into our eyes, the wind tossing the kite into tangos. In the café on the beach which is dark inside, there are birds on the walls; the corrugated plastic rattles on the roof outside. We caught crabs this morning in Wells, pulling them up on orange lines out of the solemn water. The sun rushed through once in a while, turning the grey gulls white. We're just visiting, this is not our home, I'm sure of it; we are born pioneers and tourists. Watch the wildlife programmes—this is classic tourism, Planet Earth, a wonderland and a wasteland in perfect harmony. Did we choose to come here or have we been left to look for something?

Peter Owen Jones, *Small Boat Big Sea: One Year's Journey as a Parish Priest* (Oxford: Lion, 2000), pp. 141–42.

Easter morning
The stirring wildness of God
   calls brittle bones to leaping
and stone hearts to soaring.
Old women dance among the stars.

Ann Weems, *Kneeling in Jerusalem* (Louisville, Ky.: Westminster/John Knox Press, 1992), p. 93.

A difficult choosing

The difficulty of conversion is a difficulty of choosing. A choice must be made to enter into life and share in other's search for life.

Inasmuch as conversion is a matter of choice, it entails conflict. When one possesses a certain socioeconomic position, a break is inevitable if there is to be a conversion. Gustavo Gutiérrez says: "To wish to accomplish conversion without conflict is to deceive oneself and others."

Almost all who have written on the subject of conversion are in agreement on this point. It has been said that a conversion must be radical to the point "of confronting death in order to achieve a resurrection." Jon Sobrino claims that the exhortation "repent, and believe in the gospel" has an element of intimidation in it. "Now is the time to make a decision, and it will entail a conversion . . . a radical change in one's form of existence."

This inescapable break takes the form of a rejection of the present, in which death is at work or, in other words, the oppression exercised by the socioeconomic conditions in which we are caught. If conversion is what we say it is—a change of outlook that impels us inexorably to hasten the process of liberation (so that the masses may have the right to life)—then conflict is inevitable. For conversion brings with it an identification of opposites and a definitive confrontation.

Conversion is a gift of God because it shows us the way and invites us to enter the world of freedom, the world of life. But at the same time conversion is a

human task, because it demands of us an individual and collective commitment
to the building of that world.

Elsa Tamez, *Bible of the Oppressed*, trans. Matthew J. O'Connell
(Maryknoll, N.Y.: Orbis Books, 1982), pp. 80–81.

Back from the City

After three days and nights of rich food
and late talk in overheated rooms,
of walks between mounds of garbage
and human forms bedded down for the night
under rags, I come back to my dooryard,
to my own wooden step.

The last red leaves fall to the ground
and frost has blackened the herbs and asters
that grew beside the porch. The air
is still and cool, and the withered grass
lies flat in the field. A nuthatch spirals
down the rough trunk of the tree.

At the Cloisters I indulged in piety
while gazing at a painted lindenwood Pietà—
Mary holding her pierced and desiccated son
across her knees; but when a man stepped close
under the tasselled awning of the hotel,
asking for "a quarter for someone
down on his luck," I quickly turned my back.

Now I hear tiny bits of bark and moss
break off under the bird's beak and claw,
and fall onto already-fallen leaves.
"Do you love me?" said Christ to his disciple.
"Lord, you know
that I love you."
                    "Then feed my sheep."

Jane Kenyon, "Back from the City," from *Otherwise: New and Selected
Poems* (Saint Paul, Minn.: Graywolf Press, 1996). © 1996 by the Estate
of Jane Kenyon. Reprinted with the permission of Graywolf Press,
Saint Paul, Minnesota.

It is the Lord

It is the Lord, in the dawning,
        in the renewal,
        in the arrival,
        in the new day.

It is the Lord, in the crows,
        in the church,
        in the conversation,
        in the crisis.

It is the Lord, in our joys,
        in our sorrows,
        in our sickness,
        in our health.

It is the Lord, in the stable,
        in the humble,
        in the stranger,
        in the poor.

It is the Lord, risen and returned,
        alive for evermore,
        giving me new life,
        saving me in strife.
          It is the Lord.

David Adam, *Times and Seasons* (London: Triangle, 1989).

We beg you, make us really alive. Give us the spirit of light, that we may know you, the supremely true.

Serapion, Bishop of Thmuis (fourth century)

Fourth Sunday of Easter

Acts 9:36–43	Revelation 7:9–17
Psalm 23	John 10:22–30

No substitutes

To think "shepherd" might suggest an idyllic pastoral scene.

In fact, however, the term *shepherd* is political in the Bible. It means king, sovereign, lord, authority, the one who directs, to whom I am answerable, whom I trust and serve. In this simple opening line, the psalm is clear about the goal and focus, the center and purpose of life: Yahweh and no other. There is no rival loyalty, no competing claim—not economic or political, not liberal or conservative, not sexist or racist, not any of the other petty loyalties that seduce us. It is a mark of discernment and maturity to strip life down to one compelling loyalty, to be freed of all the others that turn out to be idolatrous.

Then the poet draws a stunning conclusion from this statement about God:

I shall not want.

I shall not lack anything. I shall not have any other yearnings or desires that fall outside the gifts of God. What God gives will be enough for me. This is a statement of enormous confidence in the generosity of God, the one who knows what we need and gives well beyond all that we ask or think. But notice at the same time that this phrase, "I shall not want," is a decision made against the greed and lust and satiation and aggressive ambition of a consumer society. Our consumer society is driven by the notion that we always must want one more thing, and we are entitled to it, and we will have it no matter what. . . .

Faith in this God requires a refocus of all our desires, because most of our wants are contrived and imagined and phony. This Lord will be Lord of our wants and our needs, and we need much less when we are clear about the wonder and goodness of God. No substitutes allowed or required.

Walter Brueggemann, *The Threat of Life: Sermons on Pain, Power, and Weakness*, ed. Charles L. Campbell (Minneapolis, Minn.: Fortress Press, 1996), pp. 91–92.

Lead, kindly light, amid the encircling gloom,
　Lead thou me on;
The night is dark, and I am far from home;
　Lead thou me on.
Keep thou my feet; I do not ask to see
The distant scene: one step enough for me.

　　　　　　　　John Henry Newman

Not just managers

During the Vatican Council I happened to meet Dr. Abraham Heschel, that towering Jewish rabbi, on the street in New York City. I followed him home, and we spent a few hours together. He apologized for the sad mood he was in—a heaviness of heart he could not seem to dispel.

"What made you sad, Rabbi?" I asked.

"My morning prayer," he replied.

"Oh, what were you praying about?"

"Your council."

"Why did that make you sad?"

Heschel answered that question by asking me one: "Father, how many of your bishops gathered at the council are contemplative?" Then *I* got sad.

The rabbi was right to stake the success of the council not on the managerial talents of bishops, nor on the expertise of the theologians, but on whether or not the shepherds of the flock were Christ-men, governed by the gifts of the Holy Spirit, and, therefore, in direct contact with the Living God as he is in himself.

William McNamara, *The Human Adventure: The Art of Contemplative Living* (Amity, N.Y.: Amity House, 1974), p. 19.

Eternal life

Life is our most precious gift from God, and we are called to make it most truly human. Neither a subhuman life, nor one that is simply passive, is a fully human life. The Hebrew conception of life is always one of action, movement and enjoyment. The evangelist John speaks of eternal life as the true life. But to John, eternal life is not the future resurrected life of believers; it is a life that we already presently enjoy in our earthly existence. Eternal life begins now when we live out Jesus' words of enduring life: 'Love one another.' Our life is one, so there is no division between physical life and spiritual life, between our life of food and drink and our life of relationship to God and neighbour.

The resurrection of Jesus announces that true life is available to, and the right of, all human beings; it is not something reserved for a few, or something that we await to happen on the 'last day': it is something we already live now. It is not compensation for the miseries of life, but a continuation of an earthly existence lived out according to God's will and purpose for humanity.

Virginia Fabella, "Symbols in John's Resurrection Scene: Reflection on the Garden and Mary Magdalene," in Lee Oo Chung et al., *Women of Courage: Asian Women Reading the Bible* (Seoul: Asian Women's Resource Center for Culture and Theology, 1992), pp. 189–90.

Hope awakens life

When hope does awaken, an entire life awakens along with it. One comes fully to life. It begins to seem indeed that one has never lived before. One awakens to a life that is eternal in prospect, a life that opens up before one all the way to death and beyond, a life that seems able to endure death and survive it. Wherever hope rises, life rises. When one first enters upon the spiritual adventure, hope rises where there was no hope before, where there was a life of 'quiet desperation,' and life rises too, the life of the spiritual adventure, the sense of being on a journey in time. There is *something to live for* where before there was nothing. Yet it proves not to be enough. One's heart is kindled, and yet there is a residue of darkness in it that remains unkindled. That dark residue is touched only when one discovers a new and unknown life in another person. Where one finds the other, a new hope rises and seems now to have *someone to live for*, but that hope is disappointed. The dark residue in one's heart has been heated but not to the kindling point, the 'fire point' after which it will burn by itself. It reaches the kindling point only 'when we dead awaken,' when one discovers a life that is able to live through death and loss. When the hope of living through death arises within one that appears to be the very life one is hoping for, the life that is spoken of in the words of promise 'and whoever lives and believes in me shall never die.'

John S. Dunne, *The Reasons of the Heart* (London: SCM Press, 1978), p. 120.

The background of resurrection is always impossibility. And with impossibility staring us in the face, the prelude to resurrection is invariably doubt, confusion, strife, and the cynical smile which is our defence against them. Resurrection is always the defiance of the absurd.

Harry Williams

FIFTH SUNDAY OF EASTER

Acts 11:1–18   Revelation 21:1–6

Psalm 148   John 13:31–35

Praise

Praise the Lord in his cosmos
Praise him in his sanctuary
Praise him with a radio-signal
   100,000 million light-years away
Praise him in the stars
   in inter-stellar space
Praise him in the galaxies
   in inter-galactic space
Praise him in atoms
   in inter-atomic space
Praise him on violin and flute
   on the saxophone
Praise him with clarinet and horn
   with cornet and trombone
   on alto-sax and trumpet
Praise him with viola and cello
   on piano and harpsichord
Praise him with blues and jazz
   with an orchestra
Praise him with spirituals
   with soul-music and Beethoven's fifth
   with marimbas and guitars
Praise him with discs and cassettes
   with hi-fi systems
   and quadraphonic sound
Let everything that draws breath praise him
   Alleluia!

Let all living cells praise the Lord
   Alleluia!
      Praise the Lord!

Ernesto Cardenal, *Psalms*, trans. John Griffiths (London: Sheed & Ward, 1981). Used by permission of the Continuum International Publishing Group Ltd.

Spiritual awakening

Mechtild of Magdeburg records the event in which her eyes were opened: "The day of my spiritual awakening was the day I saw and knew I saw all things in God and God in all things." And again, "The truly wise person kneels at the feet of all creatures."

Worship will not then be confined to celebration of God's mighty deeds in the past and the anticipation or discernment of those deeds in the present. It will also include the sheer rapturous enjoyment of the beauty of the creation itself. The "congregation" will be seen to be infinitely more vast, stretching to include every created thing as a vibrant, God-praising event. Look at how Psalm 148 calls the roll of those present in the congregation that worships God. . . .

The dis-ease of modern society is fundamentally spiritual, and the cure must be as well. The angels of nature invite us to reappraise our entire attitude toward the universe. We need the modern equivalent of the Native Americans' reverence for nature. We must find ways to move beyond observing nature to experiencing ourselves as a part of the nature being observed; to go beyond admiring its beauty and being caught up in the ecstasy of nature's epiphany of God. This is, after all, the experiential implication that follows from the Heisenberg principle: the observer is always a part of the field being observed. As we begin to integrate that insight into our lives, we will begin to *see* nature differently: no longer as detached and alienated observers, but as integral aspects of the cosmic dance of praise and delight in God.

Walter Wink, *Unmasking the Powers: The Invisible Forces That Determine Human Existence* (Philadelphia: Fortress Press, 1986), pp. 166, 167.

Mystery

The meaning of things, and their purpose
is in part now hidden
but shall in the end become clear.
The choice is between
the Mystery and the absurd.
To embrace the Mystery
is to discover the real.
It is to walk towards the light,
to glimpse the morning star, to catch sight
from time to time
of what is truly real
it is no more than a flicker of light
through the cloud of unknowing,
a fitful ray of light
that is a messenger from the sun
which is hidden from the gaze.
You see the light but not the sun.
When you set yourself to look more closely,
you will begin to see more sense
in the darkness that surrounds you.
Your eyes will begin to pick out
the shape of things and persons around you.
You will begin to see in them
the presence of the One
who gives them meaning and purpose,
and that it is He
who is the explanation of them all.

Basil Hume, *The Mystery of the Incarnation* (London: Darton,
Longman & Todd/Orleans, Mass.: Paraclete Press, 1999).
© 1999 Darton, Longman & Todd and Paraclete Press. Used by
permission of the publishers.

Loving people as they are

When our hearts are free from liking and judging people merely according to their natural gifts we are not held captive by external and changing charms. We are instead free to love people as they really are, and we can penetrate more easily to the core of their personality, their true goodness.

When we love in this way our love is selfless and pleasing to God.

The more this kind of love grows the more our love of God grows with it; and the deeper our love for him the more we shall love our neighbour for the principle of both is the same.

A great benefit of this way of loving people is that it fosters a large-hearted spirit, which is as necessary in God's service as is interior freedom. With it temptations against love are easily overcome, we are able to endure all things peacefully, and the virtues grow and flourish within us.

> From John of the Cross, *The Ascent of Mount Carmel*, book 3, 22, in
> *Lamps of Fire: Daily Readings with St John of the Cross*, ed. Elizabeth
> Ruth, O.D.C. (London: Darton, Longman & Todd, 1985), p. 18.

Prayer

I love you, O God,
my Love,
my Warmth,
my Solace,
my Fulfillment.
All that I am,
all that I do
finds meaning and purpose in you.
Fill me with the full force
of your Love
and its passionate splendor,
so that I might hold
and heal all those who are crying out for love.
Love through me
all the unreconciled
whose homes and hearts

are broken,
and let them know
I am able to love
because you have first loved me.

Miriam Therese Winter, *WomanWisdom* (New York: Crossroad Publishing Company, 1991), p. 274. © Medical Mission Sisters, 1991. Used by permission of The Crossroad Publishing Company.

Final word

The final word is love. At times it has been, in the words of Father Zossima, a harsh and dreadful thing, and our very faith in love has been tried through fire.

We cannot love God unless we love each other, and to love we must know each other. We know him in the breaking of bread, and we know each other in the breaking of bread, and we are not alone any more. Heaven is a banquet and life is a banquet, too, even with a crust, where there is companionship.

We have all known the long loneliness and we have learned that the only solution is love and that love comes with community.

Dorothy Day, *The Long Loneliness: Autobiography of Dorothy Day* (San Francisco: Harper & Row, 1952).

SIXTH SUNDAY OF EASTER

Acts 16:9–15   Revelation 21:10; 21:22–22:5

Psalm 67   John 5:1–9

Do you want to be healed?

Yes, we want to be healed:

as the dry well longs for water, as the exile for her home;

as the father wants his children,

and the broken house

demands its people back.

Yes, we want to be healed:

as those who live in fear of the enemy

wish they could breathe safe;

as the fence that divides the village

prefers to be torn down;

as children who dream bad dreams

need an unbroken night;

as those who have long been paralysed

now choose to move.

Janet Morley, *Companions of God: Praying for Peace in the Holy Land*
(London: Christian Aid, 1994), p. 28.

Grace

Grace strikes us when we are in great pain and restlessness. It strikes us when we walk through the dark valley of a meaningless and empty life. It strikes us when we feel that our separation is deeper than usual, because we have violated another life, a life which we loved, or from which we were estranged. It strikes us when our disgust for our own being, our indifference, our weakness, our hostility, and our lack of direction and composure have become intolerable to us. It strikes us when, year after year, the longed-for perfection of life does not appear, when the old compulsions reign within us as they have for decades, when despair destroys all joy and courage. Sometimes at that moment a wave of light breaks into our darkness, and it is as though a voice were saying:

157

You are accepted. *You are accepted*, accepted by that which is greater than you, and the name of which you do not know. Do not ask for the name now; perhaps you will find it later. Do not try to do anything now; perhaps later you will do much. Do not seek for anything; do not intend anything. *Simply accept the fact that you are accepted!*

If that happens to us, we experience grace. After such an experience we may not be better than before, and we may not believe more than before. But everything is transformed. In that moment, grace conquers sin, and reconciliation bridges the gulf of estrangement. And nothing is demanded of this experience, no religious or moral or intellectual proposition, nothing but *acceptance.*

> Paul Tillich, *The Shaking of the Foundations* (London: SCM Press,
> 1957), pp. 161–63.

When you have to make a vital decision about behaviour, you cannot sit on the fence. To decide to do nothing is still a decision, and it means that you remain on the station platform or the air strip when the train or plane has left.

> Kathleen Lonsdale

Drawing joy

Claude has the most illogical mind that I have ever encountered so this may be the first and last time that he is ever quoted in a book. He may ask such questions as 'What time is orange?' or 'How was tomorrow?' But still he does have a wisdom all his own. . . . Well, one day Claude was at the beach with Jean-Pierre and several others of the community. The ocean was at low tide so there was an immense stretch of flat, sandy beach. They began making designs in the sand. Claude drew a big circle with a couple of marks inside that could have been facial features. 'What's that?' asked Jean-Pierre. With a big smile Claude replied: 'It's Madame Sun.' 'That's good' Jean-Pierre said, 'Now let's see you draw joy.' Claude took a look around him at the wide beach that stretched out in both directions as far as the eye could see, then turned to Jean-Pierre and said with a huge smile in all seriousness: 'There's not enough room!'

> Bill Clarke, S.J., *Enough Room for Joy: Jean Vanier's L'Arche. A Message
> for Our Time* (London: Darton, Longman & Todd, 1974).

And it is good

Sometimes at dusk we see the loveliness of a doe and her fawn walking across the field, but they have stayed away from the garden, chewing instead the bark of tender new trees.

Broccoli, Brussels sprouts, carrots, don't mind the cold. We'll be picking them long after the ground is rimed with frost. We have discovered a new vegetable this summer, spaghetti squash, which we scrape out with a fork, after cooking, in long, spaghetti-like strands. Leeks are a delight, creamed, or in soup, and spinach salad. We glory in the goodness of creation every day. All that weed-pulling was worth it, though weeds have their own beauty, and, like mosquitoes and flies, are an inevitable part of the summer.

At night now the sky is clear, with no heat haze. One night we eat supper out on the little terrace which we have made with flagstones and lots of honest sweat. We linger at the picnic table through sunset and star rise, and suddenly someone says, 'How light it is on the northern horizon!' We blow out the lamps and there is the staggering beauty of the northern lights. There is something primal about those lights pulsing, in pale green and rose, upwards from the horizon. They give me the same surge of joy as the unpolluted horizon near the Strait of Magellan, showing the curve of the home planet; the same lifting of the heart as the exuberance of the dolphins sporting about the ship after we had crossed the equator.

I sit at the table as we all watch the awesome display of beauty, and there again is the promise of the rainbow covenant of Easter, radiant, affirming.

And it is good.

> Madeleine L'Engle, *And It Was Good: Reflections on Beginnings*
> (Wheaton, Ill.: Harold Shaw Publishers, 1983), pp. 210–11.

Wild, dangerous God

So, it turns out, we do not have a little tame domestic God, thank God, but we do have a huge, wild, dangerous God—dangerous of course only if we think that God ought to be manageable and safe; a God of almost manic creativity, ingenuity and enthusiasm; a Big-Enough God, who is also a supremely generous and patient God; a God of beauty and chance and solidarity.

Now I want to move on and look at some of the consequences of a belief in such a God, and I do this in the honest belief that there is no other credible God: it is a God as big and as unmanageable as this or no God at all—only the whimperings of an individualist liberal humanism, or a brave but harsh stoicism in the face of crude materialism, red in tooth and nail, busy going nowhere. I want to ask myself some 'so what?' questions; to look at some of the demands, if you like, that such a faith might make on us—as a people who are *made selves*, who are these kinds of persons, part of *this* cosmos, in *this* particular time and space. If there is any content whatsoever to this idea of matter—and ourselves as part of and within matter as co-creators, makers daily of the 'brand new thing' that we call the present, then ethics are important in a slightly more pressing and demanding way that we have been led to think. How we act and react is, in a true sense, what we make; and if we make it badly, falsely, selfishly, then that is how it will be. We will have to live in, and hand on to the future generations, a bad, false, selfish world— or at least, since we are not the sole creators, a worse, falser, more selfish world than it might otherwise be.

Sara Maitland, *A Big-Enough God: Artful Theology*
(London: Mowbray, 1996), p. 150.

God's glory is at work in all things. Everything that exists, exists because it is held, sustained, enlivened by God's wisdom and God's power. The Word of God who is God, God expressing himself towards his creation, wills at all times to work the mystery of his embodiment.

A. M. Allchin

ASCENSION

Acts 1:1–11   Ephesians 1:15–23
Psalm 47   Luke 24:44–53

A place for you

Last night there were thunderstorms: but today everything is beautiful. The leaves on the hickory tree by the cemetery are small and the flowers fill the branches with fringes of green lace. I hear the engine running down at the mill: only that, and the birds singing.

Tomorrow is the Ascension, my favourite feast. At any time in the year I am liable to find the antiphons of Ascension Day ringing in my ears and they fill me with light and peace. 'I go to prepare a place for you.'

It is the feast of silence and interior solitude when we go up to live in heaven with Jesus: for he takes us there, after he has lived a little while on earth among us.

That is the grace of Ascension Day: to be taken up into the heaven of our own souls, the point of immediate contact with God. To rest on this quiet peak, in the darkness that surrounds God. To live there through all trials and all business with the 'tranquil God who makes all things tranquil.'

God be with me this day and forever.

> Thomas Merton, *The Sign of Jonas*
> (London: Sheldon Press, 1976), part 1.

Spinning a tale, catching a vision

The Risen Christ commissions the apostles to make disciples of all nations. God's salvation, in other words, opens up like a horseshoe, and extends until the whole of creation is within its embrace. It is of universal significance and application.

But how is this to be communicated in a way which triggers people's imagination and claims their hearts and minds? What exactly is to be proclaimed and how might we live it out? The answer to these questions might be found in an unlikely source, a well-known children's nursery rhyme:

> Pussy cat, pussy cat where have you been?
> I've been up to London to visit the Queen.

Pussy cat, pussy cat what did you there?
I frightened a little mouse under the chair!

The implication in this rhyme is that the cat, despite his adventurous excursion, remains preoccupied with the usual cat routines of life, and so failed to glimpse the light of majestic glory which was the object of his journey. Unlike the cat in this rhyme, who failed to see above the skirting board, Christians are invited at Ascensiontide to raise their sights above their daily preoccupations, to see the whole picture and then to regard everything else in its light. Ascensiontide, with its imagery of the glorified Christ 'seated at the right hand of the throne of the Majesty in heaven' (Hebrews 8:1), summons Christians to raise their sights, to cast off the blinkers of prejudice, and to contemplate the final scene, the full picture of our human flesh borne and presented by Christ to the Father. As Lewis Carroll, who enchanted and intrigued his audience by his spinning of tales and word games, said: 'That's glory for you!'

> Christopher Irvine, "Spinning a Tale and Catching a Vision: Preach-
> ing on the Ascension" in *Celebrating the Easter Mystery: Worship
> Resources for Easter to Pentecost,* ed. Christopher Irvine (London:
> Mowbray, 1996), p. 111.

The beauty of God

The glory of God, the splendor, the fullness of God—I prefer to translate this mysterious word with 'the beauty of God.' To be comforted does not mean that we receive something, a thing, an object from God but that we catch sight of the beauty and splendor of God. Where, then, do we see that? Where can we find that?

The Bible is quite clear on this point. The beauty, the splendor of God is visible in all those who prepare God's way. The messianic work of liberation awaits us. God entrusts us with preparing the way of the Messiah. God does not say to anyone, 'You are just a simple housewife or a mere employee and understand nothing of complicated necessities.' Prepare the way of God, comfort the people in their weakness, make them into street workers on God's way. No man is too small or too large, no woman is too young or too old, too educated or too ignorant. God has given all of us a part, God comforts us, and we prepare God's way. God's voice calls to us and we answer. God's spirit wants to make us courageous and capable of truth. God wants to be born in us.

> Dorothee Soelle, *Theology for Sceptics*, trans. Joyce L. Irwin (London:
> Mowbray, 1995; Minneapolis, Minn.: Fortress Press, 1995), p. 126.

A legend

There is a very old legend, and all legends that persist speak truth, concerning the return of the Lord Jesus Christ to heaven after his Ascension. It is said that the angel Gabriel met him at the gates of the city.

'Lord, this is a great salvation that thou hast wrought,' said the angel. But the Lord Jesus only said, 'Yes.'

'What plans hast thou made for carrying on the work? How are all to know what thou hast done?' asked Gabriel.

'I left Peter and James and John and Martha and Mary to tell their friends, their friends to tell their friends, till all the world should know.'

'But Lord Jesus,' said Gabriel, 'suppose Peter is too busy with the nets, or Martha with the housework, or the friends they tell are too occupied, and forget to tell their friends—what then?'

The Lord Jesus did not answer at once; then he said in his quiet wonderful voice: 'I have not made any other plans. I am counting on them.'

George MacLeod, *Daily Readings with George MacLeod*,
ed. Ron Ferguson (Glasgow: Wild Goose Publications, 2001).

Our extra bonus

Although it may seem odd, the experience of God is our extra bonus, our reward—it is the pleasure and joy of religion.

We trundle along the ground like planes about to take off. But, if we do not resist it, there is a mysterious upward thrust, and—good Lord!—we are airborne. This experience is the wine of religion, the joy which lies at its heart.

We search for God in our clumsy ways and, sometimes, we despair. But if we really search, a hand, as it were, comes down and pulls us up. We find to our surprise that we are not the only searchers. We are half-heartedly searching for God, but God is whole-heartedly searching for us.

This may seem a personal experience, some say disparagingly 'subjective.' But it is an experience witnessed again and again in the history of our people, by housewives and prophets, by rebbes and rabbis, by the ignorant and the learned, in every religious book of our history.

Lionel Blue, "God and the Jewish Problem," in *A Genuine Search*, ed.
Dow Marmur (1979), p. 43. © Reform Synagogues of Great Britain.

Ascension

Stretching Himself as if again,
   through downpress of dust
      upward, soul giving way
to thread of white, that reaches
   for daylight, to open as green
      leaf that it is ...
Can Ascension
   not have been
      arduous, almost,
as the return
   from Sheol, and
      back through the tomb
into breath?
   Matter reanimate
      now must relinquish
itself, its
   human cells,
      molecules, five
senses, linear
   vision endured
      as Man—
the sole
   all-encompassing gaze
      resumed now,
Eye of Eternity.
   Relinquished, earth's
      broken Eden.
Expulsion,
   liberation,
      last
self-enjoined task
   of Incarnation.
      He again
Fathering Himself.
   Seed-case
      splitting.

He again
  Mothering His birth:
    torture and bliss.

Denise Levertov, *A Door in the Hive* and *Evening Train* (New York: New Directions Publishing Corporation, 1992, and Newcastle upon Tyne: Bloodaxe Books, 1993), p. 207. Used by permission of Pollinger Ltd. and the Estate of Frieda Lawrence Ravagli.

The Ascension is a festival of the future of the world. The flesh is redeemed and glorified, for the Lord has risen for ever. We Christians are, therefore, the most sublime materialists.

Karl Rahner

SEVENTH SUNDAY OF EASTER

Acts 16:16–34	Revelation 22:12–14, 16–17, 20–21
Psalm 97	John 17:20–26

What kind of kingdom will this be?

What kind of kingdom will this be?

It will be a kingdom where, in accordance with Jesus' prayer, God's name is truly hallowed, his will is done on earth, human beings will have everything in abundance, all sin will be forgiven and all evil overcome.

It will be a kingdom where, in accordance with Jesus' promises, the poor, the hungry, those who weep and those who are downtrodden will finally come into their own; where pain, suffering and death will have an end.

It will be a kingdom that cannot be described, but only made known in metaphors: as the new covenant, the seed springing up, the ripe harvest, the great banquet, the royal feast.

It will therefore be a kingdom—wholly as the prophets foretold—of absolute righteousness, of unsurpassable freedom, of dauntless love, of universal reconciliation, of everlasting peace. In this sense therefore it will be the time of salvation, of fulfilment, of consummation, of God's presence: the absolute future.

Hans Küng, *On Being a Christian,* trans. Edward Quinn (William
Collins, 1977), p. 215.

New creation

The child (full of anxiety and bliss) sees itself in the power of what 'future things' will bring, and for that reason, it can only live in the present. However, they who are mature, who desire to be defined by the present, fall subject to the past, to themselves, death and guilt. It is only out of the future that the present can be lived. . . . Baptism is the call to the human being into childhood, a call that can be understood only eschatologically. . . . The child is near to what is of the future. This is the new creation of the human being of the future, which here is an event already occurring in faith, and there perfected for view. It is the new creation of those who no longer look back upon themselves, but only away from themselves to God's revelation, to Christ. It is the new creation of those born from out of the world's confines into the wideness of heaven, becoming where they were or never were, a creature of God, a child.

Dietrich Bonhoeffer, *Act and Being,* trans. Bernard Noble (London: William Collins; New York: Harper and Row, 1961), pp. 159–61.

Prayers of intercession

Risen and glorious Christ,
Come among us, restore and remake us.

Forgiving Lord, you restored Peter into fellowship and call us all to be one people: take from our hearts the spirit of retaliation; grant us the grace to forgive others, and the desire to build community with those with whom we live, and work, and worship.

Risen and glorious Christ,
Come among us, restore and remake us.

Ascended Lord, you gather up all things in heaven and earth; grant to all who govern the nations, and those who shape and implement economic and social policy a vision of the new Jerusalem, that our lives may be peaceably and justly ordered, and all people dwell in freedom and integrity.

Risen and glorious Christ,
Come among us, restore and remake us.

Living Lord, you meet us with your abundance and call us into the fullness of life; hear our prayer for those who lack food and clean water, and prosper the work of those who bring relief to those in need.

Risen and glorious Christ,
Come among us, restore and remake us.

Lord of all life, in your risen body you bear the marks of suffering; look with compassion upon all who are maimed and scarred by the violence of others. Speak your word of peace and dispel the anxiety of those bearing physical pain, and those suffering mental anguish.

Risen and glorious Christ,
Come among us, restore and remake us.

First born of the new creation, strengthen with your Spirit those who in this season have been joined to you in baptism, and incorporated into your Body the Church; through your grace may the fruits of the Spirit come to maturity in our lives, and may all our prayers and praises be joined to the prayers and praises of the saints in light.

Risen and glorious Christ,
Come among us, restore and remake us.

Christopher Irvine, ed., *Celebrating the Easter Mystery: Worship Resources for Easter to Pentecost* (London: Mowbray, 1996), pp. 63–64.

Give us hearts of flesh

Face to face we sit—
the silence, like a stone wall,
separating us.

It is not enough
to sit in proximity
if we have no trust.

Give us hearts of flesh
to grieve our hostility:
then grant us laughter

and let us reach out.
Even if we do not see
eye to eye clearly

dare us open up
our hands, be hospitable:
bare us, soul to soul.

Kate Compston, in Geoffrey Duncan, comp. and ed., *Dare to Dream* (London: Fount, 1995), p. 143. © Kate Compston.

What is mine is thine

The only way the world will recognize the mission of Jesus is by the unity of his Church. But this unity of the Church must be translated into real community.

Jesus spoke of the absolute unity between his Father and himself. And his prayer for us is that we be just as united (John 17:21–22). Can there still be mine and thine between us? No. What is mine is thine, and what is thine is mine. In the Spirit of the Church everything we have belongs to all. First and foremost we have community in the innermost values of the common life. But if we share the treasures of the Spirit, which are the greater ones, how can we refuse to share the lesser things?

Eberhard Arnold, God's Revolution: Justice, Community, and the
Coming Kingdom (Farmington, Pa./Robertsbridge, E. Sussex: Plough
Publishing House, 2d ed., 1997), pp. 33–34.

If believers in Christ are one, wherever one member seems to be to the natural eye, there indeed is the whole body by the sacramental mystery. Whatever belongs to the whole in some way seems to fit in with any part.

Peter Damian (1007–72)

Prayer used in the Ecumenical center, Geneva, Switzerland, on the occasion of the visit of Pope John Paul II.

> O God, the giver of life,
> we pray for the Church throughout the world:
> sanctify its life; renew its worship;
> empower its witness; restore its unity.
> Remove from your people all pride
> and every prejudice that dulls their will for unity.
> Strengthen the work of all those who strive to seek
> that common obedience that will bind us together.
> Heal the nations which separate your children from one another,
> that they may keep the unity of the Spirit in the bond of peace.

John Carden, ed., With All God's People (Geneva: World Council of
Churches Publications, 1989). Used by permission.

PENTECOST

Acts 2:1–21
Psalm 104:24–34, 35b

Romans 8:14–17
John 14:8–17 (25–27)

The light is so bright and warm. It is **overwhelming** and **so welcoming.** I walked in and felt your power, God. Thank you.

Jenny, Saint Matthias High School, Chicago, Ill., in *Life Can Be a Wild Ride: More Prayers by Young Teens,* ed. Marilyn Kielbasa (Winona, Minn.: St. Mary's Press, 2001), p. 88.

Heaven

Heaven is glory, and heaven is joy; we cannot tell which most; we cannot separate them; and this comfort is joy in the Holy Ghost. This makes all Job's states alike, as rich in the first chapter of his book, where all is suddenly lost, as in the last, where all is abundantly restored. This consolation from the Holy Ghost makes my midnight noon, my executioner a physician, a stake and pile of fagots, a bonfire of triumph; this consolation makes a satire and a slander and libel against me into a panegyric and an elegy in my praise; it makes an 'Away with him!' an 'All hail!', a 'Woe!' a 'Bravo!', a 'Crucify!' a 'Hosanna!'. It makes my deathbed a marriage bed, and my passing-bell an epithalamium [a wedding song].

John Donne (1572–1631), from a sermon delivered in St. Paul's Cathedral on Whitsunday 1625 (slightly modernized).

God the guest

If I asked any one of you whether you love God, you would answer me with entire confidence and complete conviction: "I do." But . . . "If anyone loves me, he will keep my word." The proof of love is its manifestation in our actions. That is why John says in his first letter that "one who says, I love God, and does not observe his commandments is a liar."

. . . My friends, consider the greatness of this solemn feast that commemorates God's coming as a guest into our hearts! If some rich and influential friend were to come to your home, you would promptly put it all in order for fear something there might offend your friend's eyes when he came in. Let all of us then who are preparing our inner homes for God cleanse them of anything our wrongdoing has brought into them.

> Gregory the Great, from Homily 30, in *Be Friends with God: Spiritual Reading from Gregory the Great,* trans. John Leinenweber (Cambridge, Mass.: Cowley Publications, 1990), pp. 145–46.

Our Stand on Strikes

Let us be honest, let us say that fundamentally, the stand we are taking is not on the ground of wages and hours and conditions of labor, but on the fundamental truth that men should be treated not as chattels, but as human beings, as "temples of the Holy Ghost." When Christ took on our human nature, when He became man, He dignified and ennobled human nature. He said, "The Kingdom of Heaven is within you." When men are striking, they are following an impulse, often blind, often uninformed, but a good impulse—one could even say an inspiration of the Holy Spirit. They are trying to uphold their right to be treated not as slaves, but as men. They are fighting against the idea of their labor as a commodity, to be bought and sold.

> Dorothy Day, *Selected Writings,* ed. Robert Ellsberg (Maryknoll, N.Y.: Orbis Books, 1992), p. 241 [July 1936].

Freedom from fear

The discovery of Pentecost, in recent years, as suitable for "political" witness is not, as some believers and non-believers alike must think, either curious or weird. It is liturgically fitting and theologically to the point. Pentecost signifies freedom. Freedom now. Public freedom. Freedom from fear. It's not coincidence that various of the resurrection occurrences transpire behind closed doors....

The question to which Pentecost comes as bold answer is this: Will the movement be ruled by fear? Will they be contained and confined? Rendered timid and silent? Pentecost says no.

The story in Acts 2 begins presumably in the upper room and ends in the streets of Jerusalem. How did they get there? Carried by the big wind? It's as if the walls dissolve. Or in a reversal of the resurrected Christ's passage into their midst, they pass through and out. The disciples take the resurrection to the streets. They go public.

To the authorities it must appear as political madness, an acute and hopefully isolated case of sanctified anarchism. Some people say that they have had too much to drink. Granted this refers in part to the inspired and ecstatic utterances, but I wager even more so to their reckless courage. After what's been done to Jesus, you'd have to be either crazy or drunk to be shouting his name in the streets and pointing accusing fingers at the executioners.

Heretofore the disciples have beheld Christ; now they experience the concrete and practical freedom of the resurrection. No political authority any place or any time can shut that down. Pentecost means speaking without confusion.

Bill Wylie Kellermann, *Seasons of Faith and Conscience: Kairos,
Confession, Liturgy* (Maryknoll, N.Y.: Orbis Books, 1991), pp. 200–201.

All that is true, by whomsoever spoken, is from the Holy Spirit.

Ambrose of Milan (340–97)

Four missionaries talk

We sit on the rock in front of the chapel tent . . . drinking sweet tea as we talk, somewhat lightheartedly, about what it means for us to be missionaries.

Sister Lwanga thinks that mission mainly consists in sharing the Good News, and she backs her argument with the Bible, quoting John 1:35–51, where Jesus called his first apostles and sends them on their way. But from the stories of Sister Martha about her youth in Uganda, it is quite clear that at times missionaries have been bad news. . . . 'Some even thought they had to bring God to Africa. They did not realize that God was there long before they arrived.'

I have heard these stories before, and in some ways I have been part of the syndrome. But here we are looking for better ways. I suggest that mission can also be seen as a dialogue where we share together, where we are sent to each other and share who we are. We can leave it open who gets converted by whom: maybe in the sharing both parties are converted. Sister Martha, who is in a bit of a provocative mood tonight, remarks that nobody is harder to convert than a missionary. If that missionary is a priest then it is even harder, she thinks. When you are a priest, or a sister for that matter, you are in a position of power in the church. She wonders whether dialogue is possible without equality. She even thinks that people are more open to each other when in some ways they are powerless.

Sister Josephine, who prefers crochet work to engaging in abstract discussion, says that she leaves it all to the Holy Spirit. 'The Spirit can sort it out. After all, mission is the work of the Holy Spirit,' someone had told her. She had liked that; it meant one less worry for her. She adds that it is all right to give the Holy Spirit a helping hand, but we should not try to take the lead. We laugh about it: four missionaries on a rock in the moonlight, unsure what their lives are really about. Sister Lwanga comes back to what Josephine said about the Spirit. We know that we should be open to that Spirit but we don't know where the Spirit will lead us.

Mathew Haumann, *The Long Road to Peace: Encounters with the People of Southern Sudan* (Leominster, Herefordshire: Gracewing, 2000), pp. 78–79.

Jesus our peace, we know very little about praying but we remember your words: "I will send you the Holy Spirit, he will be a source of comfort, remaining with you for ever."

Brother Roger of Taizé

O heavenly King, Comforter, Spirit of truth, present everywhere, filling everything, Treasury of blessings, Giver of life: come and dwell in us, cleanse us of all impurity and of your goodness save our souls.

Orthodox prayer

Trinity Sunday

Proverbs 8:1–4, 22–31

Psalm 8

Romans 5:1–5

John 16:12–15

Playtime

It takes a kind of courage
to find time for play. . . .

Thank God for the dreams
in which we mount our fiery imaginations
and ride off into the misty mountains.
Night takes to task the busy day;
but why am I ashamed to claim the right to conscious play
within the waking world?

When I can sit and let my mind catch fire
I understand how God sang for fun
calling out of nothing all creation.
Wagtails bounce and flip their feathers
salmon leap,
the world turns, the planets wheel,
tiny or vast
orchestrated into a joyful tune,
the models of all making.

Dreams, imagination and God's laughter in creation
invite me out of my industrious solemnity,
to take the task of playing seriously
until my marred manhood
is recreated in the child I have denied.

Michael Hare Duke, *Hearing the Stranger: Reflections, Poems, &*
Hymns (Sheffield: Cairns Publications, 1994), pp. 76–77.

In the daily round

For [mystics] all prayer and reflection leads into deeper exploration and understanding of the life of the Trinity, to seeing it reflected in the created world, and to sharing that life in the ordinary occupations of the daily round. Twice I have been allowed to glimpse that this is not just the high-falutin' talk of esoterics who live in a higher gear than most of us. Both were on improbable occasions, the first during an *al fresco* luncheon in a farmhouse garden when bang in the middle of the festivities the elderly French mother of the assembled family suddenly launched into a disquisition on the Trinity, its meaning and place in Christian life, that could only have issued from a lifetime's meditation on the subject. . . . The second was during a tour of the university campus in Manchester, when somewhere along the Oxford road my priest companion suddenly exposed the way in which his understanding of the Trinity had shaped and directed his own pastoral work and spiritual life. . . . Both left the strongest possible impression that the Trinity is not inescapably beyond the human horizon, but touches our human life at every point.

John Harriott, *The Empire of the Heart* (Springfield, Ill.: Templegate
Publishers/Leominster, Herefordshire: Gracewing, 1990), p. 102.

The reality of baptism

We say that in baptism we die with Christ and rise again with him, but our manner of celebrating the sacrament, by pouring a very small quantity of water on to the forehead of the person baptized, does not help us to realise the meaning of what we say. By contrast, a friend who was baptised in adult life, into the Orthodox Church, told me that at his baptism, the first time the priest pushed his head under the water—in the name of the Father—he thought, 'This is very interesting'; the second time—in the name of the Son—he thought, 'This must be what dying and rising with Christ means'; the third time—in the name of the Holy Spirit —his reaction was simply, *'Help!'*

A. M. Allchin, "The Sacraments in L'Arche," in *Encounter with
Mystery: Reflections on L'Arche and Living with Disability*, ed. Frances
Young (London: Darton, Longman & Todd, 1997), p. 104.

A new song

Though she worked in silent stone, Barbara Hepworth continually explored the power of music as she sculpted hollowed spaces and strings held in tension, suggesting, like their titles, rhythm and resonance. Her chosen epitaph for herself was *Cantate Domino* (1958), a bronze sculpture of two wings soaring upwards in bird-like transcendency, one pointing beyond the other as if to an unattained destiny. The base has a rooted network and the parted wings are linked by a flowing loop, indicating an openness to new life. The whole figure gives the impression of God at our roots and God beyond us, to whom we reach out, the God in whom heaven and earth are one. The psalms of her title sing of the God who comes to make of us a new creation and whose wonder may cause us, at any time, on any day, to exclaim

Sing to the Lord a new song!

Brian Pickett, *Songs for the Journey: The Psalms in Life and Liturgy*
(London: Darton, Longman & Todd, 2002), p. 177. © Darton,
Longman & Todd Ltd., 2002. Used by permission of the publishers.

God as father and mother

Trinitarian theology and the rediscovery of its feminine traits has . . . its basis in the Holy Scriptures and in the traditions of the Church. For this reason, it is inscribed in the heart of a people who can count on the constant companionship of a God who desires liberation from all kinds of oppression. The Church in Latin America today, the Church that has made a preferential option for the oppressed, proclaims the God of life. This God is a strong, protective Father and at the same time a loving, eternal Mother. The human image of this God is found within the community of liberated men and women who, side by side, are building the kingdom of God. They hope and pray for the promised time when all domination, whether patriarchal or matriarchal, will be overcome, and a future day will know neither lords nor slaves. In the messianic humanity there is "neither Jew nor Greek, neither slave nor free, neither male nor female" (Gal. 3:28). In Latin America today, we are called to construct such humanity from, and find its destination in, the great mystery of Love, which we call Father, Son, and Holy Spirit, which, in its infinite mercy, is revealed both as a generative and a creative force, and as a womb that gives birth and stirs with compassion.

María Clara Bingemer, from "Reflections on the Trinity," in *Through Her Eyes: Women's Theology from Latin America*, ed. Elsa Tamez (Maryknoll, N.Y.: Orbis Books, 1989), p. 80.

The force of evil

[I visited] a refugee camp called Jalazon in the occupied West Bank. Here, in the most stifling and repressive conditions, about 6,000 people attempt to maintain family life and community against all the odds. We had spent the afternoon visiting nursery schools and a women's centre, and walking the streets, being shown the bulldozed and sealed-up houses. Now we had been invited to the home of a woman whose 13-year-old son had been shot dead. There were about ten of us, sitting in this bare and utterly impoverished household. Yet even here, the duty of hospitality had to be observed. I saw the bottles of lemonade being passed in the back window from where I was sitting, and in a minute all of us were graciously served with refreshing glasses. We were sipping our drinks appreciatively because it was very hot and dusty, when suddenly there was a loud crack followed by another. A minute later, an elderly man rushed into the house, choking and spitting, and then the tear-gas began to drift into the room, making us cough and our eyes smart and run. We had to put down our drinks and move into an inner room, and then, hurriedly, out of the house and back to our car, just as a fully armed army patrol came racing down the hill towards us. There was disarray, the moment of hospitality and the sharing of grief was shattered, and the women who were our hosts were distressed and embarrassed—for our sake, because for them this was a regular occurrence. A moment of grace was terminated in fear and confusion. I experienced this as a diabolical moment, a moment when things fell apart. This is how we recognize the force of evil at work in the world—it causes things to fall apart.

Kathy Galloway, *Getting Personal: Sermons and Meditations (1986–94)* (London: SPCK, 1995), pp. 67–68.

Who is the Trinity?

You are music.
You are life.

Source of everything,
creator of everything,
angelic hosts sing your praise.

Wonderfully radiant,
deep,
mysterious.

You are alive in everything,
and yet you are unknown to us.

Hildegard of Bingen, in *Meditations with Hildegard of Bingen,* trans. Gabriele Uhlein (Santa Fe, N.M.: Bear & Company, 1983), p. 28.

PROPER 4

Ordinary Time 9

*Sunday between May 29 and June 4
inclusive (if after Trinity Sunday)*

1 Kings 18:20–21 (22–29) 30–39   Galatians 1:1–12
Psalm 96   Luke 7:1–10

Desperate measures

I wasn't sure what [treatment] to try next. I thought of the Emperor Menelik II, the dynamic and resourceful creator of modern Ethiopia, who was in the habit of nibbling a few pages of the Bible whenever he became ill. In December 1913, while recovering from a stroke, he ate the entire Book of Kings and died.

> Michael Mayne, *A Year Lost and Found* (London: Darton,
> Longman & Todd, 1987), p. 17.

Authority and obedience

Authority and obedience can never be divided, with some people having all the authority while others only have to obey. This separation causes authoritarian behaviour on the one side and doormat behaviour on the other. It perverts authority as well as obedience. A person with great authority who has nobody to be obedient to is in great spiritual danger. A very obedient person who has no authority over anyone is equally in danger.

> Henri J. M. Nouwen, *Bread for the Journey: Reflections for Every Day of
> the Year* (London: Darton, Longman & Todd, 1996), p. 119.

The spiritual authority of God is that which he exercises by displaying not his power, but his character. Holiness, not omnipotence, is the spring of his spiritual authority.

> William Temple

Dutch missionary priest: Sudanese layman

For years Ongwech and I have been conducting workshops together: with others we search for ways of further growth. . . . The participants in this workshop are a mixed bag: priests and laity, white and black, religious of various origins, tired and frustrated people, and others full of enthusiasm who want to get cracking. Tonight Ongwech conducted the last session and made a fine job of it. Many matters that had been bottled up for years were voiced. . . . After the session was over, the discussion continued outside. The atmosphere was charged and painful. . . .

Now Ongwech and I are talking about tomorrow morning's session. Ongwech is relaxed. . . . I [am] uneasy. I don't thrive in crisis situations, and at times it seems as if Ongwech is trying to provoke them. He often points out to me that every crisis creates new opportunities. Now he is suggesting that I conduct the next session. . . . 'To them I'm "only" a layman,' he says with a smile.

How are we to get this group closer together again? I ask. . . . 'Not in the Dutch way,' he responds with a smile. . . . 'What's wrong with our way?' I ask. . . . Ongwech knows our kind; he has worked together with many Dutchmen, he visited our country, had Dutch teachers at school. 'You see,' he says, 'you people think that honesty is the greatest virtue. One must always tell the truth. But you use truth as a weapon, and if someone takes offence you shrug your shoulders and say, "Well, that's the truth, isn't it?" As if that justifies hitting someone over the head with it.' . . .

I ask if he is suggesting I should let all truth go by the board. At times I get the impression truth is not always taken seriously in Africa. Ongwech reflects on this, then answers, 'You must tell the truth, but not every truth must be told. And if you have to tell the truth, a little subtlety is better than a lot of force.'

> Mathew Haumann, M.H.M., *The Long Road to Peace: Encounters with the People of the Southern Sudan* (Leominster, Herefordshire: Gracewing, 2000), pp. 103–5.

The promise of baptism

The promise of baptism is that the Spirit will conform women, men, and children into communities of disciples who become a living remembrance of the one who created inclusive communities and open table-sharing, who welcomed children and attended to the needs of the poor and outcast, who sought out those who were lost or abandoned. We recognize Christ in ministers of the gospel who bring hope to the helpless, who preach unlimited forgiveness, who bind up wounds and offer new possibilities to those who do not believe in themselves or God's power. To image Christ is to enflesh the life of the one who celebrated life in all its fullness and who exercised mercy even in the midst of his own dying.

Mary Catherine Hilkert, *Speaking with Authority: Catherine of Siena and the Voices of Women Today* (New York/Mahwah, N.J.: Paulist Press, 2000), p. 49.

What the "good news" is really about

Narrow understandings of salvation not only cause great pain to the many persons who are burdened with guilt but also lead the church to false pride and arrogance in its claim to be the "place" of God's salvation. . . . [Salvation's] gospel meaning is often illuminated most clearly by those whose struggles with death and hopes for life help us understand what good news is all about. This is because salvation is a story and not an idea, a word that describes God's mending and reconciling action in our lives and in the whole of creation. As we respond in faith to God's saving action, we are drawn into the story and God's gift of justice and love is revealed in our lives.

Letty M. Russell, *Church in the Round: Feminist Interpretation of the Church* (Louisville, Ky.: Westminster/John Knox Press, 1993), pp. 114–15.

God is Spirit

In the final analysis, the power of God *is* God. That which dwells in us is the Spirit of God, the Spirit of Christ. . . . This dominion of the Spirit as source of life is so powerful, in Paul's view, that in many passages it is impossible to decide whether "spirit" refers to the human person under grace or to the Holy Spirit.

Gustavo Gutiérrez, *We Drink from Our Own Wells: The Spiritual Journey of a People* (London: SCM Press, 1984), p. 64. Translation © Orbis Books, Maryknoll, N.Y., 1984.

Thou art the great God, of whose greatness there is no end, and thus I perceive thee to be the immeasurable measure of all things, even as the infinite end of all.

Nicolas of Cusa

Source of life

Leader: Lord God, source of life,

All: **we rejoice that through the power
of your love we are alive;
breathing, thinking, feeling creatures,
made in your likeness
and for your glory.**

Leader: Lord God, source of life,

All: **recognising that our life exists
through your desire,
we thank you and praise you
and glorify you.**

Susan Sayers, *To Worship in Stillness: Thirty Reflective Services* (Bury St. Edmunds: Kevin Mayhew, 1991), p. 16. © Susan Sayers. Reproduced by permission of the publisher, Kevin Mayhew Ltd., Buxhall, Stowmarket, Suffolk, IP14 3BW.

PROPER 5

Ordinary Time 10

*Sunday between June 5 and 11
inclusive (if after Trinity Sunday)*

1 Kings 17:8–16 (17–24)   Galatians 1:11–24
Psalm 146   Luke 7:11–17

The oddness of Elijah

The trouble in Israel was structural and systemic. There was no rain. The drought brought with it death. Drought is an ancient form of energy crisis. The energy crisis means that the government has failed. The king could not cause rain, could not give life. The king was impotent, the government was discredited. The world had failed. The situation was right for despair and dismay.

Such an energy crisis affected everyone, rich and poor. As usual, however, the crisis impinged upon the poor first, and most decisively. Our attention is focused on a nameless woman. Such women are always nameless. She had nothing, neither name, nor food nor hope. Actually, she had one thing, her beloved son. He was her only hope, her welfare system, her lean link to life.

The story begins in the failed royal system with this nameless, forlorn widow. Elijah enters the story. He is another kind of character. He is uncredentialed, uncontaminated by the system, uncompromised by government plans for rain. He is also untested, because nobody knows what he can do. He works through no royal arrangements. He is simply dispatched by Yahweh, an abrupt, unexplained command: "Go to the widow" (v. 9). He goes. He goes to meet the widow. Oddly, he gives her an unending supply of food (v. 16). He does for her what the king cannot do.

The plot now thickens. . . . The boy, the widow's only hope in this age or in the age to come dies. . . . Elijah acts in a remarkable way. He prays. He turns the problem of death over to the reality of God. He speaks to make death be a concern for God. His words open the problem of death to the power of God. . . .

God yields to Elijah. Elijah has compelled God to act. . . . God has done what the king cannot do.

This is a story about the oddness of Elijah. Elijah is shown to have the power for life. That power is not explained; it is only witnessed to. It is linked to faith and to prayer, to a refusal to accept the widow's little faith or the king's little power. The world enacted by Elijah breaks all such convention, routines, and stereotypes: New news has come. The boy lives! The news given us in this story is that the power for life is offered. It is carried by a human agent.

Walter Brueggemann, *The Threat of Life: Sermons on Pain, Power, and Weakness,* ed. Charles L. Campbell (Minneapolis: Fortress Press, 1996), pp. 42, 43, 44.

Resurrection and faith

We cannot fully know what resurrection is like; we must live into it in faith. Yet the New Testament is filled with analogies for realities we can know only through faith: parables that tell us what God's compassion is like, images of banquet feasts that suggest the qualities of the reign of God, metaphors from planting and harvest to describe transformation. Revelation reaches us through images and symbols; it comes to us primarily on the level of the imagination. Symbols bring us meaning and at the same time preserve its context of mystery. They are transparent to the divine. This is important to remember, for it frees us to imagine what resurrection might be like, knowing that the Bible itself can never fully describe or literally encompass it. In this area as in all others, we live by analogy.

The imagination is especially important when we are dealing with the body/spirit paradox, for it is the imagination that spans the difference between matter and spirit, holding them together in one act of experience and knowledge. It alerts us to the poetry found in the material world.

Kathleen Fischer, *Moving On: A Spiritual Journey for Women of Maturity* (London: SPCK, 1996; Mahwah N.J.: Paulist Press, 1995), pp. 96–97.

This time

(*originally written as opening responses for a liturgy for healing*)

If you come
in certainty or in confusion
in anger or in anguish

THIS TIME IS FOR US

If you come
in silent suffering or hidden sorrow
in pain or promise

THIS TIME IS FOR US

If you come
for your own or another's need
for a private wound or the wound of the world

THIS TIME IS FOR US

If you come,
and do not know why,
to be here is enough

THIS TIME IS FOR US ALL

Come now, Christ of the forgiving warmth
Come now, Christ of the yearning tears
Come now, Christ of the transforming touch

THIS TIME IS FOR YOU

Giles David, in *The Pattern of Our Days: Liturgies and Resources for Worship*, ed. Kathy Galloway (Glasgow: Wild Goose Publications, 1996), p. 108. © Giles David.

A parent's feelings

What is it that makes the death of a child so indescribably painful? I buried my father and that was hard. But nothing at all like this. One expects to bury one's parents; one doesn't expect—not in our day and age—to bury one's children. The burial of one's child is a wrenching alteration of expectations.

But it's more than that. I feel the more but cannot speak it. A child comes into the world without means of sustenance. Immediately we parents give it of our own. . . . We take it on ourselves to stay with this helpless infant all the way so that it has a future, a future in which we can delight in its delight and sorrow in its sorrow. Our plans and hopes and fears for it. . . . That future which I embraced for myself has been destroyed. He slipped out of my arms. For twenty-five years I guarded and sustained and encouraged him with these hands of mine, helping him to grow and become a man of his own. Then he slipped out and was smashed.

David Lockwood, *Love and Let Go* (Great Wakering, Essex: Mayhew-McCrimmon, 1975).

Wrestling with God

Get off my back, God.
Take your claws out of my shoulder.
I'd like to throw you off
like I would brush off some particularly repellent insect!

Sometimes I get the feeling that if I could turn round quick enough
I would see you
grinning at me,
full of glee, plotting, scheming, devious, challenging.

The hell with all this rubbish about fire and storm
and still, quiet waters.
I've got your number.
I've unmasked you.

I'd like to throw you off
like I would brush off
some particularly repellent insect.

You're a daemon!
Unfortunately, you seem to have this great attachment to me.

Actually, being honest, I know in my heart
I'd miss you if you weren't there,
leering at me, reminding me of
death and dread and destiny,
winding me up and puncturing
my pretensions.

I know, with a sinking feeling in my gut
that all the best of me—
the fire and storm, and even, now and then, still waters,
are born out of the death-defying struggle

that we wage,

my dearest daemon.

Kathy Galloway, *Love Burning Deep: Poems and Lyrics* (London: SPCK, 1993), p. 27.

Another wrestler

We are all different, and as the old Puritans said, God does not break all hearts in the same way. But it is a central strand of most Christian living that everybody needs, from time to time, to wrestle privately with God and his will. It is necessary, too, that Christian leaders should be seen to be telling their own story truly. For Paul, his story was closely linked with God's unveiling of Jesus as the true messiah, the crucified and risen Lord of the world. His life, his vocation, his whole identity was stamped with the gospel message.

Tom Wright, *Paul for Everyone: Galatians and Thessalonians* (London: SPCK, 2002), p. 9.

PROPER 6

Ordinary Time 11

*Sunday between June 12 and 18
inclusive (if after Trinity Sunday)*

1 Kings 21:1–10 (11–14) 15–21a   Galatians 2:15–21
Psalm 5:1–8   Luke 7:36–8:3

Tyndale in exile: 'Princes have persecuted me without a cause'

What can you do with power except misuse it?
Being so mighty makes these men afraid
That we, their subjects, might guess they're men too.
That I can understand. It's the followers
Who turn my stomach. The glib climbers
Greedy for money, land, influence, jobs for the boys.
They're drawn by the power and the glory,
And kings aren't fastidious. Consider Henry's men—
Cuthbert the cloth-eared Bishop of London;
Wolsey the Suffolk wolf; and foul-mouthed More,
The bitterest tongue in England. Consider also
Their noble master Henry, the subject-harrier,
Who drove me here. Well then, consider them.
They fear me. So they should. I plan
The invasion of England by the word of God.
And it will come. Just now, they burn my books.
An easy step from that to burning clerks,
Burning this clerk for doing what God wants,
Turning God's word to King's English.
                                        But not the King's;
The people's; England's English. That's where Christ is.
Not a king to do business with Popes and chancellors,
But a servant, a man beneath us, who washes our feet,
Who goes before to try out the hard things first,

188

Who opens gates so we can go easily through,
That is the king, one and only, who speaks our own words.
The powerlessness and the glory.

Princes have persecuted me. Perhaps they have a cause.

U. A. Fanthorpe, from the sequence *Tyndale in Darkness,* in *Safe as
Houses: Poems by U. A. Fanthorpe* (Calstock, Cornwall: Peterloo
Poets/Brownsville, Oreg.: Story Line Press, 1995), pp. 18–19.
Reproduced by permission of Peterloo Poets.

Another point of view

Here [1 Kings chapters 16–21] . . . sexuality is a thread in a larger thematic tapestry of gender, power, foreignness, and idolatry. . . . A fuller understanding of this powerful queen [Jezebel] must take further account of both her own social setting and the Bible's theological polemic. . . . As a Phoenician princess . . . she was accustomed to royal prerogative and unused to the democratic impulse in Israelite culture that regarded land as a gift given to each Israelite family by Yahweh, rather than at the behest of the king. Thus her brutal response to Naboth's refusal to sell his vineyard may be understood from her point of view as an appropriate royal response to insubordination, in contrast to Ahab's unconscionable weakness as a leader.

Claudia V. Camp, from "1 and 2 Kings" in *The Women's Bible
Commentary: Expanded Edition with Apocrypha,* ed. Carol A.
Newsom and Sharon H. Ringe (Louisville, Ky.: Westminster John
Knox Press, 1998), pp. 109, 110.

All are miserable offenders . . .

I am all for matters of spiritual self-esteem. If we are to love our neighbors as ourselves, which is the second commandment in Jesus' summary of the law, we must first and also love ourselves. We must remember and rejoice in the fact that we are created in the image of God and that we share in the full dignity of creation. I believe that. I affirm that. I also believe, however, that most of us are "miserable offenders." We are made miserable by the offenses we commit and by their consequences. Sin and evil make us miserable. That does not deny the dignity of creation; that simply affirms the reality of sin, and that there is no health in us; which does not mean that we are unhealthy. It means that on our own, of our own, by ourselves, there is nothing within us to cure the malady of sin and of evil. The cure of sin is not simply a matter of mind over matter; it is not pure willing that leads to goodness. . . . We need help.

. . . especially women?

[Many] . . . retained the notion that somehow the sins of the flesh got between the sinner and God. Such sins, however, were not sinful because they offended reason but rather because they gave pleasure, which in the refracted Calvinism to which they were all heirs, was itself an unacceptable end. Thus sex was only for the begetting of children, shameful for the man, painful for the woman, both part of a divine plan; and sex for any other purpose simply confounded pain and shame, especially if any pleasure without penalty was involved. Women were thus vessels of shame who, like Eve, Jezebel, and Delilah, led their men to disastrous ends.

> Peter J. Gomes, *The Good Book: Reading the Bible with Mind and Heart* (William Morrow and Company, Inc., 1996), pp. 248, 252.

God our beloved
(Simon the Pharisee and the woman who loved much: Luke 7:36–50)

God our beloved,
who alone can receive
the enormity of our love:
you embrace our yearning
and are not overwhelmed by our need.
Let us love you with all that we are,
and stretch us wider still.

When we are niggardly with our affection;
when we find refuge from fear in constraint,
and wantonly withhold our touch
from those who seek our welcome,
bless us with your shamelessness:

for though I give my body to be burned,
and have not charity,
it profits me nothing.

When what we know conceals from us our ignorance;
when we fail to discern you in those we disapprove of;

when our minds are blunted with lack of compassion,
so that we cannot see,
bless us with your tears:

for though I understand all mysteries and all knowledge,
and have not charity,
it profits me nothing.

When our generosity becomes ferocious; when we demand that others
    receive what swamps them;
when we insist on being the only giver,
so that we cannot bear we are forgiven,
bless us with your surrender:

for though I give away all that I have,
and I have not charity,
it profits me nothing.

Janet Morley, All Desires Known (London: SPCK, 1992), p. 69.

Remission of debt

It is not difficult to see how Jesus' teaching would have been understood in a world in which the life of a people under occupation, and with a quisling monarchy determined to extract the best it could from the situation, would create an environment in which taxes, tributes and rents would progressively result in the impoverishment of more and more of the rural population and the poor's reduction to a position close to slavery. In such circumstances people borrowed from each other to survive in any way they could, and the mercilessness contained in the system would infect all social relationships.

Any change in this situation must involve, as John Howard Yoder describes it, the transformation of relationships, the enactment of jubilee, at every level; there can be no jubilee for those who do not participate in it in relation to their fellow-citizens [*The Politics of Jesus* (Grand Rapids: Eerdmans, 1972), pp. 68ff]. [Douglas] Oakman makes the same point, pointing out also the contrasting situation portrayed in Luke 7:41–3, where two debtors, one owing ten times the debt of the other, are both released from their debts when they are unable to pay. Jesus, speaking in the house of Simon the Pharisee, asks which would love the creditor more, and uses the obvious answer to compare the response of the woman who had anointed him with that of Simon himself. For the remission of debt to function as so powerful and clear a means of teaching it is certain that the dire consequences of debt must have been a prevalent experience, and there are good grounds for seeing in that the reason why the jubilee of debt remission came to be so prominent an image of the liberation brought by Jesus.

Peter Selby, *Grace and Mortgage: The Language of Faith and the Debt of the World* (London: Darton, Longman & Todd, 1997), pp. 134–35.

Excerpt from Simon's letter to his superiors

When I first came to the parish, having heard stories of Mr Manuel's doings and wanting to judge for myself, I invited him, but without his companions, to meet some of the local clergy for supper, including Mgr Colquhoun, our leading moralist and president of the diocesan marriage tribunal. On arrival, Mr Manuel was treated with appropriate courtesy by the assembled clergy. Supper had hardly begun when a woman of notorious reputation in the town entered the dining room without as much as a 'by your leave' and proceeded to display her affection in a thoroughly distasteful display of sentimentality and hysteria. The assembled company, as Your Reverences might well imagine, sat in stunned silence. Manuel then had the impertinence to address me, comparing unfavourably the formal welcome which we, the clergy, accorded [him] with the lady's tearful effusions. He then had the temerity to assure the woman that her sins were forgiven because she believed in him! It was at this point that Mgr Colquhoun departed and later suffered a heart attack. As a result of this gesture of friendliness towards Manuel, I have not only had to take over Mgr Colquhoun's heavy responsibilities, but I have also lost my housekeeper, who, scandalized by the incident, could not be persuaded that I had not invited the lady personally to supper, an invitation never accorded to herself in twenty years' devoted service.

   . . . I remain,
      Yours sincerely
         (P. Simon, DD, Parish Priest of Portinstorm)

Author's comment: While writing this letter and entering into some of the blind spots of P. Simon, I began to recognize a few more of my own.

Gerard W. Hughes, *God of Surprises* (London: Darton, Longman & Todd, 1985), pp. 108, 110.

Extravagant love

It's as though someone were saying, John Baptist didn't think he was worthy to unlatch Jesus' shoes, but *she* was, and why? Because what Jesus recognized in her was that she had thrown herself on the mercy and love of God. This point above all, was central to the association of this text from Luke with Mary of Magdala, who became the symbol of penitence, a penitence flowing from complete assurance of mercy and love, and *not*, ever, from condemnation. So her apparent extravagance is matched by his generosity, his unstinting praise.

Ann Loades, from "Mary of Magdala," in *Silence in Heaven: A Book of Women's Preaching,* ed. Heather Walton and Susan Durber (London: SCM Press, 1994), p. 132.

PROPER 7

Ordinary Time 12

Sunday between June 19 and 25 inclusive (if after Trinity Sunday)

1 Kings 19:1–4 (5–7) 8–15a   Galatians 3:23–29
Psalms 42 and 43   Luke 8:26–39

Seeing the real person

Individuality, including eccentricity, ought to be an option for anyone. There is entirely too much standardized, homogenized, socially prescribed behavior at all levels of our culture. When I was a kid, the classic movie *Frankenstein* was playing in theaters. I was turned off by the idea of a monster running amok, acting irrationally, terrifying people, and creating havoc. My worst nightmare would have been to run into Frankenstein on a forbidding country lane on a dark, rainy night. What if he'd been accompanied by the Hound of the Baskervilles, the Man in the Iron Mask, or the Bride of Frankenstein?

A half century later, however, I rented the video and watched the film at home. Quickly, I grasped that the demonized creature was not so much a monster as a victim. Frankenstein, who had never asked to be created, yearned to be loved, but was demonized in people's imaginations. I realize now to what extent most of us are conditioned by forces—ranging from entrenched attitudes to mass media images—that cause us to look at fabricated stereotypes instead of real people.

Malcolm Boyd, *Simple Grace: A Mentor's Guide to Growing Older*
(Louisville, Ky.: Westminster John Knox Press, 2001), pp. 53–54.

Listening

Paleface people need to listen
to people of colour.
Don't say, "I hear you."
People of colour will tell us
when we've heard them.

Men need to listen to women.
Don't say, "Yes, I understand."
Women will tell us
what we've understood.

Adults need to listen to children,
walkers to riders in wheelchairs,
quick talkers to non-speakers.
They cannot always tell us
if we're listening:
all the more reason, then,
to listen, listen,
and more than listen.

Suburb, Main Line,
and First World people
need to listen, and more than listen,
to Inner City, Side-lined,
Third World people.

All of us need to listen,
and more than listen,

but quick talking, fast-walking,
main line, first world, paleface
Men
need the biggest ears,

because we need to listen
to everyone.

(PS. Dumbo had big ears
and learned to fly.)

Brian Wren, *Piece Together Praise: A Theological Journey* (Carol
Stream, Ill.: Hope Publishing Company/London: Stainer & Bell,
1996), No. 195, p. 182. © 1989 Hope Publishing Company for the
USA, Canada, Australia and New Zealand, and Stainer & Bell for all
other territories. Used by permission.

One in Christ

We can rejoice that behind the sacrament of baptism is the promise of Christ to make us new so that already we can begin to live beyond the former barriers that denied the full humanity of those who were of the "wrong religion, class, race, or gender." The ancient baptismal formula quoted by Paul in Galatians 3:27–28 reminds us that the divisions of old creation have been overcome, and old forms of domination no longer belong to life in Christ. Just as the original division of male and female in Genesis was overcome, that of Jew and Gentile, slave and free were understood to be overcome in the context of the early house churches. Some would argue that today the list needs to be much longer, to include heterosexual and homosexual, able-bodied and disabled, rich and poor, capitalist and socialist. It is the overcoming of these divisions, and the new life of freedom, that is the sign of Christ's presence.

Letty M. Russell, *Church in the Round: Feminist Interpretation of the Church* (Louisville, Ky.: Westminster/John Knox Press, 1993), p. 142.

Manifestations of the Reign

Compassion is the hallmark of Jesus' God. Consequently, Jesus' healings and exorcisms, which play such a major role in his ministry, are not simply patches on a body destined for death regardless; they are manifestations of God's Reign on earth now, an inbreaking of eternity into time, a revelation of God's merciful nature, a promise of the restitution of all things in the heart of the loving Author of the universe. "But if it is by the finger of God that I cast out the demons, then the kingdom of God has come to you." God's non-violent reign is the overcoming of demonic powers through non-violent means.

Exorcism especially preoccupied the early church. Baptism itself was an entry-exorcism, freeing the initiates from the delusional system that had previously held them in bondage. Exorcism was not, then, a rare and extreme intervention. It was the indispensable prerequisite for getting a "new mind" (*metanoia*). Jesus' teaching is itself a kind of exorcism, a cleaning of the mind of the misinformation that enslaves people to the Powers. And faith is a healing of blindness, humanity's trained inability to perceive God's presence and deeds even when they are happening before our very eyes.

Walter Wink, *Engaging the Powers: Discernment and Resistance in a World of Domination* (Minneapolis: Fortress Press, 1992), pp. 134–35.

Heal us

We come to you, our Loving and Healing Parent, remembering the miracles of healing from Jesus' time. We confess that sometimes we think of miracles as something that happened only long ago and far away. We admit our scientific skepticism. We recognize that our hopes for healing are often plagued by crises of faith. And sometimes, God, we're simply scared of how our lives would change if we were healed. Help us to willingly suspend our disbelief! Give us the faith to claim the healing you would have us enjoy. Help us to see your healing grace in every day of our lives, even in our dying. Open our hearts to the healing warmth of your presence.

> A. Stephen Pieters, in *Equal Rites: Lesbian and Gay Worship,*
> *Ceremonies, and Celebrations,* ed. Kittredge Cherry and Zalmon Sher-
> wood (Louisville, Ky.: Westminster John Knox Press, 1995), p. 28.

Criteria of the kingdom

The Christian confession brought a conversion in that estimation of women which was current both in Judaism and among the Gentiles. The well-known and already often cited text from Gal. 3.28 is a primitive Christian baptismal formula which is taken over and quoted by Paul: 'For as many of you as were baptized into Christ have put on Christ. There is neither Jew nor Greek, there is neither slave nor free, there is neither male nor female, for you are all one in Christ Jesus.' This formula declares that the classical human points of conflict—ethnic differences, social status and the sex war, all fields of tension which were a particular occasion for the formation of prejudice and discriminatory behaviour—are irrelevant to the Christian community.

Community life in the Christian community was thus regulated by criteria which went against the criteria customary elsewhere in the world. . . .

The reversal of values expressed by the baptismal formula in Galatians is very closely connected with the Jesus tradition. Not only the itinerant preachers but also Christians in a settled community committed themselves to the criteria of the kingdom of God that Jesus had preached, for in the last resort they were convinced that as the Risen One the Lord was alive and at work among them. In commentaries on Gal. 3.28 one keeps reading that this is an eschatological hope which will only materialize at the 'end of days' when God creates a new heaven and a new earth; here and now things remain as they were. Some exegetes also distinguish a saving significance 'before God,' which has no significance 'before men.' This is first contradicted by the context, which is concerned with baptism, with fellowship with Christ and thus with the community, concerned to arrange its praxis in accordance with the Spirit of Christ (cf. 1 Cor. 12.1ff.). Through baptism a person is already made new here and now by putting on Christ. The experience that the claim of Gal. 3.28 was not always realized does not do away with the claim, and anyone who argues that this applies only to the 'end of days' and is valid only 'before God' leaves reality to its own laws.

Susanne Heine, *Women and Early Christianity: Are the Feminist Scholars Right?* trans. John Bowden (London: SCM Press, 1987), pp. 84–85.

God our Mother and Father, be with us as we learn to see one another with new eyes, hear one another with new hearts, and treat one another in a new way.

Corrymeela Community

PROPER 8

Ordinary Time 13
Sunday between June 26 and July 2 inclusive

| 2 Kings 2:1–2, 6–14 | Galatians 5:1, 13–25 |
| Psalm 77:1–2, 11–20 | Luke 9:51–62 |

The great masquerade of evil

One may ask whether there have ever before in human history been people with so little ground under their feet—people to whom every available alternative seemed equally intolerable, repugnant, and futile, who looked beyond all these existing alternatives for the source of their strength so entirely in the past or in the future, and who yet, without being dreamers, were able to await the success of their cause so quietly and confidently. . . .

The great masquerade of evil has played havoc with all our ethical concepts. For evil to appear disguised as light, charity, historical necessity, or social justice is quite bewildering to anyone brought up on our traditional ethical concepts, while for Christians who base their lives on the Bible it merely confirms the fundamental wickedness of evil. . . . Who stands fast? Only the person whose final standard is not his or her reason, principles, conscience, freedom, or virtue, but who is ready to sacrifice all this when called to obedient and responsible action in faith and in exclusive allegiance to God—the responsible person, who tries to make his or her whole life an answer to the question and call of God.

Dietrich Bonhoeffer, *Letters and Papers from Prison*, trans. Reginald
Fuller et al. (London: SCM Press; New York: Macmillan, 1971),
pp. 3–5.

Prayer cannot be measured in terms of "usefulness." It can only be understood as a complete surrender without wanting "to get something out of it."

Peter G. van Breemen

Holiness

The Master would frequently assert that holiness was less a matter of what one did than of what one *allowed* to happen.

To a group of disciples who had difficulty understanding that, he told the following story:

There was once a one-legged dragon who said to the centipede, 'How do you manage all those legs? It is all I can do to manage one.'

'To tell you the truth,' said the centipede, 'I do not manage them at all.'

Anthony de Mello, S.J., *One Minute Wisdom* (Gujarat, India: Gujarat
Sahitya Prakash, 1985), p. 124.

Kindness

Kindness is the overflowing of self upon others. We put others in the place of self. We treat them as we would wish to be treated ourselves. We change places with them. For the time self is another, and others are self. Our self-love takes the shape of complacence in unselfishness. We cannot speak of the virtues without thinking of God. What would the overflow of self upon others be in Him the ever-blessed and Eternal? It was the act of creation. Creation was divine kindness. From it as from a fountain, flow the possibilities, the powers, the blessings of all created kindness. This is an honourable genealogy for kindness. Then, again, kindness is the coming to the rescue of others, when they need it and it is in our power to supply what they need; and this is the work of the Attributes of God towards His creatures. . . .

Moreover kindness is also like divine grace; for it gives us something which neither self nor nature can give us. What it gives us is something of which we are in want, or something which only another person can give, such as consolation; and besides this, the manner in which this is given is a true gift itself, better far than the thing given: and what is all this but an allegory of grace? Kindness adds sweetness to everything. It is kindness which makes life's capabilities blossom, and paints them with their cheering hues, and endows them with their invigorating fragrance. . . .

Last of all, the secret impulse out of which kindness acts is an instinct which is the noblest part of ourselves, the most undoubted remnant of the image of God, which was given us at the first.

F. W. Faber, *Spiritual Conferences* (Thomas Richardson
& Son, 1859), p. 2.

If God is slow in answering your request, and you ask but do not promptly receive anything, do not be upset, for you are not wiser than God.

Abraham of Nathpar

The fruits of love

Being in love with God, as experienced, is being in love in an unrestricted fashion. All love is self-surrender, but being in love with God is being in love without limits or qualifications or conditions or reservations. Just as unrestricted questioning is our capacity for self-transcendence, so being in love in an unrestricted fashion is the proper fulfilment of that capacity.

That fulfilment is not the product of our knowledge and choice. On the contrary, it dismantles and abolishes the horizon in which our knowing and choosing went on and it sets up a new horizon in which the love of God will transvalue our values and the eyes of that love will transform our knowing.

Though not the product of our knowing and choosing, it is a conscious dynamic state of love, joy, peace, that manifests itself in acts of kindness, goodness, fidelity, gentleness, and self-control (Gal. 5:22).

Bernard Lonergan, *Method in Theology* (London: Darton, Longman & Todd, 1972).

Free to minister

Implicit in [the] call for new understanding of ministry in the life of the church is the recognition that religious orders of vocation, polity, and church law can no longer be understood as static patterns set out by divine order. They are *gifts* of God rather than *givens* of God: part of the changing patterns of church life that evolve out of the function of the church in its work of service and witness to God's love and justice in the wider society. The ministries of the church are part of the organization of church life as it responds to the Spirit of Christ continually at work in its midst. This Spirit leads to a new order of freedom, in which Christ has set us free to be for others (Gal. 5:1). In this understanding, ministry is the response of each and every Christian to Christ's call to freedom. In their baptism Christians are set free to serve now, in and through many communities and situations. The call to ministry is not an option for some Christians. It is basic to the existence of all Christians as they seek to live together as partners in Christ's service.

Letty M. Russell, *Church in the Round: Feminist Interpretation of the Church* (Louisville, Ky.: Westminster/John Knox Press, 1993), p. 50.

Attachment?

Father Raymond tells the charming story of a little child whose mother was teaching him to pray. When he got to the part, 'Lord, I surrender everything to thee, everything I own,' he abruptly broke off and whispered to himself, 'except my baby rabbit.'

All of us have our baby rabbits. Sometimes it is an ugly thing, sometimes beautiful, sometimes large, sometimes small; but we are more attached to it than to anything else. But this is the thing God asks of us and that he touches upon when we sincerely ask guidance of him. God does not, however, ask us to seek out our neighbour's little rabbits.

> Paul Tournier, *Escape from Loneliness,* trans. John S. Gilmour (London: SCM Press, 1962), p. 111.

PROPER 9

Ordinary Time 14
Sunday between July 3 and 9 inclusive

2 Kings 5:1–14	Galatians 6:(1–6) 7–16
Psalm 30	Luke 10:1–11, 16–20

Not in charge

Religious knowledge is unlike any other, in that it forces us to choose and change. It does not allow us to stand still.

If we reject its truth, we are left with a ruined game, and expelled from Eden. If we accept it, then we have to allow ourselves to be changed.

I put it this way to emphasize that the centre of change is in our will; we do not change ourselves, we allow something to change us. We are not in charge and therefore it is frightening.

Like any act of love, physical or emotional, prayer and awareness require an ability to let go, trust and accept. And the most difficult thing in the world is to let go. For however we may complain about the present, change and letting go of this type are not immediately welcome, although for many of us there is not much to lose.

Perhaps, as Marx says, we have nothing to lose but our chains, but we are accustomed to these chains of habit and they have become cosy.

Lionel Blue, "God and the Jewish Problem," in *A Genuine Search*, ed. Dow Marmur (1979), p. 49. © Reform Synagogues of Great Britain.

Lose your mind!

The mystical vision of freedom, of "letting go" of the world, interprets possessing as being possessed. That vision appears to be something infinitely bigger and more unreal than such little endeavors as dealing responsibly with the power of money. But then it may well be that "that of God in us" is present in both the big crazies and the small practical ways of dealing with the principalities and powers under which we exist. The retreat of a Thomas Merton to the solitude of a Trappist monastery is not that far removed from an annual intervention in the shareholders' meeting. The craziness of giving things away is a symbol that transmits an idea of genuine freedom. The practical reason that fights against the ruling ideology of the innocence of money has part in that freedom. Craziness and reason are not nearly as far apart as technocratic education makes us believe. According to Gotthold Lessing, they who do not lose their mind over certain things have no mind to lose.

> Dorothee Soelle, *The Silent Cry: Mysticism and Resistance,* trans.
> Barbara and Martin Rumscheidt (Minneapolis: Fortress Press, 2001),
> p. 255.

Years on a mission

When we live our lives as missions, we become aware that there is a home from which we are sent and to which we have to return. We start thinking about ourselves as people who are in a faraway country to bring a message or work on a project, but only for a certain amount of time. When the message has been delivered and the project is finished, we want to return home to give an account of our mission and to rest from our labours.

One of the most important spiritual disciplines is to develop the knowledge that the years of our lives are years 'on a mission.'

> Henri J. M. Nouwen, *Bread for the Journey: Reflections for Every Day of
> the Year* (London: Darton, Longman & Todd, 1996), p. 132.

Bless us

> Our brother Jesus, you set our feet upon the way and sometimes where you
>   lead we do not like or understand.
> Bless us with courage where the way is fraught with dread or danger;
> bless us with graceful meetings where the way is lonely;
> bless us with good companions where the way demands a common cause;
> bless us with night vision where we travel in the dark, keen hearing where
>   we have not sight, to hear the reassuring sounds of fellow travellers;
> bless us with humour—we cannot travel lightly weighed down with gravity;
> bless us with humility to learn from those around us;
> bless us with decisiveness where we must move with speed;
> bless us with lazy moments, to stretch and rest and savour;

bless us with love, given and received;
and bless us with your presence, even when we know it in your absence;
Lead us into exile,
until we find that on the road
    is where you are,
and where you are is going home.
Bless us, lead us, love us, bring us home
    bearing the Gospel of life.

Kathy Galloway, in *Coracle* 3, no. 11. © Iona Community, 1992.

I thank God that now when I preach I shall be able to say instead of "dear brethren," "my fellow lepers."

Joseph de Veuster ("Father Damien")

Trust
Remember always that there are two things more easily incompatible than oil and water—trust and worry. Would you call it trust if you should give something into the hands of a friend to attend to for you, and then should spend your nights and days in anxious thought and worry as to whether it should be rightly and successfully done? If you have trusted God in a few things, and he has not failed you, trust him now for everything, and see if he does not do for you exceeding abundantly, above all that you could ever have asked or even thought.

Hannah Whitall Smith, in *A Religious Rebel: The Letters of H. W. Smith*, ed. Logan Pearsall Smith (London: Nisbet and Co. Ltd., 1949).

A new creation
If I were asked to sum up the Christian message for our time in two words, I would say with Paul: It is the message of a 'New Creation.' . . . Christianity is the message of the New Creation, the New Being, the New Reality which has appeared with the appearance of Jesus who for this reason, and just for this reason, is called the Christ. . . .

What is this New Being? Paul answers first by saying what it is *not*. It is neither circumcision nor uncircumcision, he says. For Paul and for the readers of his letter this meant something very definite. It meant that neither to be a Jew nor to be a pagan is ultimately important; that only one thing counts, namely, the union with him in whom the New Reality is present. Circumcision or uncircumcision— what does that mean for *us?* It can also mean something very definite, but at the same time something very universal. It means that no religion as such produces the New Being. . . .

The New Being is not something that simply takes the place of the Old Being. But it is a renewal of the Old which has been corrupted, distorted, split and almost destroyed. But not wholly destroyed. Salvation does not destroy creation; but it transforms the Old Creation into a New One. Therefore we can speak of the New in terms of a *re*-newal: The threefold '*re*', namely, *re*-conciliation, *re*-union, *re*-surrection. . . .

Reconciliation, reunion, resurrection—this is the New Creation, the New Being, the New state of things. Do we participate in it? The message of Christianity is not Christianity, but a New Reality. A New state of things has appeared, it still appears; it is hidden and visible, it is there and it is here. Accept it, enter into it, let it grasp you.

Paul Tillich, *The New Being* (London: SCM Press, 1956), p. 15.

If we in our human life take our surrender to God seriously; if God enters us as the strength of light, of the tree, as the elemental energy which alone makes new life possible—then we shall be able to live the new life.

Eberhard Arnold

PROPER 10

Ordinary Time 15
Sunday between July 10 and 16 inclusive

Amos 7:7–17   Colossians 1:1–14

Psalm 82   Luke 10:25–37

Compassion

Jesus in his solidarity with the marginal one is *moved to compassion*. Compassion constitutes a radical form of criticism, for it announces that the hurt is to be taken seriously, that the hurt is not to be accepted as normal and natural but is an abnormal and unacceptable condition for humanness. . . .

It is instructive that in the teaching of Jesus it is precisely his two best-known parables that contain the word [compassion] under discussion. First, in the narrative of the good Samaritan it is the Samaritan who has compassion (Luke 10:33). Second, in the story of the prodigal son, it is precisely the father who has compassion (Luke 15:20). Clearly the key person in each of these parables embodies the alternative consciousness from which the dominant consciousness is criticized. Both the Samaritan and the father are Jesus' peculiar articulation against the dominant culture, and so they stand as a radical threat. The Samaritan by his action judges the dominant way by disregard of the marginal. The ones who pass by, obviously carriers of the dominant tradition, are numbed, indifferent, and do not notice. The Samaritan expresses a new way that displaces the old arrangements in which outcasts are simply out. The replacing of numbness with compassion, that is, the end of cynical indifference and the beginning of noticed pain, signals a social revolution.

Walter Brueggemann, *The Prophetic Imagination*, 2d ed. (Minneapolis: Fortress Press, 2001), pp. 88, 90–91.

The Good Samaritan et al.

The priest, the Levite, and the man who fell among thieves meet in heaven to talk over old times. Since heaven has no past or future, they find themselves in the inn on the road to Jericho.

"I felt awful about not helping you," the priest says. "My heart wasn't open enough. But I'm working on it."

"The last time I had stopped to help a wounded man by the roadside," the Levite says, "he beat me and ran off with my wallet. I was afraid."

"It was my good fortune to be in the right place at the right time," the Samaritan says. "I didn't stop to think; the oil and wine poured themselves, the wound bound itself. My only problem came later, dealing with all the praise."

The man who fell among thieves takes another sip of wine. "Charity begins at home," he says. "If I had been kinder to myself, I wouldn't have been in that mess to begin with. But I am very grateful to all three of you. It takes great humility to step aside, for a parable's sake. And without a parable, I would never have been saved."

Stephen Mitchell, *Parables and Portraits* (New York: HarperCollins, 1990).

Who is my neighbor? The neighbor was the Samaritan who approached the wounded man and made him his neighbor. The neighbor . . . is not he whom I find in my path, but rather he in whose path I place myself, he whom I approach and actively seek.

Gustavo Gutiérrez

Rich and poor in the global village

We want the goods that unrestricted markets can bring (unrestricted in the sense that no one other than the prosperous restricts them). But we have yet to come to terms with what the greater part of humankind believes to be the corollary of this: that the prosperous will be seen as the makers of poverty. In the global village, the one who becomes rich is seen as the thief of his neighbour's goods. We will rightly say that this is a crass oversimplification. Free capital movement benefits the expansion of markets, and so benefits all producers; there is more space for the producer to move into, more room for the small economy to grow.

But the response from the poorer economies will be stony-faced. Debt and its management consume the energies of depressed economies, and often result in political regression and instability; the great corporations operate their own protectionist policies, and are able to sustain them by the prevailing protocols on intellectual property rights (the patenting by companies of regional produce).

Global economics is impressive in theory as regards its potential for regenerating local practice; but in reality it is seen as managed for the sake of those who are already victorious.

Rowan Williams, *Writing in the Dust: Reflections on 11th September and its Aftermath* (London: Hodder & Stoughton, 2002), pp. 57–58.

We sing a love*

We sing a love that sets all people free,
That blows like wind, that burns like scorching flame,
Enfolds like earth, springs up like water clear.
Come, living love, live in our hearts today.

We sing a love that seeks another's good,
That longs to serve and not to count the cost,
A love that, yielding, finds itself made new.
Come, caring love, live in our hearts today.

We sing a love, unflinching, unafraid
To be itself, despite another's wrath,
A love that stands alone and undismayed.
Come, strength'ning love, live in our hearts today.

We sing a love that, wand'ring, will not rest
Until it finds its way, its home, its source,
Through joy and sadness pressing on refreshed.
Come, pilgrim love, live in our hearts today.

We sing a burning, fiery, Holy Ghost
That seeks out shades of ancient bitterness,
Transfig'ring these, as Christ in ev'ry heart.
Come, joyful love, live in our hearts today.

June Boyce-Tillman, in *Reflecting Praise*, ed. June Boyce-Tillman and Janet Wootton (London: Stainer & Bell/Women in Theology, 1993).
© 1993 Stainer & Bell Ltd.

*TUNE: WOODLANDS

An umbrella called church

I was not born into the world of the church. I cannot consider myself deformed or neuroticized by the church. The policeman-god who checks under the bed-covers is known to me only from reports of people whom the church has damaged. I have never been employed by the church or received remuneration from it. The fact of this biographical distance from it has freed me for critique and affirmation, for anger *and* love. To put it concretely: It has freed me to distinguish between the church from above and the church from below. Beside the power-monger Pope Innocent III, I always saw the *poverello* Francis. The distinction between tendencies toward oppression and toward liberation in the history of Christianity is a hermeneutical principle that has pervaded my entire being. . . .

A friend of mine, the American Jesuit and resister Daniel Berrigan, once spoke of the church as "an umbrella." It protects us from the cold rain; sometimes it opens too slowly and we get rained on. Often it is not very efficient. Still, it is there, Dan said, and I would not want to do without it.

Many years after the conversation we had during a demonstration at the Pentagon, this image came back to me. It was at the time of the bloodless revolution in the former German Democratic Republic. There, too, the church had often been an inefficient shelter for many people in the movement for citizens' rights. On occasion, it left people out in the rain. Nevertheless, in 1989 I was proud of our paltry umbrella. After all, for the first time in 400 years, the Protestant church stood on the side of the people.

This nice picture must not minimize the difficulties and conflicts that I had, again and again, with the official church. But I never lost sight of this double image of hate, ignorance, and ill will on the one hand, and openness, readiness to learn and change on the other. For that I thank God.

Dorothee Soelle, *Against the Wind: Memoir of a Radical Christian,*
trans. Barbara and Martin Rumscheidt (Minneapolis: Fortress Press,
1999), pp. 90–91.

Blessing

May the God who dances in creation,
who embraces us with human love,
who shakes our lives like thunder,
bless us and drive us out with power
to fill the world with her justice.
Amen.

Janet Morley, *All Desires Known* (London: SPCK, 1992), p. 88.

PROPER 11

Ordinary Time 16
Sunday between July 17 and 23 inclusive

| Amos 8:1–12 | Colossians 1:15–28 |
| Psalm 52 | Luke 10:38–42 |

Affirmation of faith

There is a God
at whose feet we may sit
and gathered there is love.
There is a quiet space for safe encounters
and wiser understandings for our learning,
a robe for the touching of our hand
to share healing grace from the body of Christ.

There is a place
near to feet that have walked our dusty ways
and moved in courage among our complexities,
felt our painful choices at the crossroads,
turned themselves reluctantly towards our harder paths
and formed footsteps ahead of us
towards a truer, braver, many-coloured life.
We will sit at the feet of our God.

Dorothy McRae-McMahon, *Prayers for Life's Particular Moments*
(London: SPCK, 2001), p. 36.

Friends of Jesus

Mary and Martha have traditionally symbolized a polarization of women's roles. . . .

Rather than offering dichotomies, perhaps the two stories of Jesus and the critical sisters could provide a model for modern Christians. . . . Jesus and Mary and Martha treated each other as persons rather than assigning each other to limited functions and stereotypes. . . . Both sexes were honest and caring. Jesus was frank with both sisters, and they in turn treated him with openness. He plainly discussed his teachings and thinking with both Mary and Martha. They in turn show evidence of their understanding.

To demonstrate wholeness, Martha and Mary should not represent either-or possibilities, but the variety of human personhood in relation to Jesus. Each person, rather than limited to one function, can be not only a serving person, but one who shares the "better part" with Jesus.

Rachel Conrad Wahlberg, *Jesus According to a Woman*, rev. ed. (Mahwah, N.J.: Paulist Press, 1986), pp. 78, 83–84.

More Martha than Mary

The aim of Jewish study was not really the knowledge of God. That was too daring. It was not expected that any beatific vision would come to the intellect, or that it would be possible to take degrees in religious experience.

Theology was not at the heart of religion, nor did the rabbis make the nineteenth-century mistake of equating piety with culture. The aim of Jewish study was not to experience God, but to know his will. The former is, after all, a pleasure, but the latter is duty and work.

Law, commandments, statutes, and ordinances are the daily bread of any society, holy or otherwise. Philosophy is a decoration.

As a religion Judaism was temperamentally closer to the attitudes of Martha than to those of Mary.

Lionel Blue, *To Heaven with the Scribes and Pharisees* (London: Darton, Longman & Todd, 1975; 1984), p. 84.

"Martha and Magdalene"

"But, Jesus Christ," said Martha, "I've had it to here
with Mary Magdalene. I cannot take her
rosaries, her novenas anymore.
I open my mouth and she calls me a troublemaker.

I'm tied up day and night. I've never complained,
but I'm getting tired—I'm always on my feet;
you can't find this painted doll of a saint
except, of course, when there's something to eat."

"Look, Martha," the Savior said, "here's where it's at.
You don't deserve any explanation,
But her job's more important. It's as simple as that."

And Martha: "So says you, but I know better.
Listen, if I sat around on my salvation
The way she does, who'd be keeping this house together?"

Giuseppe Giocchino Belli (1791–1863), *Sonnets of Giuseppe Belli,*
trans. and introduction by Miller Williams (Baton Rouge: Louisiana
State University Press, 1981). Translation © 1981 by Miller Williams.
Reprinted by permission of the publisher.

Contemplation and action

Following its dualistic principles, medieval theology often established an order
that, corresponding to that of spiritual and worldly life or theory and practice,
ranked the contemplative life higher than the *vita activa* (the life of action). But it
was precisely this superordination of contemplating over acting that great mystics like Eckhart and Teresa of Avila criticized and overcame.

The test case for this view in the realm of Christian thought is the interpretation of the New Testament narrative of the two sisters, Martha and Mary. . . . One
acted as his host, the other listened to him speaking. Ever since Augustine, Mary's
quiet attention to Jesus' words and Martha's restless caring about the body's everyday needs have been interpreted as images of the *vita contemplativa* and the *vita
activa.* The former was held to be of greater value, to be more spiritual and essential, while the latter, however necessary, was of a lower order. In this tradition,
Martha is seen to be useful but somewhat limited, while her sister is seen as spiritual, refined, and more saintly. . . .

Meister Eckhart raised a bold objection [to this]. . . . He places the still uncompleted Mary at the beginning of the spiritual life while the active Martha is much
further ahead. "Martha feared that her sister would remain stuck in the feelings of
well-being and in sweetness." Then this spiritual counselor completely reverses
the sense of the biblical text that assigns "the better part" to Mary and, identifying himself with the activist Martha, says: "Therefore Christ spoke to her and said,
'Set your mind at ease, Martha, she too has chosen the better part. This [viz.
Mary's inaction] will come to an end in her . . . and she will be blessed like you!'"
This reversal is not only about rehabilitating Martha and active behavior but also

about abolishing the division of human beings into makers and dreamers, activists and introverts, and the differentiation between the productivity of action and the receptivity of piety. By not separating Martha's acting from Mary's contemplative devotion but, rather, conceiving of Mary in Martha, Eckhart does away with the false superordination as well as the compulsive choice between two forms of life, the spiritual and the worldly. In the perspective of mysticism, this hierarchy is untenable. Real contemplation gives rise to just actions; theory and praxis are in an indissoluble connection.

Dorothee Soelle, *The Silent Cry: Mysticism and Resistance,* trans.
Barbara and Martin Rumscheidt (Minneapolis: Fortress Press, 2001),
pp. 200–201.

"Praise of Martha"

Blessed are you, Martha, to whom love gave
the confidence that opened your mouth.
By the fruit Eve's mouth was closed
while she was hidden among the trees.
Blessed is your mouth that sounded forth with love
at the table at which God reclined.
You are greater than Sarah who served the servants,
for you served the Lord of all.

Ephrem (d. 373), from "Hymns on Virginity and on the Symbols of
the Lord," in *Ephrem the Syrian,* trans. Kathleen E. McVey (New
York/Mahwah, N.J.: Paulist Press, 1989), pp. 377–78. © 1989 Kathleen
E. McVey. Used by permission of Paulist Press. www.paulistpress.com.

PROPER 12

Ordinary Time 17

Sunday between July 24 and 30 inclusive

Hosea 1:2–10	Colossians 2:6–15 (16–19)
Psalm 85	Luke 11:1–13

Growing up

If children are to be allowed to be children, we have to ask about what prevents adults being adults. Not only parents, but adults in general, adults in their social organisation and their political choices, have to grasp what is involved in becoming responsible for the nurture and induction into human society of new human subjects in process of formation. A recent book by a Roman Catholic writer meditating on Rembrandt's great painting of the return of the Prodigal Son concludes with reflections on the difficulty of taking up the role of the parent in the group depicted, compared with the relative ease of identifying with the older or the younger son: 'Do I want to be not just the one who is being forgiven, but also the one who forgives; not just the one who is being welcomed home, but also the one who welcomes home?' [Henri J. M. Nouwen, *The Return of the Prodigal Son: A Story of Homecoming* (London: Darton, Longman & Todd, 1994), p. 122]. A society that pushes us towards dependent and frustrated patterns of behaviour will not enable adults to be 'at home' with their limits and their choices in a way that makes it possible to welcome or nurture those who are bound to be dependent, who are still learning their own freedom. How then do we, how are we encouraged to, understand the nature of adult choice in our environment?

Rowan Williams, *Lost Icons: Reflections on Cultural Bereavement*
(Edinburgh: T. & T. Clark, 2000), p. 31.

Receiving forgiveness

One of the greatest challenges of the spiritual life is to receive God's forgiveness. There is something in us humans that keeps us clinging to our sins and prevents us from letting God erase our past and offer us a completely new beginning.

Sometimes it even seems as though I want to prove to God that my darkness is too great to overcome. While God wants to restore me to the full dignity of sonship, I keep insisting that I will settle for being a hired servant. But do I truly want to be restored to the full responsibility of the son? Do I truly want to be so totally forgiven that a completely new way of living becomes possible? Do I trust myself and such a radical reclamation? Do I want to break away from my deep-rooted rebellion against God and surrender myself so absolutely to God's love that a new person can emerge? Receiving forgiveness requires a total willingness to let God be God and do all the healing, restoring, and renewing. As long as I want to do even a part of that myself, I end up with partial solutions, such as becoming a hired servant. As a hired servant, I can still keep my distance, still revolt, reject, strike, run away, or complain about my pay. As the beloved son, I have to claim my full dignity and begin preparing myself to become the father.

> Henri J. M. Nouwen, *The Return of the Prodigal Son: A Story of Homecoming* (London: Darton, Longman & Todd, 1994), p. 53.

A prayer to comfort

To this day I suckle at the Lord's Prayer like a child, and as an old man eat and drink from it and never get my fill. It is the very best prayer, even better than the psalter, which is so very dear to me. It is surely evident that a real master composed and taught it. What a great pity that the prayer of such a master is prattled and chattered so irreverently all over the world! How many pray the Lord's Prayer several thousand times in the course of a year, and if they were to keep on doing so for a thousand years they would not have tasted nor prayed one iota, one dot, of it! In a word, the Lord's Prayer is the greatest martyr on earth (as are the name and word of God). Everybody tortures and abuses it; few take comfort and joy in its proper use.

> Martin Luther, "A Simple Way to Pray for a good friend. How one should pray; for Peter, the Master Barber" in *Luther's Works* (American edition, ed. Jaroslav Pelikan and Helmut Lehmann, Philadelphia: Muhlenberg and Fortress Press; and St. Louis: Concordia Publishing House, 1955–), 43, p. 198.

An inexhaustible petition

Last night, going to bed alone, I suddenly found myself (I was taking off my waist-coat) reciting the Lord's Prayer in a loud, emphatic voice—a thing I had not done for many years—with deep urgency and profound disturbed emotion. While I went on I grew more composed; as if it had been empty and craving and were being replenished, my soul grew still; every word had a strange fullness of meaning which astonished and delighted me. It was late; I had sat up reading; I was sleepy; but as I stood in the middle of the floor half-undressed, saying the prayer over and over, meaning after meaning sprang from it, overcoming me again with joyful surprise; and I realized that this simple petition was always inexhaustible, and day by day sanctified human life.

Edwin Muir, *An Autobiography* (London: Hogarth Press, 1954),
p. 246.

Being present to another

Some years ago I received a letter from a missionary in a rather desolate area of Nigeria. She wrote both from a sense of shame at the ineffectualness of her intercession, and also to share a basic query. 'Let me give an example,' she said. 'There were five boys weighing on my mind at the end of last term as I knew their fees for this year were just hopelessly inadequate. They were pretty constantly in my mind, yet I do not recall that I formulated any prayer for them. However, within a month four of them had adequate financial assistance. A week later came a Christmas gift from my sister and her husband for any student needing help; so that was the fifth! I quite simply regard this as miraculous—the result of God's concern—and I do not see that formal intercession would have made any difference one way or the other.' When someone whose life is simply and sacrificially dedicated to God has any fellow human being pretty constantly in mind to the extent that the feelings of concern lead to responsible action, that, surely, is the whole of intercession. For a timeless moment it makes one totally present with the other person or persons across the intervening distances, without words and in a manner that goes beyond thought. It is simply a matter of 'being there for them' in a concentration upon the other which obliterates all awareness of self and yet is not strung up but totally relaxed. In that stillness which lies beyond thought we are to let the presence of that other person impinge upon our spirit across the distance, with all their rich reality and all their need and burden. Their presence matters more than our own.

John V. Taylor, *The Go-Between God* (London: SCM Press, 1972),
pp. 242–43.

When the world was lying sick

O Godhead,
my love,
I have one thing to ask of you. When the world was lying sick
you sent your only-begotten Son as doctor,
and I know you did it for love.
But now I see the world lying completely dead—
so dead my soul faints at the sight.
What way can there be now
to revive this dead one once more?
For you, God, cannot suffer,
and you are not about to come again
to redeem the world but to judge it.
How then
shall this dead one be brought back to life?
I do not believe, O infinite goodness,
that you have no remedy.
Indeed, I proclaim it:
your love is not wanting,
nor is your power weakened,
nor is your wisdom lessened.
So you want to, you can,
and you know how to
send the remedy that is needed.
I beg you then,
let it please your goodness
to show me the remedy,
and let my soul be roused to pick it up courageously.

Catherine of Siena, *The Prayers of Catherine of Siena,* trans. and ed.
Suzanne Noffke (Mahwah, N.J.: Paulist Press, 1983), Prayer 19,
Passion Sunday, 27 March 1379. © Suzanne Noffke, 1983. Used by
permission of Paulist Press. www.paulistpress.com.

The Lord's Prayer

Eternal Spirit,
Life-Giver, Pain-Bearer, Love-Maker,
Source of all that is and that shall be,
Father and Mother of us all,
Loving God, in whom is heaven:

The Hallowing of your Name
  echo throughout the universe!
The Way of your Justice
  be followed by the peoples of the world!
Your Heavenly Will
  be done by all created beings!
Your Commonwealth of Peace and Freedom
  sustain our hope and come on earth!

With the bread we need for today,
  feed us.
In the hurts we absorb from one another,
  forgive us.
In times of temptation and test,
  strengthen us.
From trials too sharp to endure,
  spare us.
From the grip of all that is evil,
  free us.

For you reign in the glory
of the power that is love,
now and for ever. Amen.

Jim Cotter, *Prayer at Night's Approaching: A Book for the Darkness*
(Sheffield: Cairns Publications, 2001), pp. 15–16.

PROPER 13

Ordinary Time 18

Sunday between July 31 and August 6 inclusive

| Hosea 11:1–11 | Colossians 3:1–11 |
| Psalm 107:1–9, 43 | Luke 12:13–21 |

Things that are above

The mould under the bushes, the moss on the path, and the little brick border, were not visibly changed. But they were changed. A boundary had been crossed. She had come into a world, or into a Person, or into the presence of a Person. Something expectant, patient, inexorable, met her with no veil or protection between. . . . This demand which now pressed upon her was not, even by analogy, like any other demand. It was the origin of all right demands and contained them. In its light you could understand them; but from them you could know nothing of it. There was nothing, and never had been anything, like this. And now there was nothing except this. Yet also, everything had been like this; only by being like this had anything existed. In this height and depth and breadth the little idea of herself which she had hitherto called *me* dropped down and vanished, unflutter-ing into bottomless distance, like a bird in a space without air. . . .

The largest thing that had ever happened to her had, apparently, found room for itself in a moment of time too short to be called time at all.

> C. S. Lewis, *That Hideous Strength* (London: Macmillan 1947),
> chap. 14.

> Poverty is having nothing, wanting nothing,
> And possessing all things
>   in the spirit of freedom.

> Jacopone da Todi (c. 1230–1306)

Love redeems all

Don't be afraid of anything. Do not ever be afraid. And don't worry. So long as you remain sincerely penitent, God will forgive you everything. There's no sin, and there can be no sin in the whole world which God will not forgive to those who are truly repentant. Why, a person cannot commit so great a sin as to exhaust the infinite love of God. Or can there be a sin that would exceed the love of God? Only you must never forget to think continually of repentance, but dismiss your fear altogether. Believe that God loves you in a way you cannot even conceive of. He loves you in spite of your sin and in your sin. And there's more joy in heaven over one sinner that repents than over ten righteous persons. This was said a long time ago. So go and do not be afraid. Do not be upset by people and do not be angry if you're wronged. . . . [I]f you are sorry for what you did, then you must love. And if you love, you are of God. . . . Everything can be atoned for, everything can be saved by love. If I, a sinner like you, have been moved by your story and am sorry for you, how much more will God be. Love is such a priceless treasure that you can redeem everything in the world by it, and expiate not only your own but other people's sins. Go and do not be afraid.

Fyodor Dostoyevsky, *The Brothers Karamazov,* vol. 1, trans. David
Magarshack (Harmondsworth: Penguin Books, 1963), p. 56.

True freedom

My freedom does not mean my ability to do what I like as and when I like: it means my ability to choose some goal or end, and to unify all my powers in the consistent pursuit of that goal or end.

That is a freedom for the whole person, a freedom which involves an ideal *for* which one is free; a freedom which involves restraints which a person makes for themselves, but which the community can also help them make in a common pursuit of freedom. It is, above all, not only a freedom *from* this and that and the other, but a freedom *for* something greater than oneself. And in so far as it is a freedom *from*, it is freedom from oneself, from the arbitrary tyranny which the self can impose upon itself.

Michael Ramsey, in *Through the Year with Michael Ramsey,* ed.
Margaret Duggan (London: Hodder & Stoughton, 1975), p. 212.

When you are compelled to weave barbed wire around yourself as a protection against your fellow-citizens, your security is a form of imprisonment—you can only shut others out at the price of shutting yourself in.

Colin Morris

Simple happiness

Communities which live simply and without waste, and which do not use television all the time, help people to discover a whole new way of life, which demands fewer financial resources but more commitment to relationships and to celebration. Is there a better way to bridge the gulf which widens daily between rich and poor countries? It is not simply a question of generous people going to work in developing countries. Rich countries themselves have to be awakened to the fact that happiness is not to be found in a frantic search for material goods, but in simple and loving relationships, lived and celebrated in communities which have renounced that search.

Jean Vanier, Community and Growth (London: Darton, Longman &
Todd, 1991), p. 309.

Faith sets us free

Faith enables us to get free from:

The domination of place and time, for it gives the additional dimension of the spiritual and the eternal.

The domination of happenings, for we are not at the mercy of circumstances, but can draw upon the inexhaustible wisdom and grace of God.

The domination of the written word, for we do not identify it with the inerrant word of God, but test it by the incarnate word.

The domination of theology, for our thoughts about God change, and our theories, however good, are seen to be imperfect.

The domination of puritanism, for we see that truth and love must be decisive about action.

The domination of conscience, for conscience constantly needs educating from our growing knowledge of God.

George Appleton, Journey for a Soul (London: William Collins Sons &
Co., 1976), p. 182.

Love's faithfulness

You offer comfort
in affliction.
Within the wasteland of
my pilgrim heart
You stand radiant
moving forward,
dustblown through the years
facing every onslaught
wiping every tear
defusing every deception
disarming vanity
confronting pride—
idolatry of every kind.
Seemingly lost amidst unbelief
and the pain and turmoil
of past years
and recent grief,
yet here you stand

With you I emerge
burnt
yet more vulnerable
more real.

Kathy Keay, in *Laughter, Silence and Shouting: An Anthology of Women's Prayers,* comp. Kathy Keay (London: HarperCollins, 1994), p. 128. © Kathy Keay, 1994. Used by permission of the estate of Kathy Keay.

Proper 14

Ordinary Time 19
Sunday between August 7 and 13 inclusive

Isaiah 1:1, 10–20	Hebrews 11:1–3, 8–16
Psalm 50:1–8, 22–23	Luke 12:32–40

The givenness of things

Eucharist means thanksgiving, gratitude, appreciation. A total response to God for receiving all things at his hands. We cannot celebrate the Eucharist out of context with our total attitude to possessions and ownership.

The Eucharist is also an explicit denial of any form of dualism: that material things don't matter, that it is the spirit alone that is relevant. God presents himself to us as things, things to be eaten and to be drunk. This is incarnation in its full expression and should be a dire warning against making Christian faith 'spiritual', of thinking for instance that Jesus was really talking about being poor in spirit in a way that makes no demands on our life style.

When poverty is talked about people immediately think of St. Francis. In general we have inherited quite a developed theology and tradition of giving everything up for the freedom of the kingdom—even if few of us are any good at doing so, and even if more of us are probably called to that total handing over than in fact ever have a go. But to complement that poverty of go-sell-give-come-follow we also need a theology of ownership (which we have not at all inherited). Most people are in no position to relinquish all, because of family and other responsibilities. But all of us need to theologise contemplatively on: What does it mean for me to *own* this car, this house, to *have* this talent, this skill, to be able to enjoy and indulge in so many things?

Thomas Cullinan, *The Passion of Political Love* (London: Sheed & Ward, 1987), pp. 82–83.

The Mirage

My wife and I stayed in a Las Vegas hotel once on the first night of a vacation trip to Idaho. We spent an hour or so on a walking tour. Entering one casino, we came upon a family in turmoil. The father had just discovered that his wallet was missing. A look of horror came over him, and suddenly he began to run. His wife screamed after him hysterically; the two children, one a teenager, began to cry. As we walked away, I looked up and saw a sign bearing the name of one of Las Vegas's establishments—"The Mirage."

Richard J. Mouw, *Consulting the Faithful: What Christian Intellectuals Can Learn from Popular Religion* (Grand Rapids: Wm. B. Eerdmans, 1994), p. 22.

Thanksgiving for the real riches

Thanksgiving is a feast that was instituted only after the pilgrims had withstood great sacrifice and difficult living. It was not a feast of baubles; it was a recognition of the glory of survival. What have you survived this year that is worth your gratitude? Forget all the fixtures and gadgets and extras in which you're steeped. Give thanks for the real riches of life, the things that make you what you are deep down.

Joan D. Chittister, O.S.B., *The Psalms: Meditations for Every Day of the Year* (New York: Crossroad Publishing Company, 1996), p. 126.

Far from being saints

The image of Abraham as the exemplary man of faith has come to dominate our thinking about him, and Sarah sometimes basks briefly in this glory. . . . For in truth, Abraham is far from being a saint in Genesis, and the same goes for Sarah. Abraham was turned into a saint by the Jewish theologians of the period between the Old and New Testaments, and sometimes Sarah was given something of a halo herself. That thinking had a profound influence on the writers of the New Testament, and led to the two-dimensional pictures of Abraham and Sarah we find in the Epistles. In Genesis itself they are fully rounded characters, subtly drawn, with their strengths matched—one is tempted to say *more* than matched—by their weaknesses. They are, in a word, all too "human" there, and the narrator rarely tells us explicitly what to make of them.

Trevor Dennis, *Sarah Laughed: Women's Voices in the Old Testament* (London: SPCK, 1994; Nashville: Abingdon Press, 1994), p. 35.

Making sacred

And what is sacrifice? To sacrifice is literally "to make a thing sacred"; it is to take something out of common use and make it over to God. It is a symbolic act by which we recognize that everything in this world derives from another order of being and seeks to enter into communion with that other world. But the outward thing which is sacrificed can never be more than a sign of an inward offering; what we desire is to offer ourselves. The essential sacrifice has to take place in the center of our own being, in the darkness of the interior where alone we can encounter the God who is hidden in the depths of the soul. We have to pass beyond all the images of the senses, beyond all the concepts of the mind, beyond ourselves, if we are really to find God.

> Bede Griffiths, O.S.B., *The Golden String* (New York: The Harvill
> Press Ltd., 1954), p. 163.

Living religion

Mentally we have made religion into a *thing*. What used to be the possessive and progressive experience of a people has become a circumscribed entity. Instead of flowing with the water's current, we have crawled out of the stream, sat on the bank, and begun to study the stream.

. . . It is as Christians' faith in God has weakened that they have busied themselves with Christianity, and as their personal relationship with Christ has waned that they have turned to religion. So many Christians today speak about believing in Christianity rather than believing in Christ himself and God his Father. They preach Christianity instead of the good news of Jesus Christ and practice Christianity instead of love. They talk about being saved by Christianity rather than by the bloody anguish and self-sacrificing love of Jesus of Galilee.

> William McNamara, *The Human Adventure: The Art of Contemplative
> Living* (Amity, N.Y.: Amity House, 1974), pp. 91, 93.

Listening

The most difficult and decisive part of prayer is acquiring [the] ability to listen. Listening is no passive affair, a space when we happen not to be doing or speaking. Inactivity and superficial silence do not necessarily mean that we are in a position to listen. Listening is a conscious, willed action, requiring alertness and vigilance, by which our whole attention is focused and controlled. Listening is in this sense a difficult thing. And it is decisive because it is the beginning of our entry into a personal and unique relationship with God, in which we hear the call of our own special responsibilities for which God has intended us. Listening is the aspect of silence in which we receive the commission of God.

Mother Mary Clare, S.L.G., *Encountering the Depths* (London: Darton, Longman & Todd, 1981), p. 33.

On the edge

They say that Abraham is a great example of faith. I sometimes wonder. It says that 'he went out not knowing. . . .' I sometimes fancy that he had left faith far behind; that he was way away out on the edge of things, where only a sliver of hope sustains. When we can join him out there on that edge, in hope sacrificing hope— only then may we see light, and be satisfied.

Henry McKeating, *God and the Future*
(London: SCM Press, 1974), p. 84.

PROPER 15

Ordinary Time 20
Sunday between August 14 and 20 inclusive

| Isaiah 5:1–7 | Hebrews 11:29–12:2 |
| Psalm 80:1–2, 8–19 | Luke 12:49–56 |

God, could you leave us alone?

Zealous God, we confess, like your people Israel, that we tire of being "the cho-sen." Could you not just leave us alone every once in a while? Sometimes this "Christian stuff" gets a bit much. Life goes on and we have lives to live. Yet, unrelenting, you refuse to leave us alone. You are, after all, a zealous God. You startle us from our reveries by gathering us into your dream time, into your Church. May we, thus gathered, be so inspired by your Spirit that our lives never tire, that we have the energy now to wait, to rest, in the goodness and beauty of your truth. Amen.

Stanley Hauerwas, *Prayers Plainly Spoken* (Grove, Ill.: InterVarsity
Press, 1999; London: Triangle, 1999), p. 26.

In it together

Our individualistic culture has lost the sense that traditional societies all retained: that personal aberrations are integrally connected with the breakdown of right social relations in the community. The demoniac was his society's deviant. What do deviants tell us about their societies?

... When I was a pastor near Galveston, Texas, in the early 1960s, the local press carried the story of Major Claude Eartherly, the navigator of the plane that dropped the atom bomb on Hiroshima. He had been involved in a series of petty crimes which he committed apparently for the sole reason of getting himself arrested, and was now in the Galveston jail. The newspaper dismissed him as suffering from a personal guilt complex. My own reaction was to want to go visit him and try to communicate to him God's forgiveness. He was later committed, on the "expert" witness of psychiatrists, to a mental institution on the grounds of "lunacy."

They did well, for he carried in his heart a bomb that could have exploded and shattered all our sleep. He had been trying to make the nation face the immorality of this act in which he had played a small but significant part. Failing that, he had sought, by increasingly bizarre behavior, to see that at least *he* was punished, thereby forcing the guilty to punish him.

Walter Wink, *Unmasking the Powers: The Invisible Forces That
Determine Human Existence* (Philadelphia: Fortress Press, 1986), p. 48.

The obedience of God?

We are able to obey, to give ourselves in glad response to God in person after person, in situation after situation, because we know God has promised to be there for us, that God's great self-consistency underlies all these. With that revelation, in that confidence, we know whom we must obey. . . .

Is there also a . . . way in which we can turn that original definition of covenant on its head? The promise of God, the obedience of human beings, the promise of human beings—and, surely, the *obedience of God.* Can we dare to say that as well? The faithfulness, the self-consistency of God is nothing other than loving attention and responsiveness to the world he has made; a kind of obedience.

Rowan Williams, *Open to Judgement: Sermons and Addresses*
(London: Darton, Longman & Todd, 1994), pp. 40–41.

The pain of God

Our wrongdoing and sin, in both attitude and in specific acts, caused our separation from God: God's love has reached across this break to us who are broken away, so that the relationship shall not be broken. In this reaching out, his love fully experiences, in a way we can barely comprehend, the rejection and refusal of the sinner, the rending disjunction in the fabric of his universe of love. Although God promised to blot out our sins, he does not 'forget' in the usual sense of the term. Omniscience has to know what has been done, and 'always' will, but he loves the repentant sinner just as though it had not been done, loves fully, openly and graciously. The knowledge of the sin, of the denial and refusal, remains in him fully, alongside the full love. That is the pain of God.

Dorin Barter, *Grace Abounding: Wrestling with Sin and Guilt*
(London: Darton, Longman & Todd, 1993), p. 165.

World of contradictions

This poem may be sung as a hymn, to the tune "ST. CLEMENT."

O God of peace, your beauty calls us
While conflicts rage and cares dismay:
How can we smile when love impels us
To strive and bleed to end the fray?

When healing flees as pain consumes us
Or pity fires our angry eyes,
How dare an opening leaf beguile us
Or birdsong taunt the thundery skies?

How dare you, God, assault our grieving
With tender buds and radiant stars?
The gossamer grass and pearly sunset
Make mock of justice's call to arms.

You set before us calm and beauty,
Truth, justice, mercy—where is peace?
How can we choose when torn by tension
When blessings soothe while hates increase?

Creator God, your gift of freedom
Reveals you trust us; come what may
We walk this world of contradictions
In steadfast anguish, Jesus' way.

Mary Ann Ebert, in *The Way of Peace*, ed. Hannah Ward and Jennifer
Wild (Oxford: Lion Publishing, 1999), p. 87. Used by permission
of P. A. Ebert.

Love in action is a harsh and dreadful thing compared to love in dreams.

Dorothy Day

PROPER 16

Ordinary Time 21
Sunday between August 21 and 27 inclusive

Jeremiah 1:4–10   Hebrews 12:18–29
Psalm 71:1–6   Luke 13:10–17

Physicians to each other

In dealing with deeply ill patients, a prerequisite is the establishment of proper relations with the world, and—in particular—with other human beings, or *one* human being, for it is human relations which carry the possibilities of proper being-in-the-world. Feeling the fullness of the presence of the world depends on feeling the fullness of another *person,* as a person; reality is given to us by the reality of people; our sense of reality, of trust or security, is critically dependent on a human relation. A single good relation is a lifeline . . . and we see, again and again in the histories of these patients, how a single relation can extricate them from trouble. Kinship is healing: we are physicians to each other.

Oliver Sacks, *Awakenings* (London: Duckworth, 1973), pp. 194–95.

Hope and despair

Hope and despair are not opposites. They are cut from the very same cloth, made from the very same material, shaped from the very same circumstances. Most of all, every life finds itself forced to choose one from the other, one day at a time, one circumstance after another. The only difference between the two is that despair shapes an attitude of mind; hope creates a quality of soul. Despair colors the way we look at things, makes us suspicious of the future, makes us negative about the present. Hope, on the other hand, takes life on its own terms, knows that whatever happens God lives in it, and expects that, whatever its twists and turns, it will ultimately yield its good to those who live it well.

When tragedy strikes, when trouble comes, when life disappoints us, we stand at the crossroads between hope and despair, torn and hurting. Despair cements us in the present; hope sends us dancing around dark corners trusting in a tomorrow we cannot see. Despair says that there is no place to go but here. Hope says that God is waiting for us someplace else. Begin again.

Joan D. Chittister, O.S.B., *The Psalms: Meditations for Every Day of the Year* (New York: Crossroad Publishing Company, 1996), p. 44.

Often we shall have to change the direction of our thinking and our wishing and our striving. That is what repentance really means—taking our bearings afresh and trying a new road.

Harry Williams

Repentance

It seems a characteristic of one's later years that whilst the wrongs one has suffered fade in one's memory towards vanishing point, the wrongs one has inflicted on others stand out ever more distinctly. It is not that one is consumed with guilt over sins long since confessed but rather that the undoubted effects and the suspected effects of one's actions upon others really strike to the heart. But it is a joy-bringing revelation as well because it reveals how one's heart is longing as never before for repentance. Old age, therefore, as many cultures teach and as Christendom once knew, is the age of repentance. And in that joyful repentance there is also a deep poignancy because, inevitably, many of those one feels to have harmed, in one way or another, are dead. As a result direct reparation towards them is no longer possible. However, the burning regret that one cannot now make reparation towards them only intensifies one's desire and determination to behave with all the more kindness and compassion towards anyone who comes across one's path during whatever time is left.

At the same time, if that desire and determination are not themselves to become a burdensome duty but a source of joy, then they have to be accompanied by a real hope that in some way our acts of kindness and compassion will, within the economy of salvation, touch those who have gone before us even though we ourselves can no longer touch them directly. That is a matter of hope—not of hopefulness.

Donald Nicholl, from "Growing Old," article in
Priests and People (1973).

Christ calls us to repentance, not so that we shall remain at this introspective stage, but so that, forgiven and set free, we can throw ourselves into action, and bring forth fruit, as he himself insists.

Paul Tournier

My name is known to you

God of many names,
my name is known to you.
I am held in the hand of your life,
and I do not know what you will make of me.
All I know is that I cannot make myself
any more than I could in my mother's womb.
But this I can do,
this I choose,
to give myself into the hand of your continuing creativity.
My past, with its joys and triumphs, its failures and regrets.
My present, with its struggles and accomplishments, its hopes and setbacks.
My future, with its fears and freedom, its pain and promise.
To loose and to bind, to stretch and to shape,
to become what I will,
trusting the hand that made the world
trusting the spirit that breathes life
trusting the love that will not let me go
trusting the promise of the Word made flesh.

Kathy Galloway, from *Talking to the Bones*
(London: SPCK, 1996), p. 82.

Wherever you lead

God, take me by Your hand, I shall follow You dutifully, and not resist too much. I shall evade none of the tempests life has in store for me, I shall try to face it all as best I can. But now and then grant me a short respite. I shall never again assume, in my innocence, that any peace that comes my way will be eternal. I shall accept all the inevitable tumult and struggle. I delight in warmth and security, but I shall not rebel if I have to suffer cold, should You so decree. I shall follow wherever Your hand leads me and I shall try not to be afraid.

Etty Hillesum, *Etty: A Diary 1941–43,* trans. Arnold J. Pomerans
(London: Jonathan Cape, 1983; New York: Pantheon Books, 1984).

PROPER 17

Ordinary Time 22

Sunday between August 28 and September 3 inclusive

| Jeremiah 2:4–13 | Hebrews 13:1–8, 15–16 |
| Psalm 81:1, 10–16 | Luke 14:1, 7–14 |

Listening with the heart

Responsive listening is the form the Bible gives to our basic religious quest as human beings. This is the quest for a full human life, for happiness. It is the quest for meaning, for our happiness hinges not on good luck; it hinges on peace of heart. Even in the midst of what we call bad luck, in the midst of pain and suffering, we can find peace of heart, if we find meaning in it all. Biblical tradition points the way by proclaiming that God speaks to us in and through even the most troublesome predicaments. By listening deeply to the message of any given moment I shall be able to tap the very Source of Meaning and to realize the unfolding meaning of my life.

To listen in this way means to listen with one's heart, with one's whole being. The heart stands for that center of our being at which we are truly "together." Together with ourselves, not split up into intellect, will, emotions, into mind and body. Together with all other creatures, for the heart is that realm where I am paradoxically not only most intimately myself, but most intimately united with all. Together with God, the source of life, the life of my life, welling up in the heart. In order to listen with my heart, I must return again and again to my heart through a process of centering, through taking things to heart. Listening with my heart I will find meaning. For just as the eye perceives light and the ear sound, the heart is the organ for meaning.

David Steindl-Rast, *A Listening Heart: The Art of Contemplative Listening* (New York: Crossroad, 1983), pp. 9–10.

Confession

God, whose costly life in the world often challenges our small ideas
about what it means to be your people,
we make our confession before you.
If we have become so engrossed in many activities
that it is a long time since we stopped
and asked whether our gods are now false gods:
Forgive us, O God.
Forgive us, O God.

A silence is kept

If we are so confident of our place at your table
that we have not searched our lives
to see whether we are excluding the very people who need you most:
Forgive us, O God.
Forgive us, O God.

A silence is kept

If we refuse to enter the banquet
because we cannot imagine that we could share
in your celebration of life,
rejecting your offer of forgiveness for the past,
and your kind invitation to be present now with you:
Forgive us, O God.
Forgive us, O God.

Dorothy McRae-McMahon, *Prayers for Life's Particular Moments*
(London: SPCK, 2001), p. 82.

Loving diversity

When people are in need, whatever the cause may be, we too often show an illiberal and judgemental desire to hold the fort, to keep the rules at whatever the cost, time and again making the best the enemy of the good; and as a result the God revealed as Christlike is popularly perceived to be not only remote but easily upset, judgemental and even somewhat prim.

Nowhere is this truer than in matters of human sexuality. We have loved definitions; we have felt safe knowing what are the proper bounds, even though they carry dangerous overtones of exclusion. But life for most people is not like that. Life is about exploring, hoping, struggling, yearning, longing for love and experiencing grief. It is often messy. It is about being knocked flat. It takes courage. We frequently get it wrong. At a time of rapid social change we need more than an appeal to moral codes that are so rigid that they fail to allow for human diversity, do not have a realistic understanding of sexual orientation, and apply generalised precepts to individual circumstances. We have to find ways of responding to the universal human need to find and give love that will keep faith with what we believe about the true worth of every human being; an approach that meets the unchanging test of what love of God and love of neighbour demands of us in terms of compassion, justice and forgiveness.

> Michael Mayne, *Learning to Dance* (London: Darton, Longman
> & Todd, 2001), p. 199.

Children of God

The Christian gospel declares that people are of inestimable value because they are the children of God, the concern of his love, created for an eternal destiny; not just people in general, but individual men, women and children, each with a name, each having priceless worth. This was made startlingly plain by Jesus when he told his disciples 'the very hairs of your head are all numbered': an extravagant piece of imagery to drive home what he was saying. When we take his words seriously, we begin to realize how far-reaching their significance is. If they are true, if that is how things really are, if God really does care for every single man, woman and child in the teeming millions that inhabit the globe, not to speak of the countless generations of the past and those as yet unborn, we cannot dismiss anyone as of no consequence; nor are we entitled to suppose that some are more important than others or that any should be sacrificed to serve some interest which takes precedence over their inherent worth. The consequences of accepting this basic presupposition are shattering, calling in question not only the way in which we commonly behave towards many of our fellow human beings, but the international, military, political, economic and social policies which have been and still are considered reasonable by those who are responsible for them.

> Paul Rowntree Clifford, *Government by the People?*
> (London: SCM Press, 1986).

Hospitality is about a relationship—one cannot be hospitable without guests. God not only plays the host for us and becomes the banquet for us: God also has become guest for us. This is one of the deep meanings of the incarnation, that God let go of hosting long enough to become a guest as well.

Matthew Fox

The quality of silence

One Thursday, I passed a Quaker meeting-house when a meeting was about to take place. It was not for undergraduates who came on a Sunday but for Quaker farmers in the country round about.

I walked in, sat down, and was sucked into the silence. It is the only mystery the Quakers possess, but it is a very powerful one. Some people got up from time to time and said the normal things, reminding the Almighty of the more distressing current events as if he did not know them.

I did not bother about them. I wanted to go deeper into that silence, because I knew that something was in it. It was the same silence I had felt in synagogue after my Bar Mitzvah. I had picked up an old thread, and I was jolly well going to follow it and unravel it.

I attended that meeting every week for about two months, and the silence became deeper and more profound. It began to have a face, a personality and a voice.

Lionel Blue, *A Backdoor to Heaven*
(London: Darton, Longman & Todd, 1979), p. 29.

The call to justice jars on many ears.

David Sheppard

PROPER 18

Ordinary Time 23

Sunday between September 4 and 10 inclusive

Jeremiah 18:1–11	Philemon 1–21
Psalm 139:1–6, 13–18	Luke 14:25–33

Solidarity with all humankind

Jesus appealed . . . for a loving solidarity which would exclude nobody at all.

Solidarity with humankind is the basic attitude. It must take precedence over every other kind of love and every other kind of solidarity. 'Whoever comes to me and does not *hate* father and mother, wife and children, brothers and sisters, yes, and even life itself, cannot be my disciple' (Luke 14:26).

The commentators always point out that because of the paucity of the Hebrew and Aramaic languages, the word 'hate' is used to cover all the attitudes which are not love. Thus it could mean hating, being indifferent to, detached from, or not preferring, someone. In this context, we are told, Jesus is asking for detachment: that one should not give preference to one's families and relatives. This is true but it does not do justice to the mode of thinking of Jesus and his contemporaries.

If love means solidarity then hate means non-solidarity. What Jesus is asking for is that the group solidarity of the family be replaced by a more basic solidarity with all humankind. This obviously does not mean that one's kith and kin are to be excluded—as enemies! They are included in the new solidarity because they too are human beings. Nor does this mean that one should love them any the less. It is the *basis* of the love that is being altered. They are not to be loved just because they happen to be your family and relatives but because they too are persons. They are to be loved with an inclusive love. In the end this will mean that they are loved all the more. They will be *loved*, not merely preferred.

All the other references to the family in the gospels confirm this interpretation.

Albert Nolan, *Jesus before Christianity: The Gospel of Liberation*
(London: Darton, Longman & Todd, 1977), pp. 61–62.

Prayer

Let us not die from poverty of caring,
>   let us not starve, where love is to be shared.
Come, break us open to receive your healing:
>   your broken body be our wine and bread.

> Shirley Erena Murray, *In Every Corner Sing* (Carol Stream, Ill.: Hope
> Publishing Company, 1992), no. 28 ("God of All Time"), verse 4.
> © CopyCare International for the UK. © Hope Publishing Company
> for all other territories. Used by permission.

What kind of church?

A Church founded on unmerited and unconstrained mercy may not at times be the Church we would like; but it is the only Church we have been given. It may fail to guarantee our proud entitlements or protect our vulnerabilities; but it is the only kind of Church that could make space for the new life, the rejected perceptions or the unexpected love on which our shared future depends. Above all, it is the kind of Church there would have to be if God really means to love the unwanted more than those whom human structures of power would reward, the only kind of Church that could carry life that comes from the Cross.

Such, then, is the belonging we have in God. The moments when we experience it, and know ourselves held in that love, are also times when we know there is more to desire, more than we could name. It is a belonging held open to a universe whose splendour is still to be disclosed. It asks of us that we recognize that what we have desired and experienced may also appear in the lives of our sisters and brothers in ways that are full of surprise and disturbance and which we nevertheless can welcome as promises fulfilled.

> Peter Selby, *BeLonging: Challenge to a Tribal Church*
> (London: SPCK, 1991), pp. 78–79.

Going beyond ourselves

Adoration is the first and greatest of life's responses to its spiritual environment; the first and most fundamental of spirit's movements towards Spirit, the seed from which all other prayer must spring. It is among the most powerful of the educative forces which purify the understanding, form and develop the spiritual life. As we can never know the secret of great art or music until we have learned to look and listen with a self-oblivious reverence, acknowledging a beauty that is beyond our grasp—so the claim and loveliness remain unrealized till we have learned to look, to listen, to adore. Then only do we go beyond ourselves and our small vision, pour ourselves out to that which we know not, and so escape from our own pettiness and limitations into the universal life.

Evelyn Underhill, *The Golden Sequence*
(London: Methuen & Co., 1932), p. 162.

Abandonment

Abandonment is not just hanging loose.
It is letting go.
It is a severing of the strings by which one
manipulates
controls
administrates
the forces of one's life.
Abandonment is receiving things the way one receives
a gift
with opened hands
and opened heart.
Abandonment to God
is the climactic point in anyone's life.

Sheila Cassidy, *Good Friday People* (London: Darton, Longman & Todd; Maryknoll, N.Y.: Orbis Books, 1991). © 1991 Darton, Longman & Todd Ltd. and Orbis Books. Used by permission of the publishers.

Religion's radical protest

We are afraid of religion and of the community that goes hand in hand with it. It is difficult to control. We are afraid of the emotions that religion helps to articulate. We do not object to emotions so long as they are private and restrained. Nor do we object to a group dynamic that is totally wrapped up in itself. But the kind of religious emotions that are expressed in ways critical of the world are regarded as dangerous. For us such emotions are as much taboo as was conversation about sexual matters to our grandparents. To pray, to experience common aspirations, to share with one another our fears as well as our hopes—such acts we find constricting and not bourgeois, indeed quite unappealing. Prayers and songs and rituals such as lighting candles, distributing bread, kneeling, and embracing are quickly disparaged. The intellectual can easily dismiss them with a contemptuous smile and the observation that religion, even when practiced to a small extent, is a fraud.

We are afraid of the kind of experiences that challenge our sense of security. We are afraid to allow the petty bourgeois individual we were and are to be shaken and disturbed by such experiences. . . . We want to prevent religion from doing this. We do not want religion to do what its most radical critic says it has done and in spite of his criticism still does—protest and comfort. We are afraid of religion's inherent radical protest against the death-ridden life we live and cultivate. We do not want to hear the protest and outcry that religion raises. So we say that religion is not an outcry of protest but the babbling of addicts or, as Marx put it, the opiate of the masses. Actually, however, Marx knew full well that religion is an outcry of protest. And we can know that we are afraid of religion because we are afraid of the absolute demands religion lays upon us. . . . The very word 'absolute' . . . unleashes thoughts of relativity. We can look at anything from a number of points of view. We can even look at the effect of horrible weapons upon the flesh of children from several points of view. We refuse to accept any absolute standards for our lives because if we did life would be unendurable for us.

Dorothee Soelle, *The Inward Road and the Way Back,* trans. David L.
Scheidt (London: Darton, Longman & Todd, 1979), pp. 21–22.

Human life gains the greatest part of its richness from the capacity for ecstasy, by which I do not mean the alleged experiences of the mystic, but any experience of stepping outside the taken-for-granted reality of everyday life, any openness to the mystery that surrounds us on all sides.

Peter L. Berger

PROPER 19

Ordinary Time 24

Sunday between September 11 and 17 inclusive

Jeremiah 4:11–12, 22–28	1 Timothy 1:12–17
Psalm 14	Luke 15:1–10

In [chapter 15] Luke tells three Jesus stories that show how God is concerned for the lost. He will seek the lost, no matter how obscure the lost one is, no matter how much patience or persistence it takes.

We are all familiar with the stories—the lost son, the lost coin, and the lost sheep. In each story, someone represents God . . . the woman, as well as the father and the shepherd, is in the God-position of looking for the lost.

"Oh, I never thought of that," most people are inclined to say. This aspect of the story has traditionally gone unnoticed. For centuries we have been deluged with sermons about the prodigal son and the lost sheep. But among the three stories, the poor woman sweeping for the coin gets swept under the carpet. Her story takes three verses; the prodigal son's takes thirty-three.

Why is the God-woman obscured?

First, because she is a woman. When we read or hear the story, our perception of it is immediately limited to the sex role implications we have all internalized. A person is a woman—*therefore* we look for significance in ways we are accustomed to thinking of women.

Women sweep. Women lose things. Women call together their neighbors for a celebration. These are familiar thought patterns. But we do not think: *the woman, like God, is seeking the lost.*

The seeking father of a son is a God/father symbol. The seeking shepherd is a God/caretaker symbol. And the woman is a God/housemanager symbol. . . .

To see woman as God is to see the story in terms which shake up our familiar categories. To see a woman as God is to break out of our lots for women—our condition categories. Jesus did not have our hangups about picturing God as either sex. But because of our trained God-perceptions—the traditional association of God with the male sex—we have been unable to see in this story the woman as deity. We don't have room in our heads for that kind of woman.

Rachel Conrad Wahlberg, *Jesus According to a Woman,* rev. ed.
(Mahwah, N.J.: Paulist Press, 1986), pp. 27–29.

God cares

The whole creation is beloved by God. Like the woman who swept and cleaned her house in search of a lost coin, we affirm that God cares for even the last detail of this, God's household, into which we are placed. Women who care for life and nurture it in the daily events of their lives have always been part of that loving relationship towards all that is and the whole of creation.

Women's statement to a World Council of Churches Conference on
Justice, Peace, and the Integrity of Creation

It is allowable to mourn the loss of earthly things, the ruin of something for which one has worked all one's life long. But we need not and must not despair. It is a loss for only a short moment, as short as the duration of life, and our happiness is not in the least affected by it. Happiness lies in the hands of God alone. It lies beyond life, and the gate that brings us to it is death.

Ewald von Kleist-Schmenzin

Closer to God than we think

"My God, my God, why have you forsaken me?"

He is not forsaken, but Christ does feel the pain and anguish that our hearts must sometimes suffer.

It's the psychology of suffering: to feel alone, to feel that no one understands, to feel forsaken. . . .

God is not failing us when we don't feel his presence.

Let's not say: God doesn't do what I pray for so much, and therefore I don't pray any more.

God exists, and he exists even more, the farther you feel from him.

God is closer to you when you feel he is farther away and doesn't hear you.

When you feel the anguished desire for God to come near you because you don't feel him present, then God is very close to your anguish.

When are we going to understand that God is not only a God who gives happiness but that he tests our faithfulness in moments of affliction?

It is then that prayer and religion have most merit: when one is faithful in spite of not feeling the Lord's presence.

Let us learn from that cry of Christ that God is always our Father and never forsakes us, and that we are closer to him than we think.

Oscar Romero, from a homily given on Good Friday, 13 April 1979,
The Church Is All of You: Thoughts of Archbishop Oscar Romero, comp.
and trans. James R. Brockman, S.J. (London: Collins Fount
Paperbacks, 1985), p. 90.

Awareness of sin

One morning, while I was walking as usual in a solitary place, I at once saw that all my contrivances and projections to effect or procure deliverance and salvation for myself were utterly in vain. I was brought quite to a stand as finding myself totally lost. The tumult that had been before in my mind was now quieted, and I was something eased of that distress which I felt while struggling against a sight of myself and of the divine sovereignty. I had the greatest certainty that my state was forever miserable, for all that I could do. I wondered that I had never been sensible of it before.

In the time I remained in this state, my notions respecting my duties were quite different. Before this, the more I did in duty, the more I thought God was obliged to me. But now, the more I prayed, the more I saw I was indebted to God for allowing me to ask for mercy; for I saw it was self-interest that had led me to pray, and that I had never once prayed from any respect to the glory of God. I saw that I had been heaping up my devotions before God, fasting, praying, pretending; whereas I never once truly intended to aim at the glory of God, but only my own happiness. I saw that, as I had never done anything for God, I had no claim to lay to anything from him.

David Brainerd, *The Diary and Journal of David Brainerd*
(London, 1902).

Prayer for healing

Leader: O God, we cry to you in our anger
that people hurt each other.

People: **Be with us and heal us, O God.**

Leader: We feel the fear and pain
of the innocent and trusting child.

People: **Be with us and heal us, O God.**

Leader: We carry with us the things
that have been done to us
which hurt and destroy.

People: **Be with us and heal us, O God.**

Leader: They stand before us
and weigh us down.
They stop us living with joy and hope.

People: **Be with us and heal us, O God.**

Leader: Lift us up
on the wings of your Spirit.

People: **Set us free with your peace
and your power.**

Leader: For you are stronger
than all the forces that stand against us.

People: **Set us free,
heal our wounds,
O God who never leaves us
nor forsakes us.
Amen.**

Dorothy McRae-McMahon, from "Service of Healing," in *Echoes of
Our Journey: Liturgies of the People* (Melbourne: Joint Board of
Christian Education, 1993), pp. 82–83. © Dorothy McRae-McMahon.

He that saves you, the same saves your horse and your sheep; to come to the very least, your hen too.

Augustine of Hippo (354–430)

PROPER 20

Ordinary Time 25

Sunday between September 18 and 24 inclusive

Jeremiah 8:18–9:1   1 Timothy 2:1–7
Psalm 79:1–9   Luke 16:1–13

The prayer of compassion

In 1938 a man died on Mount Athos. He was a very simple man, a peasant from Russia who came to Mount Athos when he was in his twenties and stayed for about fifty years.... For a long time he was in charge of the workshops of the monastery. The workshops of the monastery were manned by young Russian peasants who used to come for one year, for two years, in order to make some money ... in order to go back to their villages with a few pounds ... to be able to start a family by marrying, by building a hut and by buying enough to start their crops.

One day other monks, who were in charge of other workshops, said 'Father Silouan, how is it that the people who work in your workshops work so well while you never supervise them, while we spend our time looking after them and they try continuously to cheat us in their work?' Father Silouan said 'I don't know. I can tell you what I do about it. When I come in the morning, I never come without having prayed for these people and I come with my heart filled with compassion and with love for them, and when I walk into the workshop I have tears in my soul for love of them. And then I give them the task they have to perform in the day and as long as they will work I will pray for them, so I go into my cell and I begin to pray about each of them individually. I take my stand before God and I say "O Lord, remember Nicholas. He is young, he is just twenty, he has left in his village his wife, who is even younger than he, and their first child. . . ." 'And so,' he said, 'I spend my days, praying for each of them in turn, one after the other, and when the day is over I go, I say a few words to them, we pray together and they go to their rest. And I go back to fulfil my monastic office.'

Anthony Bloom, *School for Prayer* (London: Darton,
Longman & Todd, 1970).

If I could live in a tiny dwelling on a rock in the ocean, surrounded by the waves of the sea and cut off from the sight and sound of everything else, I would still not be free of the cares of this passing world, or from the fear that somehow the love of money might still come and snatch me away.

Cuthbert of Lindisfarne

Pressures of taxation

There were marked tensions between Jerusalem and Galilee and between city and country.

I shall demonstrate this crisis situation more closely in terms of the burden of taxation, though I would not want to make taxes exclusively responsible for everything. Nevertheless it is always economic crises which increase tensions of many kinds, since here the most vital interests are infringed. At the time of Jesus the Jews lived in a territory occupied by the Romans and had to pay a mass of taxes to the occupying authorities: every year about a quarter of the crop, land and poll tax ... and in addition offerings in kind ... and unpaid services for the occupation forces, customs duty, and tolls for using the roads. Agriculture and therefore land was the economic basis of Palestine, so it was here that most was to be had. That applied not only to taxes but also to the confiscation of property, a practice carried out by both the Roman and the Jewish authorities, dependent on Roman favour, and necessary for gifts, bribes or for the settlement of retired Roman legionaries. The increasing impoverishment of the small farmers and the accumulation of possessions in the hands of the great landowners meant that the poor got increasingly poor and the rich got increasingly rich. There is some such experience behind the statement in the Gospel of Luke (19.26): 'I tell you, to all those who have, more will be given; but from those who have nothing, even what they have will be taken away.'

Political tensions could lead to remissions in taxes but also to increases in taxes, and this was rightly understood by the Jews as punishment for their intractability. The pressure of taxation also makes it clear why publicans were so hated. As tax farmers they worked for the Romans; they not only levied the taxes for them, but in so doing also betrayed the Jewish resistance against Rome. The burden of taxation and debt was further 'enhanced' by bad harvests, famine and epidemics, especially in the 20s and 60s of the first century. So it is not surprising that criticism of the rich runs through the Jesus tradition like a scarlet thread, and that the remission of debts is given a positive interpretation, indeed becomes a parable for the grace of God (e.g. Luke 16.1ff.).

Susanne Heine, *Women and Early Christianity:*
Are the Feminist Scholars Right?, trans. John Bowden
(London: SCM Press, 1987), pp. 56–57.

[Jesus] praises the swindler. Are you indignant? Apply the lesson to yourselves. . . . For you, too, the challenge of the hour demands prudence; everything is at stake!

Joachim Jeremias

A proper detachment

Christians have to be clear where they stand with regard to property and goods. They should not condemn them, since they are good things. But they should be ruthless and radical towards the possessive instinct in themselves. There Christ asks for everything and rejects any compromise—surely because the facts of the case themselves reject compromise. If I do not act ruthlessly against my possessiveness, I will be possessed by it. It will lead me and govern me. I will be caught up in an unending spiral of desire, fulfilment and greater desire and soon both my surrender to God and my openness to my neighbour will have been thrown aside. In fact these two gospel commands of love presuppose an attitude of poverty and detachment from self which are incompatible with the acquisitive spirit. Perhaps the reason we so often fail to love as we should is not because of a defect of loving in us, but because we are unwilling to conquer our spirit of greed and so, inevitably, put ourselves before others. When it comes to a final count we cling to our own self's needs and put our neighbour second. This is true of families as well as individuals.

The surrender to God in adoration and to one's neighbour in availability imply a 'letting go' which is the opposite of the acquisitive 'hanging on.' We have to be very honest with ourselves about the possessive instinct. Unless we root it out from the depths, it will take charge and oust every fine feeling in our hearts and leave only selfish concern. Jesus really meant it when he said 'You cannot serve God and Mammon.'

John Dalrymple, *Costing Not Less Than Everything* (London: Darton,
Longman & Todd, 1975), pp. 106–7.

Doing God's miracles

I think we tend sometimes to look simplistically towards God to correct all our weaknesses and restore the consequences of our wrong. My view is that this prayer reflects God's will and our request to God to be given this type of will. But we must not forget that God looks to his people to perform his miracles, and live in a way which is conducive to those standards he sets us. Any faults there are in our world today cannot be placed at the door of God, but rather at the door of the people who populate this world, and possibly those leaders within the world who should be leading in different and better directions.

God is God, and he is everlasting. I have no belief in the sanctity of life for individuals, because the evidence of that in places of starvation, deprivation and disease show that there is no sanctity for so many people who are equal in the eyes of God. My clear belief is that it is the people who are more favoured, more blessed, or more fortunate because of the area in which they live or the circumstances of their living who should be doing more for the underprivileged to even this out. That is God's will.

> O God, creator and preserver of all humankind;
> bless the people of all nations,
> reconcile those who are divided,
> relieve the hungry and oppressed,
> bring joy to the sorrowing,
> and peace and hope to all;
> through Jesus Christ, our Lord.

John Hermon (formerly Chief Constable, Royal Ulster Constabulary, Northern Ireland), in James Whitbourne, *A Prayer in the Life: Selections from BBC Radio 4's Prayer for the Day* (London: Triangle, SPCK, 1993), p. 56. (Prayer [slightly adapted with permission] from *The Alternative Prayer Book 1984* (London: William Collins, 1984), © The General Synod of the Church of Ireland.)

PROPER 21

Ordinary Time 26

Sunday between September 25 and October 1 inclusive

| Jeremiah 32:1–3a, 6–15 | 1 Timothy 6:6–19 |
| Psalm 91:1–6, 14–16 | Luke 16:19–31 |

Worlds apart

The parable of Dives and Lazarus is very disturbing. There is no suggestion that Dives persecutes or oppresses Lazarus. Dives may well have been a believer in the Gospel of Prosperity, thanking God for the many blessings bestowed on him. He might even have held prayer meetings in his mansion. Dives simply does not notice Lazarus, and it is his failure to notice which brings him to torment in Hades. If we think that this is a very unfair punishment, it is worth pondering our reaction.

Why do I think the punishment unfair? Because Dives has not deliberately wronged Lazarus? Here we come up against the difference between our thinking and God's thinking. We see ourselves as individuals struggling to live as best we can. The effort to do so can so preoccupy us that we simply do not notice what is happening to others. One political party promises a reduction in taxes, while the opposition threatens to raise them, so why not vote for the party offering the tax cut?

Jesus's thinking is different. He thinks not in terms of 'me,' but of 'us,' and 'us' includes all human beings. What glorious breadth of thinking, and how very awkward for those of us whose security depends upon our ability to ignore the plight of others. The gap between the rich and poor of the world is widening rapidly, not primarily because of lack of resources, but because of their unfair distribution.

Gerard W. Hughes, *God of Compassion* (London:
Hodder & Stoughton, 1998), pp. 79–80.

Jesus never speaks of wealth *in itself* or poverty *in itself* but of rich and poor as they are, historically.

José Miguez-Bonino

Ballad of Dives and Lazarus

Two men lived in the same street
But they were poles apart
For Lazarus had crippled bones
But Dives a crippled heart
That made him stare both night and day
At a production chart.

The springtime came, the springtime went,
The tide flowed up the sand;
Lazarus murmured to himself,
'It is a pleasant land;
The sun that shines upon my coat
Is the comfort of God's hand.'

But Dives in anger cried aloud,
'I spend too much on you!
A blind man cannot watch the dials
That help my engines go;
A deaf man cannot hear the whistle
To tell the end of smoko;

'A lame man cannot fetch and carry
The cheques that I must write—
The graph of my production chart
Is lovely in my sight
As Jacob's ladder was to him
Upon a starry night.

'And you will live, since live you must,
But at a cheaper rate;
A cripple cannot ask the World
To carry his dead weight—

My engines run too slowly
Because of the Welfare State.'

God spoke to Dives upon the hour
(Since God and God alone
Knows what can turn a human heart
Into a heart of stone)–
'My poor blind crippled son,' He said,
'Sit here beneath My Throne,

'Why force My Hand? I did not make
Man for the gap of Hell;
I gave the wild sea and the wind
And limbs that serve him well,
And a heart that is My dwelling place
Where none may buy or sell.

'Go back and learn from Lazarus
To walk on My highway
Until your crippled soul can stand
And bear the light of day,
And you and Lazarus are one
In holy poverty.'

James K. Baxter. Reproduced by permission of the James K. Baxter
Foundation. First published in *Collected Poems* by James K. Baxter
(Australia and New Zealand: Oxford University Press, 1988),
pp. 34–35.

The love of money

'The love of money is the root of all evils,' says 1 Timothy, and certainly, some of the things that have been done in pursuit of wealth make a very convincing argument in favour of original sin. Curiously, though, for such a strong biblical statement, these words have been somewhat ignored by many who have a great dedication to other parts of the Pauline canon (on personal morality and the role of women, for example). Perhaps that's because it's quite socially unacceptable to say that we love money—we are 'creating wealth,' or 'realizing our assets' or 'protecting our interests', or 'investing in the future.' If we don't actually love money, but only what it can do for us, then there's no theological problem—or at least, it's someone else's problem.

And it's certainly that. Western economic policies, sometimes known as development, have signally failed the countries of the Third World. . . .

People's innate sense of justice and fair play leads them to see that 'something is rotten in the state of Denmark.' But we need a framework, a story, to give us words of advocacy. The biblical story is of sufficiency—discerning what is 'enough' is an ongoing task. And we need practical beginnings to help us translate our sense of wrongness from despairing paralysis into political will.

> Kathy Galloway, *Getting Personal: Sermons and Meditations (1986–94)*
> (London: SPCK, 1995), pp. 40–41.

Unless the widening gap between the rich and poor is arrested, and if possible reversed, the very peace and stability of any society will be seriously jeopardized.

> Akin J. Omoyajowo

A litany of confession

Lord, we confess our day-to-day failure to be human.
Lord, we confess to you.

Lord, we confess that we often fail to love with all that we have and are, often because we do not fully understand what loving means, often because we are afraid of risking ourselves.
Lord, we confess to you.

Lord, we cut ourselves off from each other and we erect barriers of division.
Lord, we confess to you.

Lord, we confess that by silence and ill-considered words
we have built up walls of prejudice.

Lord, we confess that by selfishness and lack of sympathy
we have stifled generosity and left little time for others.

Holy Spirit, speak to us. Help us listen to your word of forgiveness, for we
are very deaf.

Come fill this moment and free us from our sin.

Cathedral Church of St. George, Cape Town, South Africa, in
Celebrating One World: A Worship Resource Book on Social Justice, ed.
Linda Jones, Annabel Shilson-Thomas, and Bernadette Farrell
(London: HarperCollins in association with CAFOD, 1998),
pp. 60–61. © The Very Revd the Dean, St. George's Cathedral,
Cape Town.

I used to think when I was a child that Christ might have been exaggerating when
he warned about the danger of wealth. Today I know better. I know how very hard
it is to be rich and still keep the milk of human kindness. Money has a dangerous
way of putting scales on one's eyes, a dangerous way of freezing people's hands,
eyes, lips, and hearts.

Helder Camara

PROPER 22

Ordinary Time 27
Sunday between October 2 and 8 inclusive

| Lamentations 1:1–6 | 2 Timothy 1:1–14 |
| Psalm 137 | Luke 17:5–10 |

What did I dream?

You ask me, what did I dream?
I dreamt I became
a bird.
You ask me, why did I
want to become a bird?
I really wanted to
have wings.

You ask me, why did I
want wings?
These wings would
help me fly back to
my country.
You ask me, why did I
want to go back there?
Because I wanted to
find something
I missed.

You ask me, what
do I miss?
I miss the place where
I lived as a child.
You ask me, what was
that place like?
The place was happy,

my family was close
together.

You ask me, what do I
remember best?
I still remember my
father reading the
newspaper.
You ask me, why do I
think of him?
I miss him and
I'm sad.

You ask me, why
I am sad?
I'm sad because all my
friends have fathers.
You ask me, why does
this matter?
Because my father is
far away.
I want to fly to him
like a bird.

Fourteen-year-old Vietnamese boy living in Australia, from *Borders
and Barriers*, © Uniya/Jesuit Refugee Service, Sydney, Australia. Used
by permission of Uniya Jesuit-Social Justice Centre.

Bound for heaven

An old church member says, "I have so many dark days. I do want to get to
heaven."

Keep your seat! The train goes through. If you want to get to the good world,
get on God's excursion train, and you will run in under the old car shed of heaven.
Some of you will have children there to take hold of your hand and welcome you
to the city of God. We will get there, thank God! Sister, keep your seat, it will go
through. Brother, keep your head in at the window; the train is in safe hands. I
have quit troubling myself. I have turned it all over to God.

Another says, "I am waiting for faith." Yes, you have been waiting forty years for faith. How much have you saved up? Like the fellow who had ten bushels of wheat, and was waiting till more grew before he could sow what he had. Sow it, and you will have a hundredfold. By keeping it, you will not get any more, but the rats will eat up what you have.

. . . "I want to be a blacksmith as soon as I get muscle." Why don't you go at it? There he stands until at last he has got muscle enough to lift the hammer. He is "getting it" with a vengeance. How did you get faith? By using what you had. I tell you what tickles me—to hear fellows down praying for faith. "Lord, give me faith." The next time you get any in that way, bring it over and let me see it. That ain't scriptural, that talk you are doing now. Christ rebuked those who prayed for faith. The trouble with you is not that you need more faith. You use the faith you have, and then you will get more. I would as soon pray for sweet potatoes as for faith.

Samuel P. Jones, "Waiting and Hoping," in Sermons and Sayings, by the Rev. Sam P. Jones, ed. W. M. Leftwich (Nashville: 1885).

Affirmation of faith

We believe in the gift of sorrow
which carries us back to humanness
and reminds us of the way
we dreamed life ought to be,
which marks truly
our love for people
and stills us to find new paths
through the blurred landscape
of our tears.
We believe that,
despite betrayal and deception,
in a way which we do not always understand,
we are not left alone.

And we believe that
we will not stay sorrowing forever
but that our spirits will as surely lift
as the day follows night.

Despite our doubts,
we believe that it is always better

to hope than to despair
to build anew rather than to destroy
and to accept that
life will not confirm our worst fears
but will surprise us
with unforeseen revelations.

God is above us
God is below us
God is between us
God is within us.
We will not be afraid.

> Dorothy McRae-McMahon, *Echoes of Our Journey: Liturgies of the People* (Melbourne: The Joint Board of Christian Education, 1993), p. 53. © Dorothy McRae-McMahon.

It is the combination of both power and love which makes a community workable and sustainable. It is the combination of power and love which Christians call the Spirit, and which empowers us to shape our common future for the good of all.

> Anne Primavesi

As big as a mustard seed

Loving God,
we confess that we have failed,
we have not been what you intend us to be,
we have not been what we want to be:

We would touch the world with goodness,
but we chase after our own salvation.
We would care for your creation,
but we squander it with little thought for those still to come.
We would meet the needs of others,
but we find ourselves reluctant to share.
We would stand for truth,
but we remain silent in the face of evil.

We would live with love and compassion,
but we take on the values of this world.
We would share our faith joyfully,
but we lack courage to trust in you.

We need you, God,
if we are to become who you want us to be.
Transform us by the power of your Spirit.
Renew our faith day by day
and make it as big as a mustard seed,
full of promise and possibility,
so that we may live with courage and purpose
and see the signs and parables
you have for us
in the world today.

Francis Brienen, in *A Restless Hope: Prayer Handbook 1995* (London:
United Reformed Church, 1995), 15 October. © Francis Brienen.

Every painful event contains in itself a seed of growth and liberation.

Anthony de Mello

Proper 23

Ordinary Time 28
Sunday between October 9 and 15 inclusive

Jeremiah 29:1, 4–7	2 Timothy 2:8–15
Psalm 66:1–12	Luke 17:11–19

God's design

A narrow-minded nationalist hardened by religious centrism could not have written such words. The eyes of Jeremiah, however, were opened to God's design for the nations as well as for his own nation. No one single nation could contain the power of God that moves history. And with the fall of the kingdom of Judah, Jeremiah must have sensed the history-moving power of God operating in Babylon. It has continued for more than two thousand years. It has been a long way from the Tower of Babel and from the call of Abraham. Through disruption and dispersion, nations and peoples are led to realize that God is greater than one's own nation, one's own religion and culture.

One particular nation alone, even that of Israel and Judah, cannot make a total picture of what God is doing in the world. It is only after Assyria and Babylon were brought into the arena of history that a more complete picture of God's design for the world began to appear. In the same way, one particular culture alone, even that which is called Christian culture, cannot reveal the entirety of God's thoughts for the world. Until Hindu culture or Confucian culture is consulted, [for example,] the God of Christians remains a partial God.

> Choan-Seng Song, *The Compassionate God: An Exercise in the
> Theology of Transposition* (Maryknoll, N.Y.: Orbis Books/London:
> SCM Press, 1982), p. 38.

International community

The convergence of *Yahweh's intention for the nations* and *Yahweh's intention for Israel* is perhaps best voiced in the "letter of Jeremiah" to the exilic community:

But seek the welfare of the city where I have sent you into exile, and pray to Yahweh on its behalf, for in its welfare you will find your welfare. (Jer. 29:7)

There is for Israel no "separate peace," no private "welfare" by withdrawal from the world of international reality. This could perhaps be taken as common sense. It is, however, more than common sense. It is an insistence that Israel is a member of a larger community of nations over which Yahweh rules. Israel's future is in the midst of a Yahweh-practicing world community and not apart from it. For that reason, these unaccommodating witnesses to Yahweh adamantly insist that all members of that community—Israel and every other member—must attend to the news of the new Governance. It is the *doing* and not the *naming* of Yahweh that matters to these prophets.

Walter Brueggemann, *Cadences of Home: Preaching among Exiles*
(Louisville, Ky.: Westminster John Knox Press, 1997), p. 90.

The Church in any country fails to be the Church if it forgets that its members in one nation have a fellowship with its members in every nation.

George Kennedy Allen Bell

Healing the rejected

Healing God, we praise you for the Christ
who, without fear, met those with leprosy
and gave them new life.
May that healing touch
reach the fears and darkness of our world.

Touch us, caring Jesus,
to take from our hearts
that fear which makes us keep our distance
from all deep agony.

Touch us, caring Jesus,
to heal that fear for ourselves
which bars us from understanding
mental illness, disfigurement and the approach of death.

Touch those, caring Jesus,
>who have been segregated, rejected, cast adrift
>because they offend our competitive society.

And touch with hope, healing Jesus,
>those who give themselves to combat
>grim illness and all that threatens life.

**I am come that they may have life
and may have it in all its fullness.**

Even so, come, Lord Jesus.

Bernard Thorogood, in *A Restless Hope: Prayer Handbook 1995*
(London: United Reformed Church, 1995), 9 July.
© Bernard Thorogood.

Probably no word better summarizes the suffering of our times than the word "homeless." It reveals one of our deepest and most painful conditions, the condition of not having a sense of belonging, of not having a place where we can feel safe, cared for, protected, and loved.

Henri J. M. Nouwen

The joys of a garden

For many years I had a dream: I wanted to plant *my* garden. Not a garden but *my* garden. I say *my* garden because it had to be able to evoke the stories and images I love. Many gardens are delights to the senses but they are dumb. They say nothing. They lack the power to evoke. I walk through their alleys and my inner garden continues to sleep. Yes, there is an inner vegetal world inside our bodies. . . .

I dreamed about planting *my* garden because I couldn't. The plot where my house was built was too small. But one day I managed to buy the vacant plot by the side of my house, and my dream came true.

For those whom I have not told my dreams, my plants are only plants: vegetal entities which offer a bit of pleasure to the body. For me, however, they are magical: they have the power to conjure up the past. The lilac was given by my father. Every time I smell its odour I see my father's face and hear his voice. The myrtle takes me back to the public garden of my home town. The emperor's jasmin grew in the backyard of my grandfather's huge colonial house, filled with mysteries, where I played as a boy. I walk by my plants. There are invisible presences in their midst. The past becomes present. My garden is a text. Each plant is a poetic metonymy. Many other plants give me pleasure. But my garden gives me joy.

Rubem A. Alves, *The Poet, The Warrior, The Prophet* (London: SCM
Press/New York: Trinity Press International, 1990), p. 46.

Gratitude is a fruit of great cultivation; you do not find it among gross people.

Samuel Johnson

PROPER 24

Ordinary Time 29
Sunday between October 16 and 22 inclusive

Jeremiah 31:27–34   2 Timothy 3:14–4:5
Psalm 119:97–104   Luke 18:1–8

The country of our soul

All this beauty that haunts us comes by revelation to those who are able to hear it. It is all around us, pressing in upon us, if only we could hear, if only we could learn to listen. And news of that other country we are born trying to remember comes the same way. We are homesick for something that lies beyond the universe yet strangely affects the movement of the sea. Our sense of regret points to a primordial homesickness—a sorrow that afflicts us precisely because we turn ourselves away from God who is the country we long for, the land of lost content. Most of us are mildly aware of this, but we are more than half afraid of the consequences of really finding God—'Lest, having Him, we must have naught beside,' in the words of Francis Thompson. The saints have a raging sense of their need for God. He is the country of their soul, and tidings from that far country break in upon them. That is the meaning of Christ, who brought tidings, news of that country. He brought the very air of it into our land of exile. And there have been other moments of revelation, brief glimpses beyond the curtain. The world rolls back, and we are left forlorn, but sustained by the memory of it and the sense we have that history, including our own private history, is the story of a return.

Richard Holloway, *Paradoxes of Christian Faith and Life*
(London: Mowbray, 1984), p. 25

We must not therefore be hesitant and lacking in faith. We must persist in our prayers, and our persistence will quite certainly win us, as God has told us, everything we ask for. No doubt about this at all!

John Cassian

266

Scripture's fountain

Who is capable of comprehending the extent of what is to be discovered in a single utterance of yours [Christ]? For we leave behind in it far more than we take from it, like thirsty people drinking from a fountain.

The facets of his word are more numerous than the faces of those who learn from it. God depicted his word with many beauties, so that each of those who learn from it can examine that aspect of it which he likes. And God has hidden within his word all sorts of treasures, so that each of us can be enriched by it from whatever aspect he meditates on. For God's word is the Tree of life which proffers to you on all sides blessed fruits; it is like the Rock which was struck in the Wilderness, which became a spiritual drink for everyone on all sides: 'They ate the food of the Spirit and they drank the draft of the Spirit.'

Anyone who encounters Scripture should not suppose that the single one of its riches that he has found is the only one to exist; rather, he should realize that he himself is only capable of discovering that one out of the many riches which exist in it.

Nor, because Scripture has enriched him should the reader impoverish it. Rather, if the reader is incapable of finding more, let him acknowledge Scripture's magnitude. Rejoice because you have found satisfaction, and do not be grieved that there has been something left over by you. A thirsty person rejoices because he has drunk: he is not grieved because he proved incapable of drinking the fountain dry. Let the fountain vanquish your thirst, your thirst should not vanquish the fountain!

Ephrem the Syrian, *Commentary on the Diatessaron,* trans. Sebastian
Brock, in *The Luminous Eye: The Spiritual World Vision of St. Ephrem*
(Kalamazoo, Mich.: Cistercian Publications, 1992), pp. 50–51.

We cannot segregate God's word from the historical reality in which it is proclaimed. It would not then be God's word. It would be history, it would be a pious book, a Bible that is just a book in our library. It becomes God's Word because it vivifies, enlightens, contrasts, repudiates, praises what is going on today in this society.

Oscar Romero

Hymn of the ten words

The great commandment of our Lord:
translating language into deed
and giving shape to spoken word,
creating life from clay of creed.
Praise God, whose word and deed are one,
creative Spirit, human Son!

Ten times, for every finger once,
he spoke and all things came to be.
Ten times the Lord of life pronounced
the words that set his people free.

Chorus

The hands of God create and guide;
he goes before us on our way.
He gives his Word to take our side
and hallow each surprising day.

Chorus

Lord, use our hands to care and bless,
and make us fluent in your speech.
Help us to be what we profess,
to re-present your love to each.
Bring through us all the day to birth
when word and deed are one on earth.

Feed on God's word

I was sitting one day, in the New Forest, under a beech tree. I like to look at the
beech, and study it, as I do many other trees, for every one has its own peculiari-

ties and habits, its special ways of twisting its boughs, and growing its bark, and opening its leaves, and so forth. As I looked up at that beech, and admired the wisdom of God in making it, I saw a squirrel running round and round the trunk, and up the branches, and I thought to myself, 'Ah! this beech tree is a great deal more to you than it is to me, for it is your home, your living, your all.' Its big branches were the main streets of his city, and its little boughs were the lanes; somewhere in that tree he had his house, and the beech-mast was his daily food, he lived on it. Well, now, the way to deal with God's word is not merely to contemplate it, or to study it, as a student does; but to live on it, as that squirrel lives on his beech tree. Let it be to you, spiritually, your house, your home, your food, your medicine, your clothing, the one essential element of your soul's life and growth.

Charles Haddon Spurgeon, sermon preached at the Tabernacle,
London, *Autobiography*, rev. ed. (London: Banner of Truth
Trust, 1973), p. 218.

Righteous God

Righteous God,
you plead the cause
of the poor and unprotected.
Fill us with holy rage
when justice is delayed,
and give us the persistence
to require those rights that are denied;
for your name's sake, **Amen.**

Janet Morley, *All Desires Known* (London: SPCK, 1992), p. 24.

For the Christian people there are no people beyond the power of God's word. Christians know no "barbarians," but only strangers whom we hope to make our friends.

Stanley Hauerwas

PROPER 25

Ordinary Time 30
Sunday between October 23 and 29 inclusive

Joel 2:23–32	2 Timothy 4:6–8, 16–18
Psalm 65	Luke 18:9–14

Understanding love

How many of us, at first reading, stop to wonder why the Pharisee feels the need to pray in this way? It can at times be easier to simply judge the actions of others rather than look at what may drive those actions. To act towards others out of love often requires us to look beyond the obvious. What is it that compels the Pharisee to compare himself favourably to the tax collector before God? A more loving response to this parable might be to try to understand the underlying needs and hurt of both the Pharisee and the tax collector.

It is only when we regard others out of love that true humility follows. Love and humility are essential partners. From self love and acceptance arises the ability to put aside the need for both self promotion and the false humility of self abasement. Love of others allows us to build relationships on acceptance rather than criticism and comparison. Such love allows us to walk alongside each other. To achieve true humility therefore we should put love at the centre of our lives. If we focus on being humble and striving for humility, on the other hand, then we may achieve quite the opposite affect.

Jayne Hoose, in <i>Fruits of the Earth: The CAFOD/DLT Lent Book 2002</i>
(London: CAFOD/Darton, Longman & Todd, 2001), pp. 50–51.

Steadfast love

Gracious God,
for your love for us,
gentle as a shower,
healing our pain,

binding up our wounds,
we give you thanks.

For your love for us,
sure as the dawn,
transforming our darkness,
revealing your truth,
we give you thanks.

For your love for us,
mercifully steadfast,
calling us to you,
raising us up,
we give you thanks.

For your love for us,
encouraging questions,
open to our doubts,
making us vulnerable,
we give you thanks.

For your steadfast love
has brought us to faith.
Your steadfast love
has cradled a new creation.
Your reconciling power
has brought to birth
a new ministry.
> Urge us on, O Christ,
> to find wholeness
> through serving you
> by serving others,
> in the power of the Spirit.

Kate McIlhagga, in *Encompassing Presence: Prayer Handbook 1993*
(London: United Reformed Church, 1993), Week 31.
© Donald McIlhagga.

An outrageous verdict

It is difficult for us to imagine the shock with which the parable of the publican and the Pharisee must have been received (Luke 18:9–14). The Pharisee is depicted as an exemplary man of religion. He does even more than is required of him by the law: he fasts twice a week. There is no suggestion that he was a hypocrite. He does not take the credit for his own virtue; he thanks God for it. The publican or tax collector on the other hand, although he asks God for mercy, makes no attempt to mend his ways and to make restitution for all the money he has stolen.

Jesus' verdict on these two men must have sounded outrageous. The sinner is pleasing to God and the virtuous man is not. Why? Because the sinner did not exalt himself and the virtuous man did. The Pharisee dared to regard himself as superior to men like the tax collector. . . . This is not so much a matter of pride as an inability to share God's compassion for all. Without compassion all religious practices and beliefs are useless and empty (1 Cor. 13:1–3). Without compassion all politics will be oppressive, even the politics of revolution.

One of the basic causes of oppression, discrimination and suffering in that society was its religion. . . . And nothing is more impervious to change than religious zeal. The piety and good works of the dutiful religious man made him feel that God was on his side. He did not need God's mercy and forgiveness; that was what others needed. The sinner, on the other hand, was well aware of his desperate need for mercy and forgiveness (Luke 18:13) and of his need to change his life. . . . Jesus soon discovered that it was the dutiful religious man, rather than the sinner or pagan Roman, who was an obstacle to the coming of the kingdom of total liberation.

> Albert Nolan, *Jesus before Christianity: The Gospel of Liberation* (London: Darton, Longman & Todd, 1977), p. 98.

The last decade of the twentieth century and the ushering in of the twenty-first century are golden moments when the renewal and transformation of society, humanity and of the earth can take place. It may be our last chance, and so, by God's grace, we have to make the most of it.

> Jose P. M. Cunanan

From Psalm 65

O God, it is right for us to praise you:
you are the one who answers our prayers.

You care for the land and water it:
you make it rich and fertile.

You fill the running streams with water:
you irrigate the land.

You soften the ground with showers:
you make the young crops grow.

You crown the year with your goodness:
you give us a plentiful harvest.

The pastures are filled with flocks:
the hillsides are clothed with joy.

The fields are covered with grain:
they shout for joy and sing.

Michael Perry, *Bible Prayers for Worship* (London: Marshall Pickering,
1997), p. 88. Reprinted by permission of HarperCollins Publishers
Ltd. © Michael Perry 1997.

O taste and see*

Now is the time for the good wine
Pressed from the fruit of the tree
Now is the time for rejoicing
In the place where the feast will be
O taste and see
And refresh us with love.

Leave all the cares of the growing
Just let the mystery sing
Magic of ripening and pruning
And the fullness that time will bring
O taste and see
And refresh us with love.

*Tune: FRANKIE AND JOHNNIE

Sweet-tasting cup of our loving
Promise of pleasure and pain
Take it and drink of it deeply
For the new life it will contain
O taste and see
And refresh us with love.

Kathy Galloway, in *Celebrating Women,* ed. Hannah Ward, Jennifer Wild, and Janet Morley (London: SPCK/Harrisburg, Pa.: Morehouse Publishing, 1995), p. 134. © Kathy Galloway.

PROPER 26

Ordinary Time 31

Sunday between October 30 and November 5 inclusive

Habakkuk 1:1–4; 2:1–4	2 Thessalonians 1:1–4, 11–12
Psalm 119:137–144	Luke 19:1–10

Jesus the disturber

In Christian memory and tradition Zacchaeus is portrayed as either fraudulent or as a collaborator with the occupying Roman government. . . . The reaction of the crowd bears this out. They all 'murmured' that Jesus had gone to be the guest of a 'sinner.' Zacchaeus, meanwhile, has responded to Jesus' visit by giving half his goods to the poor. Then comes the hidden sting in the story, for he adds that if he has defrauded anyone of anything he will restore it fourfold. If. That 'if' must be one of the most important two-letter words in the Gospels. That Zacchaeus is despised by the crowd is not in doubt. But nowhere in the story does it say that he was dishonest. He is simply hated for what he does, but he almost certainly acts with honesty and integrity.

What then does Jesus' action signify? Simply this: that in the midst of a crowd bestowing their adulation he refuses to side with their base prejudices. Zacchaeus is affirmed for who he is. He does not repent, contrary to how the story is usually read: he has no need to. Rather, a person who is despised is allowed to flourish, and he is now seen as a person of generosity. He has, after all, given away half of what he has. Consistently, Jesus sides with the ostracized, the rejected, the unclean, the impure, the (alleged) sinner, and the half-breeds. He is no crowd pleaser, he is their confounder. Even before the palm branches are stripped from the trees, and the cries of 'Blessed!' are heard, Jesus is a disturber of crowds. He does not want their praise: he wants their commitment. And they will make him pay for this, his failure to deliver what they promised themselves.

Martyn Percy, from "Sensing the Crowds," in Rowan Williams et al.,
Darkness Yielding: Angles on Christmas, Holy Week, and Easter
(Sheffield: Cairns Publications, 2001), pp. 77–78.

Godly curiosity

Praiseworthy to a high degree
Is godly curiosity;
To search the Lord, above, around,
If haply he may yet be found.
Short-sighted reason, dwarf desire,
Are faith and zeal when lifted high'r.
Then on the Tree of Life sublime
With hand and knees devoutly climb;
Catch mercy's moments as they fly,
Behold! The Lord is passing by.

Christopher Smart (1722–71), from "The Story of Zacchaeus."

"Who is Jesus Christ for us today?"

The question of Christ turned out, in our discussion of Bonhoeffer, to entail the three linked questions of deciding who we are (the question of identity), who 'us' is (the question of solidarity), and whose 'today' it is to be (the challenge of discernment). . . .

Who is Christ and who are we? Consumer? Depositor? Usurer? Debtor? Where, that is to say, do we place ourselves and where do we place Christ in the international networks . . . ? For some, clearly, Christ is where we are, exercising the freedom that those who have money enjoy to do what they will with their own. The Christ of this selective freedom enjoys the choices and responsibilities that the world of money provides for those who have it, seeking within that to exercise as much compassion as he can without at any point confronting the results of the exercise of that freedom in the lives of those who have nothing. Or is Christ where they are, the ally of the penniless and the indebted? And in that case, what is his word and where do his actions lead? . . .

The question of 'us' raises again the limits of our solidarity. We have seen money as having a power to render ineffective many of the inherited loyalties, the patriotism and the national pride, that are the assumptions behind many of our constitutional mechanisms. That is, we have seen that money bestrides the world, uncontrollable as it seems by national powers. . . .

Above all, though, we have to ask about our commitment to 'today,' and to the today of those for whom it may be the last. Unlike the strong in the world of the market, most of the world's people cannot bank on a future income, for the future is being devoured already by a market and the way it works. They cannot look to future profit, for that only comes to those who have today's riches to invest, and who by doing so claim in advance the harvest that the future will yield. Christ's question is, whose 'today' concerns you?

> Peter Selby, *Grace and Mortgage: The Language of Faith and the Debt of the World* (London: Darton, Longman & Todd, 1997), pp. 119–20.

If a person gets his attitude toward money straight, it will help straighten out almost every other area in his life.

> Billy Graham

"Destruction and violence are before me"

I go apart to pray, and feel a resistance even before I have tried. I know I will have difficulty praying about this war. I don't know how to begin.

When I intercede for a troubled person, I visualize holding her in my arms before God—until God stretches out to take her from me: then I can step back and leave her where the love and strength are a billion times greater than mine. . . .

But I can't hold this war: when I try, everything and everyone caught up in its vast network spills out of my arms. It is too hot—and too huge—to handle. I arrive before God and am empty-handed. No prayer wells up in me—just horror and helplessness. And then—tears.

At first I am ashamed. The tears go on and on. Not much of my praying is saying these days: none the less I feel I ought now to have some words to offer.

And then slowly it comes to me that just 'sitting with it' . . . being struck dumb and shedding this fountain of tears . . . is not a failure to pray. Being horrified and helpless and sad and frightened and spiritually smashed up in the presence of God . . . feeling in every cell, as it were, the pain, violence, futility and guilt of war . . . maybe this, of itself, is prayer.

And I stay with that for a while.

Then something else comes. The conviction that, having sat in the mud, I can maybe now lift my eyes to the stars. In the past, prayer has taken me beyond the 'is' of a situation to the 'what has not yet come to be.' Might it not do so now?

Kate Compston, in Michael Hare Duke (ed.), *Praying for Peace: Reflections on the Gulf Crisis* (London: Fount, 1991), pp. 58–59.

When love is stamped on every coin*

When love is stamped on every coin
the market with the cross shall meet,
while bulls and bears with angels join
to dance along Threadneedle Street.

But cash has meaning here and now:
it measures work and time and care;
it buys a bomb; it buys a plough;
it pays for hope; it funds despair.

Remind us always, dearest Lord,
of what you said in Galilee:
that where we keep our treasure stored
our hearts and minds will surely be.

So shall our dealings speak your word,
your values keep our souls alive,
while dreams that well may be absurd
assist Creation to survive.

Elizabeth Cosnett, in *Hymns for Everyday Saints* (London: Stainer & Bell, 2001). © 2000 Stainer & Bell Ltd.

Lord, you seek and save

Lord, we give thanks that you sought us out and brought us to yourself.
We pray for all who are newcomers to the faith: the newly converted, the
    baptized, the confirmed;
for all who are seekers and exploring the meaning of life.
Lord, may the church help to show that you seek for and welcome all;

*Tune: ANGELS' LAUDS (LM) by Ian Sharp

may your church be an accepting church, a hospitable church.
We ask that you will guide us in our stewardship,
that we may use our gifts to the benefit of others and to your glory.
Lord, you seek and save that which is lost.
Have mercy on us and hear our prayer.

We ask your blessing on all who work in commerce, upon financiers and
    bankers, upon tax-collectors and accountants.
We pray for individuals and countries that are deeply in debt,
for the world's poor and for all who have suffered because of the greed,
    corruption and deceitfulness of others.
We pray for the liberation of all who arc impoverished.
Lord, you seek and save that which is lost.
Have mercy on us and hear our prayer.

. . .

We pray for all who have been belittled by others,
all who have been squeezed out of their community,
all who are despised or rejected, all who have to do unpopular work.
We remember all who are feeling hurt, all who are despairing or desolate,
all who feel lost and have nowhere or nobody to turn to.
We pray for friends and loved ones suffering at this time.
Lord, you seek and save that which is lost.
Have mercy on us and hear our prayer.

We rejoice that you welcome us into your presence and your kingdom.
We give thanks for the forgiveness of sins and opportunity to amend our
    lives.
We ask your blessing upon all whom you have welcomed in love and into
    eternal life, especially _____
Lord, you seek and save that which is lost.
Have mercy on us and hear our prayer.

David Adam, *Glimpses of Glory* (London: SPCK, 2000), pp. 146–48.

PROPER 27

Ordinary Time 32

Sunday between November 6 and 12 inclusive

| Haggai 1:15b–2:9 | 2 Thessalonians 2:1–5, 13–17 |
| Psalm 145:1–5, 17–21 | Luke 20:27–38 |

The sacrifice of praise

Bible and liturgy use the metaphor of the 'sacrifice of praise'; as if the language of ascribing worth, beauty and desirability to God represented some sort of *cost* to us. So it does: praise is nothing if not the struggle to voice how the directedness of my regard depends on, is moulded by, something irreducibly other than itself. It is my speech seeking to transmute into its own substance something on whose radical difference that very substance depends; so that it must on no account *absorb* it into itself, as that would be to lose the object's generative power. The transmutation is a reforming of the language, not the disappearance of the praised object into existing patterns of words, foreordained responses. It is, as David Jones said of all art that is in any sense representation, a 'showing forth under another form'; and for this to be serious, it entails some sense at some stage of loss of control, unclarity of focus. A celebratory work that simply uses a repertoire of stock techniques that direct our attention not to what is being celebrated but to the smooth and finished quality of its own surface is a failure. . . .

The praise of God is . . . not a matter simply of euphoric fluency; because of its attempt to speak to and of the reality of God and not simply to collapse back upon itself as a mere articulation of religious emotion, it involves 'the labour, the patience and the pain of the negative,' a dispossession in respect of what is easily available for religious language. This dispossession is, at its simplest, the suspension of the ordinary categories of 'rational' speech; at a more pervasive level, it is a dispossession of the human mind conceived as central to the order of the world, and a dispossession of the entire identity that exists prior to the paschal drama, the identity that has not seen and named its self-deception and self-destructiveness. In praise, God is truthfully spoken of by learning to speak of the world in a certain way, and of the self in a certain way; by giving over what is said to the pattern of creation and redemption, a pattern moving through loss and disorder to life.

Rowan Williams, *On Christian Theology* (Oxford: Blackwell, 2000),
pp. 9, 10–11.

The praise of God should be the object of our meditation in this life, because in the life to come it will be for ever the object of our rejoicing.

Augustine of Hippo

God gives us a future

God gives us a future,
daring us to go
into dreams and dangers
on a path unknown.
We will face tomorrow
in the Spirit's power,
we will let God change us,
for new life starts now.

We must leave behind us
sins of yesterday,
for God's new beginning
is a better way.
Fear and doubt and habit
must not hold us back:
God gives hope, and insight,
and the strength we lack.

Holy Spirit, teach us
how to read the signs,
how to meet the challenge
of our troubled times.
Love us into action,
stir us into prayer,

till we choose God's life, and
find our future there.

Images of heaven: reunions in heaven?

There is simply no doubt that the blessed individual dead, who dropped out of the Protestant official picture with the end of Purgatory as a doctrine, reappear in the nineteenth century as welcoming presences. The reappearance of dead family members in afterlife imagery is not surprising given the focus on intense personal relationships within an increasingly small and isolated family unit. What is astonishing to us is how absent such figures and anticipations are from earlier sources. The angels in the medieval woodcut of the *Ars Moriendi* held up a curtain to exclude the family members from the dying person and the real drama. In contrast, family reunions in Heaven became the central core around which other elements of middle-class life were projected in nineteenth-century North American popular writings. An acknowledged expert on Heaven, Elizabeth Stuart Phelps, wrote a best-selling book, *The Gates Ajar* (1868), based on the principle that anything good or pleasing in this life would also be found on the other side. While official orthodox Christian thinkers bewailed the trivialization of last things in the consolation literature, Phelps' Heaven was filled with everything—human relationships, nice scenery, piano—except work. It resembled a Florida retirement community, minus ill health and mortality. While it is easy to poke fun at the exploitation of religious imagery that mingles sentiment and materialism, *The Gates Ajar* was intended as consolation, to comfort those who have lost loved ones. The official teachings were thought to be too cold, too vague, too remote from what nineteenth-century persons really cared about and hoped for in their spiritual lives.

Lucy Bregman, *Beyond Silence and Denial: Death and Dying Reconsidered* (Louisville, Ky.: Westminster John Knox Press, 1999), pp. 33–34.

Reflecting on death

Death awareness, or reflection on death and dying, can bring harmony and peace to our life. We tend, however, to avoid thinking about death because we have not come to terms with our fears. . . .

A simple reflection on death can help us recall the important values of our life and redirect our energy. Knowing that we have a limited time gives us a chance to regain an authentic sense of our relationship with self, others, and God, and places us fully in the moment.

Take some time tonight. Calm yourself, perhaps with a breathing technique, and say to yourself, "I will die." Let that awareness awaken you to the depth of the present moment and perhaps lead to a conversation with yourself on the richness of the day and the people that you are grateful for. Close with this prayer: *Eternal God, grant me an awareness of my death so that I may be open to the true values of my life and learn gratitude for all your blessings. Let me experience my life in a new way through the mindfulness that death is as common as life. May I find strength in the promise of the resurrection.*

Wayne Simsic, *Pray without Ceasing: Mindfulness of God in Daily Life*
(Winona, Minn.: St. Mary's Press, 2000), pp. 108–9.

Different perspectives

The proclamation of the resurrection of Jesus had coincided with decades of growing estrangement between his supporters and their fellow Jews. Many followers lost the sense that there should be a natural, undisrupted continuity between the present social structures of Israel and those of the new kingdom. Rather than a miraculous return to married stability, with all 'hardness of heart' banished from society, many disciples now saw a stark contrast between 'that [coming] age' and the life of the 'sons of this age,' who 'marry and are given in marriage' (Luke 20:34–36). The frankly extraordinary lives of the few preachers of the kingdom came to be thought of as standing for the nature of life itself within the kingdom: in such a kingdom, even the accustomed landmark of marriage was absent.

On the other hand, the silent majority of those who awaited the coming of the kingdom were careworn and decent householders, long used to the punctilious rhythms of Jewish life. Secure in their moral horizons, they were in no position to allow the painfully assembled fabric of their social person—their wives, their children, their kinfolk, and the few ancestral fields that they would inherit when they buried their father—to evaporate at the call of the wandering few. Christian communities where such men came to the fore would look at the world around them in a very different manner from those who imagined that, on the open road, they already breathed the heady air of the kingdom.

Peter Brown, *The Body and Society: Men, Women and Sexual Renunciation in Early Christianity* (London: Faber and Faber, 1989; Boston: Columbia University Press, 1988), p. 44.

They live in our hearts

The Christian message about the death of Jesus as the beginning of new life gave deeper meaning and clarity to our own indigenous beliefs through the vivid imagery of the scourged, crowned-with-thorns, crucified Jesus of Nazareth. Our ancient icons were now assumed by the suffering Jesus. At the same time, the Christian belief in the communion of saints gave a deeper and more exciting meaning to our ancient belief of the continuity of the ancestors. Far from dwelling in some far-off mysterious place, they were now enjoying the eternal and unending feast! Our own *mitotes* (Indian word for community-wide feasts) were now seen to be the images and foretaste of the future unending feast in heaven. In this religious *mestizaje*, the elements of our new identity were being forged and shaped.

For a people who have consistently been subjected to injustice, cruelty and early death, the image of the crucified is the supreme symbol of life in spite of the multiple daily threats of death. If there was something good and redemptive in the unjust condemnation and crucifixion of the God-man, then, as senseless and useless as our suffering appears to be, there must be something of ultimate value in it. We don't understand it, but in Jesus, the God-man who suffered for our salvation, we affirm it and in this very affirmation receive the power to endure it without its destroying us. Even if we are killed, we cannot be destroyed. This is the curious irony of our celebrations of the dead: they appear to be dead, but they are not really dead! For they live not only in God but in our hearts and in our memory. Those whom the world thinks are dead, those who have been killed by society, defy death and are alive in us.

Virgil Elizondo, "Popular Religions as Support of Identity," in *Spirituality of the Third World* (Maryknoll, N.Y.: Orbis Books, 1994), p. 61.

Prayer is praise of God; our whole life is that constant prayer, and I wish to know no other; it can be inspired by love, by distress, or by humility. I should like it to spring only from love.

André Gide

PROPER 28

Ordinary Time 33

Sunday between November 13 and 19 inclusive

| Isaiah 65:17–25 | 2 Thessalonians 3:6–13 |
| Isaiah 12 | Luke 21:5–19 |

Heaven and earth will rejoice

I invite you to entertain for a moment this poem [Isaiah 65:17–25], and let it seep into your bones and into your heart and into your vision. God speaks: "New heaven, new earth, new Jerusalem." It will be a world of rejoicing when the newness comes. And do you know why?

Heaven and earth will rejoice because, in that new world wrought by God, there will be no more sound of weeping, no more homeless folks to moan, no more broken folk to whimper, no more terrorized folk to cry out.

Heaven and earth will rejoice, because in that new world wrought by God there will be no more infant mortality, no more infants who live but a few days, and no more old people who will die too young or live too feebly or continue as a shell while the life is gone.

Heaven and earth will rejoice, because in that new world wrought by God there will be no more usurpation of people's homes. Those who build will stay around to inhabit, those who plant will survive to harvest and enjoy their produce. No more people being taxed out of their homes, no more losing their vulnerable homes to the right of eminent domain, no more rapacious seizure by war, no more the big ones eating the little ones. When the newness comes, every person will live safely under a vine and fig tree, safe, unafraid, at peace, no more destructive threat nor competitive anxiety.

Heaven and earth will rejoice, because in that new world wrought by God, there will be no more labor in vain, no more birthing into anguish, no more nurturing children in anxiety and dread and fear, because God will bless and make the force of life everywhere palpably available. Persons and families will live in well-being, without jeopardy or grief.

Heaven and earth will rejoice, because in the new world wrought by God, God will be attentive. God will be like a mother who hears and answers in the night, knowing before we call who is needed and what is needed. And we shall never be left alone again.

Walter Brueggemann, *The Threat of Life: Sermons on Pain, Power, and Weakness,* ed. Charles L. Campbell (Minneapolis: Fortress Press, 1996), pp. 65–66.

The world is not like a picture painted by an artist centuries ago which now hangs untouchable in a museum. It is more like a work of art in constant process of creation, still in a studio.

Ernesto Cardenal

Harvest home

Psalm 126 is almost certainly a "harvest home" song. It speaks of those who "come home with shouts of joy, carrying their sheaves" (Ps. 126:6). It was probably sung as travelers went up to Jerusalem for one of the harvest festivals. The psalm celebrates both past and future: it is a song of thanksgiving for God's deliverance and a prayer for a reversal of fortune (which might refer to the crops of the coming year) that will bring joy to lips and tongues. . . .

In Isaiah, there is a suggestion of a harvest-home festival in the banquet that will take place when the messiah comes, when the Lord will make for all people "a feast of rich food, a feast of well-aged wines, or rich food filled with marrow, of well-aged wines strained clear," and at which God "will wipe away the tears from all faces" (Isa. 25:6, 8). A later passage [Isa. 65:17, 21–22] contains a more complete description of the joyful fulfillment of the harvest home to come. . . . This is the promise of a joyful harvest, of a garden that brings full satisfaction, of life lived in all the fullness of God's grace. This "new earth" will be a place not of idleness but of satisfying work that is not vain and pointless. True shalom will reign as it did in the original garden.

Sara Covin Juengst, *Like a Garden: A Biblical Spirituality of Growth* (Louisville, Ky.: Westminster John Knox Press, 1996), pp. 94–95.

Shalom

The Hebrew word for peace is "shalom." Shalom is the substance of the biblical vision of one community embracing all creation. Shalom implies well-being and the wholeness of all life—material, spiritual, physical, personal, corporate. Shalom is the reality of Paradise. Shalom is eternal life in the holy caring and sharing community of God's Spirit, the blessing promised to Abraham for the salvation of all the families of the earth.

God created us for shalom—he created us to abide in harmony with his Spirit and all creation for eternity. But shalom cannot be forced upon us against our will. Shalom is a gift freely given that must be freely received.

> From Howard Goeringer, *He Is Our Peace: Meditations on Christian Nonviolence,* in *The Writings of Howard Goeringer, Eberhard Arnold, Christoph F. Blumhardt, & Others,* ed. Emmy Barth (Farmington, Pa./Robertsbridge, E. Sussex: Plough Publishing House, 1994).

Liberator Lord*

To those whose lives are bitter, the poor and dispossessed
your word is one of justice, of balances redressed,
the riches of creation a commonwealth possessed.
May your spirit be upon us, our Liberator Lord.

To those who live in bondage of body and of mind
who are prisoners of ignorance or the hatred of their kind
your word is one of liberty, the captive to unbind.
May your spirit be upon us, our Liberator Lord.

To those whose eyes are blinded, who will or dare not see
your word is calling softly, come, face reality
and find in it the dearest truth, your lives will precious be.
May your spirit be upon us, our Liberator Lord.

To those who know the anguish of love that cannot flower
whose race or class or gender define another's power,
your word is one of freedom to grow and not to cower.
May your spirit be upon us, our Liberator Lord.

*Tune: CORMAC, *The Church Hymnary,* 3d ed., no. 365 (Oxford University Press, 1988)

You have spoken through the prophets and saints of history
through the sobbing of the voiceless and the groans of the unfree
and your voice is still proclaiming, 'now, you must speak for me.'
May your spirit be upon us, our Liberator Lord.

Kathy Galloway, *Love Burning Deep: Poems and Lyrics*
(London: SPCK, 1993), p. 34.

Refusing newness

The Church has most often either removed itself from culture, been assimilated to culture, or subsumed culture into itself. The tensive prophetic relationship, that is, genuine, ambiguity-ridden, two-way, Gospel-infused cultural participation, is something we as a Church community have not yet managed to imagine into existence. And when some person or some local community does manage it, the result is often enough martyrdom or suppression. The Church can deal with Mother Teresa but not with Jeannine Gramick; it can embrace Opus Dei but struggles with liberation theology. One might say that the Church is either stereotypically male, fiercely independent and even condemnatory of culture, refusing any entangling commitments to it, or stereotypically female, merged to the point of innocuous invisibility into its cultural surroundings. Critical participation, that is, a genuinely prophetic presence, is difficult to sustain.

Sandra M. Schneiders, *With Oil in Their Lamps: Faith, Feminism, and the Future* (New York/Mahwah, N.J.: Paulist Press, 2000), p. 97.

PROPER 29

(Christ the King or Reign of Christ)
Ordinary Time 34

Sunday between November 20 and 26 inclusive

| Jeremiah 23:1–6 | Colossians 1:11–20 |
| Luke 1:68–79 | Luke 23:33–43 |

Remember me!

What we should observe here is Jesus' acceptance of the repentant thief, and the glorious promise that carried him over the river and into the garden of God's paradise. And all this is not on the ground of merit, good works or human goodness, but simply because he recognized himself as a sinful and helpless soul in the hour of his mortal agony, with no one else to turn to, and only Jesus before him. If any soul manifests the joy of salvation by faith, the lost sheep being found by the shepherd, the prodigal son returning to his yearning father—it is this one!

He called Jesus by his first and saving name—the name of Jesus is the symbol and meaning of our salvation. Every novice who enters Orthodox monastic life on Mount Athos receives a prayer rope and simple instructions on saying the Jesus Prayer: 'Lord Jesus Christ, Son of God, have mercy on me, a sinner.'

This is the basic prayer I have been saying for over twenty-five years, and the one which will carry me into the arms of my Lord Jesus in life and in death. It is the prayer that sounds continually in my heart, and which enfolds me to his heart—the prayer that lays hold on the saving name of Jesus, and proves it to be the name of the Saviour of the world.

Brother Ramon, *When They Crucified My Lord: Through Lenten
Sorrow to Easter Joy* (Oxford: The Bible Reading Fellowship, 1999),
p. 142.

Like the thief I cry to you,
    "Remember me";
Like Peter I weep bitterly;
Like the publican I call out,
    "Forgive me, Savior";
Like the harlot I shed tears.
Accept my lamentation,
    as once you have accepted
The entreaties of the woman of Canaan.
Have mercy on me, O God,
    have mercy on me.

Andrew of Crete

The penitent thief

. . . You, hanging on his right; on his left, your brother;
Writhing like skinned frogs,
Flea-bitten petty thieves thrown in as a retinue to his shame,
Courtiers to a mock king in his pain.

O master of courtesy and manners, who enlightened you
About your part in this harsh parody?
'Lord, when you come into your kingdom, remember me,'—
The kingdom that was conquered through death. . . .

O thief who took paradise from the nails of a gibbet,
Foremost of the *nobilitas* of heaven,
Before the hour of death pray that it may be given to us
To perceive him and to taste him.

Saunders Lewis, from "The Penitent Thief," in *Byd a Betws*
(Llandysul, Wales: Gomer Press, 1941).

A life of service

Jesus' originality does not lie in his spiritualization of the kingdom, but rather in the fact that he saw the true fulfillment of its earthly hopes in a more radical way than many of his contemporaries. He did not see the struggle against injustice and oppression primarily as a holy war against the Romans. This does not mean that deliverance from oppression did not include deliverance from the Romans. But Jesus looked deeper than the oppression of Israel by Rome to the fundamental roots of oppression itself. He sees this as the love of prestige, power and wealth that causes people to seek domination and to lord it over each other. Unless this fundamental lust for domination is overcome, a successful war of liberation will only replace one domination with another. Jesus seeks to model, in his own life, a new concept of leadership based on service to others, even unto death. This is the model that he wishes to impart to his followers. In the new community based on the life of service to others, the lust for domination will be overcome at its source.

Rosemary Radford Ruether, *To Change the World: Christology and Cultural Criticism* (New York: Crossroad, 1988), p. 15.

Problems with kingship

This imaginative picture [of God as king] is so prevalent in mainstream Christianity that it is often not recognized as a picture. Nor is it immediately perceived as oppressive. More often it is accepted as the natural understanding of the relationship of God and the world—and one we like. Think for a moment of the sense of triumph, joy, and power that surges through us when we join in singing the "Hallelujah Chorus" from Handel's *Messiah*. Probably we do not think about the implications of the images we sing, but we know they make us feel good about our God and about ourselves as his subjects. . . .

My criticism of [this monarchical model] focuses on its inability to serve as the imaginative framework for an understanding of the gospel as a destabilizing, inclusive, nonhierarchical vision of fulfillment for all of creation. . . .

The relationship of a king to his subjects is necessarily a distant one: royalty is "untouchable." It is the distance, the difference, the otherness of God that is underscored with this imagery. God as king is in his kingdom—which is not of this earth—and we remain in another place, far from his dwelling. In this picture God is worldless and the world is Godless: the world is empty of God's presence, for it is too lowly to be the royal abode. Time and space are not filled with God: the eons of human and geological time stretch as a yawning void back into the recesses, empty of the divine presence; the places loved and noted on our earth, as well as the unfathomable space of the universe, are not the house of God. Whatever one does for the world is not finally important in this model, for its ruler does not inhabit it as his primary residence, and his subjects are well advised not to become too involved in it either. The king's power extends over the entire universe, of course, but his being does not: he relates to it externally, he is not part of it but essentially different from it and apart from it.

Sallie McFague, *Models of God: Theology for an Ecological, Nuclear Age* (Philadelphia: Fortress Press, 1988), pp. 63–65.

Dying love

Dying love has been my birth
    undeserved and undisguised;
Christ declares me full of worth,
    valued, loved, accepted, prized!

Love that bore and understood
    all my emptiness and sin,
recreates me new and good,
    healed, and beautiful within.

Let this love my love release,
    hopeful through defeat or loss,
peaceful, as I work for peace,
    faithful, though I bear the cross.

All are worthy, full of worth,
    loved, whoever would despise.
Tell and show it here on earth!
    Shout hosanna to the skies!

Brian Wren, *Piece Together Praise: A Theological Journey* (London: Stainer & Bell; Carol Stream, Ill.: Hope Publishing Company, 1996), no. 43. © 1983, 1995 Hope Publishing Company for the USA, Canada, Australia and New Zealand, and Stainer & Bell Ltd. for all other territories. Used by permission.

ALL SAINTS

November 1 or the first Sunday in November

Daniel 7:1–3, 15–18	Ephesians 1:11–23
Psalm 149	Luke 6:20–31

Thanksgiving for those who preceded us

Our Father, you who have mothered us by giving us good forebears, we thank you for those who have preceded us. Without them, faithful and unfaithful, we would not be. Often we little understand what they must have been like, yet they passed on to us a sense of how wonderful it is to be your people. May we be capable of producing yet new generations born of your hope. Amen.

Stanley Hauerwas, *Prayers Plainly Spoken* (Grove, Ill.: InterVarsity Press, 1999; London: Triangle, 1999), p. 44.

In communion

We have to choose: but *these,* no other, nothing easier, are the choices. If *all* time is to be redeemed, it must be by means of the giving up of self in all times and places, accepting the horror and the darkness and not trying to evade it by fantasy or by philosophy. And the way has been shown by the action of the world's maker and lord emptying himself and taking a servant's form, putting aside his lordship to suffer our wounds, so that his compassion becomes the food by which we live.

If we can consent to this, to making out of chaos a network of compassion, of giving to others, then there *is* redemption and reconciliation in the world of history. Past and present alike may be folded into this; we shall be able to see ourselves as living from the love of previous generations, in communion with living and dead. We shall be able to give ourselves for the life of the living and the unborn. 'Little Gidding' [T. S. Eliot's poem] pictures unforgettably this fusion of death and life, by offering it for the world. The pain will not go away, the horror will remain; yet it is shot through with the hope and possibility of compassion and reconciliation, a simplicity, 'Costing not less than everything.'

Rowan Williams, "Lazarus: In Memory of T. S. Eliot," in *Open to Judgment: Sermons and Addresses* (London: Darton, Longman & Todd, 1994), pp. 218–19.

Are saints special?

Human beings are not always good enough to honour one another wholeheartedly. It feels safely sophisticated to enjoy the old pictures of saints wearing haloes and to think how inconvenient it would be to go about with a gold saucepan lid on one's head.

So of course the saints are special: other-worldly, heads in the clouds, 'holier than thou.' To call somebody 'only human' has almost turned into a compliment. It is more comfortable to be with people who make no claims to extraordinary virtue. When the preacher at a funeral says, 'of course, he was no saint,' this may be simply less embarrassing than 'Lord have mercy': but it may be a way of positively praising our departed friend for not being a prig. St Paul would have been horrified by this notion that sanctity is something which needs apology. When he wrote to the Corinthians 'All the saints greet you,' he expected his correspondents to feel encouraged, not put down.

Helen Oppenheimer, from "Are Saints Special?" *Theology* 105, no. 828 (November 2002): pp. 444–45.

A vast horde of souls

There was only a purple streak in the sky, cutting through a field of crimson and leading, like an extension of the highway, into the descending dusk. [Ruby Turpin] raised her hands from the side of the pen in a gesture hieratic and profound. A visionary light settled in her eyes. She saw the streak as a vast swinging bridge extending upward from the earth through a field of living fire. Upon it a vast horde of souls were rumbling toward heaven. There were whole companies of white-trash, clean for the first time in their lives, and bands of black niggers in white robes, and battalions of freaks and lunatics shouting and clapping and leaping like frogs. And bringing up the end of the procession was a tribe of people whom she recognized at once as those who, like herself and Claud, had always had a little of everything and the God-given wit to use it right. She leaned forward to observe them closer. They were marching behind the others with great dignity, accountable as they had always been for the good order and common sense and respectable behavior. They alone were on key. Yet she could see by their shocked and altered faces that even their virtues were being burned away. She lowered her hands and gripped the rail of the hog pen, her eyes small but fixed unblinkingly on what lay ahead. In a moment the vision faded but she remained where she was, immobile.

At length she got down and turned off the faucet and made her slow way on the darkening path to the house. In the woods around her the invisible cricket choruses had struck up, but what she heard were the voices of the souls climbing upward into the starry field and shouting hallelujah.

Flannery O'Connor, from "Revelation," in Flannery O'Connor,
Everything That Rises Must Converge (New York: Farrar, Straus
and Giroux, 1956).

Love rooted in the pain of God

The heart of the gospel was revealed to me as 'the pain of God.' ... I am filled with gratitude because I was allowed to experience the depth of God's heart with Jeremiah. . . .

We dare to speak about this 'pain of God,' for, to use Calvin's words, 'God does not express his great love for us in any other way!' We dare to see with Jeremiah God's grace in his 'pain.' Are not the eyes which saw God's pain frozen? '. . . his appearance was so marred, beyond human semblance, and his form beyond that of the sons of men . . .' (Isa. 52:14). We cannot behold his pain without risking our life. We must pronounce the words 'pain of God' as if we are allowed to speak them only once in a lifetime. Those who have beheld the pain of God cease to be loquacious, and open their mouths only by the passion to bear witness to it. Those who have seen the pain of God can live without dying, because the 'pain' is at once 'love.' By this 'love,' [our] pain is purified and becomes like God's 'pain.'

'Love rooted in the pain of God' cannot be observed objectively outside of our human experience. There is no way to see it other than experiencing it in our own life.

Kazoh Kitamori, *Theology of the Pain of God* (London:
SCM Press, 1966), pp. 19–20, 167.

Bare humanity

Rilke has a story called 'Why God Wants Poor People.' God wants to see what human beings are like, he says, when they are stripped down to their bare humanity. If I were to write a converse story called 'Why Poor People Want God,' it would have to be a story of heart's desire. Poor people want God not because they are poor, I would have to say, not because they are naked human beings but because they are human beings. If human beings are like the earth, the simile I have been using, they want God as the earth wants the sun. The earth does not plunge into the sun, but it orbits around the sun while turning on its own axis. Poor people, and people generally, if I am right, want to orbit around God, have a relationship with God, while turning on their own axis, living a human existence. God then is not simply an escape from a human existence that has been stripped of everything that makes it desirable. Rather, God makes existence desirable even when people have been stripped to their bare humanity. It is true, as Rilke implies, that riches conceal that bare humanity and poverty reveals it. So also poverty reveals the desire for God.

> John S. Dunne, *The Church of the Poor Devil: Reflections on a
> Riverboat Voyage and a Spiritual Journey* (London: SCM Press;
> New York: Macmillan, 1982), p. 57.

I hold you by love

I hold you by love, most loving Jesus,
and I will not let you go.
for your blessing will never be enough for me
unless I hold you
and keep you as my best part, all my hope and longing.
O Love, life-giving Life,
you are the living word of God: bring me to life.
Whatever of God's love is broken or extinguished,
repair in me by your grace.

My Love, my God, you created me:
recreate me by your love.
O Love, you redeemed me:
whatever of your love has been neglected in me,
supply from yourself and redeem in me.

My Love, my God, you gained me for yourself by the blood of your Christ: make me holy in your truth.

Gertrude the Great (1256–1302), from *Exercitia Spiritualia Septem* V, trans. Brian Pickett, in *The Heart of Love: Prayers of German Women Mystics* (Middlegreen, Slough: St. Paul Publications, 1991), p. 85.

INDEX OF LECTIONARY READINGS

INDEX OF THEMES

INDEX OF AUTHORS